UNEXPLAINED
KENT

UNEXPLAINED

KM

KENT

DB
PUBLISHING

First published in Great Britain by The Breedon Books Publishing Company Limited Breedon House, 44 Friar Gate, Derby, DE1 1DA. 1997

Paperback edition published in 2011 in Great Britain by The Derby Book Publishing Company Ltd., 3 The Parker Centre, Mansfield Road, Derby DE21 4SZ

ISBN 978-1-85983-944-7

Printed and bound by CPI Antony Rowe, Chippenham.

CONTENTS

ACKNOWLEDGEMENTS

The Editor thanks the following contributors without whose efforts this book could not have been produced:

Writers: Justin Williams, Beth Mullins, Stephen Hedges, Robert Barman, Bel Austin, Sue Potter, George Ward, Melody Foreman, Neil Clements, John Guy, Ruth Spencer, Jean Bennet, Hal Williams and John Nurden.

Researchers: Margaret Kennard, Linda Evans and Ann Humphrey.

Photographic staff: Barry Hollis, Mike Whiting and Julie Tompkins.

Assistants: June George, Pamela Paine and Sue Sturgess.

Chapter One

UNIDENTIFIED FLYING OBJECTS

The West Malling Incident

IN the early 1950s an extraordinary encounter took place in the skies over Kent. It was to lead to a debate in the House of Commons and interest by Prince Philip, the Duke of Edinburgh. For a remarkable nine days the Air Ministry allowed the media free access to a pilot and his navigator after they reported seeing an unidentified circular object while flying at 30,000 feet.

Then the shutters came down, the incident was dismissed as a case of mistaken identification and the media's access to servicemen was ended as abruptly as it began. But recently the *Kent Messenger* was able to meet the pilot of the jet involved who talked for the first time in more than 40 years about his bizarre experience.

It all began at about 10am on 3 November 1953, over West Malling. A pilot, Flight Lieutenant Terry Johnson, and his navigator, Flying Officer Geoffrey Smythe, were in a two-seater Vampire night fighter on a reconnaissance mission. The day was bright and there were few clouds in the sky. The two airmen were flying north.

Mr Johnson spotted an unusual object dead ahead which he described as being about a mile away and about half the size of a full moon.

"It was a bright circular object which was glowing with greater intensity around its periphery than at the centre."

Mr Johnson, now a successful businessman living in Hampshire, motioned to his navigator who had not seen the object on his radar screen. He looked up and they both followed the UFO as it moved across the sky.

"After about ten seconds it moved to our right, to the east of the plane, at very high speed," said Mr Johnson. "It did not appear on Geoff's radar screen at any time, as you would have expected a normal solid object to have done."

The entire incident was over in less than 30 seconds and the two men continued with their reconnaissance before landing back at the base at RAF West Malling.

"We fully expected to have our legs pulled about the incident," said Mr Johnson.

But the opposite happened — when the two men landed they were questioned by Squadron Commander Furze about their experience and he in turn reported it to the station commander, Group Captain Hamley. The group captain's interest was aroused because he had had a similar experience to Johnson and Smythe during World War Two.

During bombing missions over Berlin, Squadron Commander Furze, like many other British and American airmen, had encountered mysterious lights flying alongside his aircraft. At first these 'foo fighters', as they became known, were assumed to be experimental German aircraft.

But after the war Luftwaffe pilots told the Allies that they, too, had seen the lights and had assumed they were British or American. Now, it seemed, the foo fighters were back and flying unchallenged over the skies of South East England.

Mr Johnson said, "We were called up to the Air Ministry to give a full report of the incident to the Duke of Edinburgh's equerry. We were told that Prince Philip was interested in flying saucers."

After 48 hours the Air Ministry voluntarily released information on the sighting to the media. Such openness was not to last long and has never been repeated since.

Mr Johnson added, "It was the first time in Britain that there was official mention made of flying saucers."

This was followed a few days later by a second astonishing announcement. In a sensational press release which appeared to back up everything the two airmen had seen, the War Office said that, on the same day at 2.30pm, an unidentified object had been tracked on ground radar based at Lee Green.

The object was circular and motionless and the radar echo appeared to show that it was up to 200 feet across. After ten minutes the object moved away slowly until it was lost from radar range. At 2.45pm the same object was also observed on radar by four men at a nearby anti-aircraft workshop. The War Office also said that it had received three other radar trackings of UFOs between 14 and 22 September.

But, in a sudden about-turn, the Air Ministry put out a second press release stating that the object tracked on radar at Lee Green had been a meteorological balloon released at Crawley, West Sussex, at 2pm. The ministry also said that what Johnson and Smythe had seen in the morning had been a balloon released earlier.

Even now, many years after the event, Mr Johnson is in no doubt that what he and Mr Smythe witnessed was not a weather balloon.

He said, "If it had been a balloon then we would have approached it very quickly. This object moved off at very great speed, something which a weather balloon was not capable of. I have no idea what it really was but we were familiar with all aircraft of the day and it was certainly nothing like anything we had ever seen. It is possible that the object was extraterrestrial."

Mr Smythe is also under no doubts about the UFO. He said, "It was not a balloon but there is every possibility that what we saw was extraterrestrial."

Their conviction is backed up by an interview given at the time by Sergeant Waller, one of the anti-aircraft workshop crew. He was convinced the object was not a balloon and that, for it to have given such a strong radar return, it had to have been metallic. Sergeant Waller also said that he had previously seen five objects flying at impossible speeds in perfect formation in a separate incident.

On 24 November, the Air Ministry's attempt to explain the sightings as balloons appeared to have succeeded. In a debate in the House of Commons, Mr Birch, Parliamentary Secretary to the Secretary of State for Defence, confirmed the Ministry's version.

Sir Isaacs, the Labour MP for Southwark, said, to laughter, "Will the minister agree that this story of flying saucers is all ballooney?"

Mr Birch said that Mr Isaacs' appreciation was 'very nearly correct'. It was leapt on by the infant UFO research community as evidence of an attempt to keep from the public the truth about the flying saucers. In fact, there have been many reported sightings of UFOs over Kent, going back over 80 years. Here is a brief selection:

January 1913 — Strange glowing disc-shaped object sighted over Dover.

October 1932 — Army captain sees two round objects like hollow rings moving at speed over Herne Bay. They make no sound.

November 1953 — Pilot and navigator in Vampire jet encounter bright disc over West Malling.

September 1963 — Strange glowing object spotted hovering over east Kent coast. The RAF at Manston investigates but can find no logical explanation.

August 1967 — Round, flat disc seen hovering over Maidstone. It makes no sound and suddenly disappears at incredible speed leaving behind four fading shafts of light.

February 1970 — Coastguard at Margate observes white and green disc at 2am for half an hour. Two police officers report seeing same object.

November 1972 — Revolving disc-shaped UFO coloured red, white and green moves at tree-top height across the Thanet Way at Whitstable and Herne Bay. More than 30 employees at Faversham Shipyard report discs and cigar-shaped objects over the Creek. Investigated by Ministry of Defence.

February 1976 — Captain Philp, flying a British Air Ferries Convair from Basle to Southend, reports bright light moving at incredible speed at Dover.

February 1977 — Six people see pulsating red oval object over Boxley Hill, near Maidstone. Object disappears at high speed.

July 1977 — Silver disc seen hovering over West Farleigh.

August 1987 — Bright disc seen travelling at high speed over the Weald. Police receive reports from residents in Charing, Biddenden and Cranbrook.

April 1991 — Captain Achille Zaghetti piloting an Alitalia MD80 passenger jet from Milan to Heathrow reports a near miss with a brown missile-shaped object over Lydd at 22,000ft.

He said afterwards, "I used the word missile because of its shape, not because I saw a missile. It was about ten feet long, light brown in colour and I said to my co-pilot, 'Look out! Look out!' and he saw what I saw."

December 1991 — Large UFO witnessed hovering low over Teynham Church, near Sittingbourne. Lynne Yates said, "At first it looked just like a huge star but something shot off from it and then lots of different beams of light started flashing. It stayed around for about half an hour. It is like nothing I have ever seen before."

April 1992 — Alsi Bassett-Burr sees a large object hovering over Herbert Road, Rainham. She said it was like a wheel with spikes and had at least 110 white lights.

March 1996 — Large dark triangular-shaped craft seen moving slowly over the Smarden area. Witnesses describe a low humming sound and banks of lights around its edges.

This list is not exhaustive. Let us look at some other instances in more detail.

Cigars, Domes, Circles and Squares

THE *Kent Evening Post* — now *Kent Today* — moved into the new year of 1979 with a story on 3 January about a housewife who saw a cigar-shaped object overhead on her way back home from shopping. It reported:

Housewife Faith Ayres is one of thousands of Britons who are convinced they had close encounters with UFOs during the holiday weekend.

Mrs Ayres, of School Lane, Higham, saw the object in the sky above the village as she walked home from the shops on Friday morning. She said, "Before I saw this thing I never believed in UFOs. But I know this wasn't a plane or balloon. It's a pity there was nobody else about at the time to confirm what I saw."

Mrs Ayres said the object was silver and about the length of three buses. Trailing behind it were silver 'rays' which seemed to propel it along.

Mrs Ayres watched it for several minutes from Forge Lane before it disappeared over the rooftops.

In June, a cigar-shaped object was seen in the night sky over Rochester. Although there were thousands of sightings throughout the county at the weekend, there were no more reports of UFOs in North Kent.

A year later, on 4 April, the *Evening Post* was telling its readers about a 'close encounter' of the eerie kind for a couple near Thurnham:

Approaching the Pilgrim's Way, near Thurnham, after spending the evening at the Windmill pub in Hollingbourne, the scene suddenly resembled an excerpt from the famous UFO movie.

Two lights, a foot across, were moving slowly towards Cliff's [Cliff Cheal] new Capri car and they appeared to be less than 100 feet in the air. His first instincts told him the mystery object must be a helicopter.

Stopping the car and switching off the lights, he opened the door and listened. Nothing, just the lights and the steady movement through silent air.

No helicopter this, he realised as the alien swept over the car. It was 25 feet across and the dark shape behind the lights appeared like 'a plane with no tail'.

The couple turned up the chance of a closer inspection and roared off into the night.

Four months later, on 26 August 1980, *the Evening Post* carried a page lead headline: 'Experts Baffled by Night Lights — UFO Spotters Report the Hovering Dome.' It recorded:

Ministry of Defence experts are baffled by the appearance of a so-called UFO over the town. It was photographed by Christopher Collins-Mackay, of Whitehall Road, Gravesend.

It first appeared last Monday night and was seen by three members of the Collins-Mackay family. They called the police who at first put the object down to a panic.

Astronomer Patrick Moore and the Royal Observatory suggested it might have been the tail end of a meteor caused by the end of a comet passing close to Earth.

But Christopher Collins-Mackay and his mother, Kay, spotted the object again early Friday morning and again on Sunday morning.

Christopher said, "It was like a ball of shimmering light with a domed shape, rather like an illuminated clock face, and there was a sort of garland of tinselly stuff around it.

"It was hovering. It must have stayed like it for several hours and only seemed to drift a little. I have never seen anything like it."

A spokesman for the Ministry of Defence said it had received no other sightings and could offer no explanation.

It was also spotted by Mrs Ethel Hammock, of Hever Farm, early Tuesday morning.

Mrs Hammock said, "It was ring-like and slightly domed at the top and had a series of lights coming out from the centre. It was definitely not a star. It was too big."

The Royal Observatory, expanding on its view in another story published in the same newspaper, offered 'space debris' from the comet Swift-Tuddle as the most likely explanation.

The comet — which passed the Earth two years later in 1982 — had previously shown itself in 1862, but the RO said the tail end of debris 120 years old was still entering the Earth's atmosphere and burning up.

"It's part of a Perseid shower," said the RO spokesman. "It's called that because the meteor is heading in the direction of the constellation Perseus. We are seeing space debris that intersected the Earth's orbit."

As 1980 drew towards its close, the spotlight switched to mid Kent where the *Kent Messenger* reported, on 9 December, that an encounter with teaching staff at Cornwallis School, Maidstone, was followed by a close encounter of a different kind for Cyril Ellen and his wife, Ivy.

Mr and Mrs Ellen, of Kenward Road, Yalding, were driving home after discussing their son's examination prospects at the school when they spotted a strange light in the sky:

"It was about nine o'clock when we saw this round object like a saucer, with a yellow light and red and green flashing lights round the outside," Mr Ellen said.

"I stopped the car and we got out to have a look. The yellow light suddenly went out and the object went at speed back towards Coxheath.

"It was definitely not an aircraft, as there was no noise."

Police could shed no light on the mystery object in the sky, which was spotted on 26 November. They said they had received no similar reports.

Still in December 1980, on Christmas Eve, farm worker John Slattery was reported by the *Kent Messenger* to have seen stars in the sky — and he believed they were UFOs.

He was working in a hop garden at East Farleigh when he saw tiny stars shooting from what he at first thought was a weather balloon.

Half an hour later, Mr Slattery, of Lower Road, East Farleigh, saw two large stars with more of the smaller stars drifting away from them. He said, "I have seen weather balloons before, but never anything like this. I'm convinced they were UFOs."

In January 1981, the seasonal festivities barely over, the *Evening Post* printed a series of reports with Maureen Hall, a leading local UFO investigator.

Mrs Hall revealed that she had taken a call from a man who wanted to report a sighting. The newspaper reporter and Mrs Hall visited the caller,

Peter Langridge, a television scriptwriter, at his home, where he told his story.

He said he saw an unidentified craft on Friday, 2 January, in the early evening after returning from a family gathering in West Sussex. He was driving back with his son, Neil — then 15 — whom he described as 'the world's worst map reader'. The newspaper reported:

They were soon lost near Petworth and found themselves travelling along a narrow, winding lane bordered with high hedges near the A272. Rounding yet another bend, Peter saw an object in the sky straddling the road at a height he estimated at 'one and a half telegraph poles'.

At first, Peter said he thought it was 'one of the hydraulic cranes they use for mending street lamps'. There were no street lamps or houses anywhere near the lane and it was dark, but the night sky was bright and clear with stars.

Peter continued his story: "I stopped the car and said to my son: 'Just look out the back window and tell me what you see. There is something in the sky behind us and it's got lights on.'"

Neil confirmed that there was something there and Peter said, "I think it's a flying saucer. I'm going to have a look."

He ignored his son's plea to refrain and got out. Neil could not follow because his passenger door was hard against the hedge. Later in the interview, Peter told Mrs Hall that, when he got out of his car, his feelings were friendly towards the object hovering above the road.

"The thing was dark but a deeper dark than night and it had lights around it — they were yellow and created a haze rather than a beam, rather like disco lights."

He described the outline of the craft as resembling two 50p pieces one above the other and connected by inward curving panels. As it hovered, it appeared to be reverberating.

The word he used to describe the effect was 'purring' but there was no audible sound coming from it.

"When I got there I was suddenly incredibly frightened, panic stricken."

He moved back to the car and his son said, "I think we should go."

Peter looked back and saw the object was still in the air, although it had shifted slightly to one side. He was then distracted by a passing car, but looked up to see the mysterious shape going away.

Peter said that moving away was not really the right description. He said the object 'faded out' gradually as though it was being erased.

He said, "It was the most amazing thing. My whole family works in television and I know people who could reproduce that thing. It was a very real experience for both my son and I. The panic feeling that I had was very frightening but I also had a sort of feeling that there was a purpose to what happened."

Peter said he felt he could have reached the object with the beam of a torch if he had had one with him.

"I very seldom have a feeling of panic, but I felt out of my depth, incredibly small and very lonely."

Five months later, on 2 June, an object like an oblong balloon was spotted in the sky over Gillingham. It was metallic with a red flashing light, said Valerie Bennett and her husband John, who saw it from the garden of their home in Lambsfrith Grove, Hempstead.

Mrs Bennett told the *Evening Post* it was faster than a helicopter, but only about one third the size:

"There was no noise — that's what was really uncanny. It was there for only a few seconds before it went behind the trees. It seemed to follow the motorway."

Gillingham police said they had no reports of unidentified flying objects.

Two days later, the mystery appeared to have been cleared up. A man, who did not want to be named, telephoned *The Post*, saying he had bought a new toy, a helium-filled balloon with a metallic silver top. The paper said:

> His granddaughter took it away with her and was walking home in Hempstead on the day when Mr and Mrs Bennett saw the object. She let it go and it flew straight up to the sky.

In July, the same newspaper reported that police had been alerted to a mystery light above the A2 at Northfleet:

> A spokesman said, "People called it a UFO, but most talked of a white light swivelling about."
>
> Police informed the Civil Aviation Authority and RAF Manston — but the UFO is believed to have been a helicopter.
>
> The police spokesman added, "There's quite a few going to and from Sandwich for the golf."

Sightings of strange lights near airports crop up whenever you look at UFO cases and Kent had its own little scare in 1983. On 5 December that year, the *Evening Post* interviewed a couple, Tom and Eileen Carter, who said they had seen a circular object 'surrounded by lights' above Rochester airport and were certain it was not a plane:

> It was the second reported sighting (earlier a woman had to be calmed by police who found her in a hedge after she had seen a UFO).
>
> The couple, from Longley Road, Walderslade, were driving down City Way on Wednesday evening at about 9pm when they saw incredibly bright lights. Their report coincides with that of the un-named woman who collapsed screaming in City Way the same evening.

Within a week, the riddle of the sightings was solved, said the newspaper. A woman, who did not want to be named, telephoned the newspaper to say the circular object was a Singapore Airlines jumbo jet. The *Evening Post* again:

> The airline has confirmed that three nights a week a jumbo flies over the Medway Towns at about 9pm, the time of the reported sightings. A spokesman said the landing and tail lights could 'possibly' be mistaken for something strange in the sky.'

Was the Shell Research Centre, Sittingbourne, the subject of interest for alien eyes in September 1984? A mystery object, described as a 'square of white light with two lines of white light running across the middle', was seen near the centre in the early hours of a Sunday morning. The *Evening Post* carried the story on 24 September:

> It was spotted by Kevin Pook (then 19), of Staplehurst Road, Sittingbourne, shortly after 2am. Kevin told the police he saw the UFO twice, once around 2.05am and then about half an hour later.
>
> The object made no noise and, shortly after Kevin saw it for the second time, it headed off over the fields towards London.
>
> He tried to follow the object in his car. The second time he noticed it, the UFO was hovering in the sky in the distance.
>
> Police telephoned RAF Manston. A police spokesman said it was a 'matter of procedure' to report all UFO sightings to the RAF.

In recent years, UFO stories have been more spasmodic. Whether that is because people have become more blasé about the subject or whether there are just fewer cases is open to question. But, in the summer of 1992, *Kent Today* reported that a Snodland couple saw two unidentified flying objects on two successive nights. Was it just another silly season story? The edition of 30 July stated:

> Sue Nye said, "We watched them for a little while and they went away. A couple of hours later we saw one again. It had flashing

lights and kept turning round as if it was watching something. We watched it for about an hour."

The next night the couple say they saw the strange shapes again. This time there were three.

She said, "We looked at them through binoculars and they had a circle of white lights with flashing coloured lights inside."

Rochester airport said it had not received any reports of UFO sightings, but there was an interesting response from a MoD spokesman. The newspaper said that 'according to Nick Pope of the secretariat to the air staff' there had already been 60 reports of UFO sightings in Britain that year.

Kent Today continued:

Mr Pope, who says he has an open mind about the existence of UFOs, said, "We think about 95 per cent of these reports can be explained away. But there will always be those reports which cannot be explained away."

Both *Kent Today* and its sister paper, *Kent Messenger*, carried stories about an odd incident in January 1995, in which an amateur photographer took a picture of lights in the sky — and captured a strange face on the only picture to come out.

The *KM* of 13 January edition, reported:

Alan Irving, of Coombe Road, Tovil and his partner, Anne Ward, first saw the lights one night in October.

Miss Ward said, "I was outside smoking a cigarette and I saw a pale light, like a lot of circles all joined together, hovering in the sky overhead.

"As I watched, they moved slowly across the sky from left to right and back again several times.

"I called to Alan to come outside and we watched them together for a while before they disappeared."

Alan Irving was puzzled by the strange face which appeared on a picture he took of lights in the sky.

The lights were observed again on several nights, usually when it was overcast, and were seen by other people in the road.

The *KM* continued:

One night, Mr Irving fixed a telescopic lens to his camera and took a series of photographs of the lights. Only one picture came out — which clearly showed the face of a man, eyes downcast, seemingly standing by an open hatch. Mr Irving was baffled. He approached the *KM* half convinced he had photographed a being from another dimension.

KM photographer John Wardley, who examined both the negatives and the print, said it was more likely that Mr Irving had inadvertently photographed someone's TV screen. But Mr Irving did not see how he could have photographed a TV screen when all the shots on the film were taken outside the house with the camera pointing at the sky.

The *KM* invited readers to help solve the mystery and a couple of weeks later it ran a follow-up piece stating that two local groups which investigated UFOs and related phenomena had offered to investigate.

Another reader wrote to say the photograph 'looks suspiciously like that of the late Raymond Massey in the film version of H.G.Wells's *Things to Come*'.

Then a night club manager came up with an explanation which seemed to fit the bill — it was nothing more than a rather spectacular light show. David Keetley, of the then newly-opened Zoots club in High Street, Maidstone, said he had a Skytrack machine which shot beams of light into the sky and it was being operated at the club during September and October.

He said, "It sends out not one but hundreds of light beams in a circular pattern which can be seen up to 15 miles away, so it's quite possible people in Tovil could have seen it."

Spectacular lights were the order of the day in *Kent Today* (24 August 1995), but this time it was unlikely that a night club was responsible. It reported:

Peter Hadden, of Gladstone Road, Deal, said he watched the mysterious lights for 15 minutes.

Mr Hadden was in his back garden just after 9pm on Sunday when he saw the UFO coming from the east.

"It was a dim light, high up and speeding almost towards me," he said. "My next door neighbour was in her garden and I pointed it out to her.

"The object kept coming towards me until it stopped, moved left and then came back up to a terrific speed, with a small wake of vapour behind.

"It went in a large, left-handed arc where another object, of the same dimness, joined it. At one stage the object split in two and flew in different directions."

Mr Hadden watched the spectacle for almost 15 minutes and then called RAF Manston to see if anyone had reported it. But no others had been received.

"The UFOs were definitely not aircraft of the conventional earthly kind," he added.

D-Day Anniversary Sighting

TEENAGER Amanda Joseph picked up her binoculars. Gazing idly through the window of her grandmother's bungalow, she had seen what looked like an unusual aircraft over the North Downs, about one and a half miles distant.

The 19-year-old turned her attention away from the sandwich she was eating in her nan's kitchen to scan the sky. She had lived with her grandparents in the village of Addington, near West Malling, since she was four.

The day 6 June 1992 — the 48th anniversary of the D-Day landings in Normandy — was bright and sunny. The chalkland downs looked beautiful.

Ever since childhood, Amanda had loved looking at the view from the kitchen window. She focused her binoculars on the hilltop transmission station at Wrotham. The pylon is a famous landmark visible for miles around. Its three red lights shine prominently in the night sky.

Beneath the downs, the endless ribbon of cars and lorries snaked and shimmered along the M20, *en route* for London, the M25 or the Channel coast. Amanda shifted her focus slightly towards the London side of the beacon. And there it was.

"It was such a sunny day, you would expect it to have been shiny on top but it was a matt grey. Underneath, it was silvery. I remember thinking this was strange. As it was a sunny day, normal logic would expect it to be the reverse.

"It was moving very slowly from left to right and parallel to the top of the downs. It inched towards the signal tower. I had watched it for ages and assumed it was a helicopter but it didn't look like it. It really wasn't so far away that I couldn't recognise it to be a helicopter if it was.

"I thought it was very odd. It was moving so slowly and in such a straight line. It was only when it stopped dead in front of the tower that I thought it was a UFO. I studied it carefully through the binoculars as I remember thinking that no one would believe me otherwise.

"Basically it appeared to be this shape [she drew a flat 'hat' outline]. I don't know if it was circular although my impression was that it was. It

Amanda Joseph spotted something 'very odd' with her binoculars while looking out to the North Downs.

could have been the length of a lorry trailer, the sort that you see on the motorway attached to a cab.

"My nan was ill in bed at the time and my boyfriend Bill was watching *Grange Hill* on television. I knew nobody would believe me. I really did have a good look at it. I was gobsmacked. I couldn't speak. Of course, I was very excited but I didn't have the voice to call anyone to witness it.

"It wasn't the right shape to be a light aircraft and, anyway, they don't hover. It definitely wasn't a helicopter."

Amanda said that, after she had watched the UFO hover for a few minutes, it retraced its steps, then suddenly sped away.

"I didn't report it. I meant to, but never got round to it. About one week later, there was a television report of a pilot seeing a UFO over the east coast. That clinched it for me."

Five years on, Amanda, now the proud mum of baby Bronwyn and living in Maidstone with Bill, tries to make sense of what happened that summer's day.

"I'd heard tales around Addington that people had seen things, but that usually happened at night. I believe there is more to the universe than just us. Perhaps beings in the UFO were looking at the pylon, or perhaps the M20 motorway.

"A psychic friend once told me there was something psychic going on between people on Earth and aliens and that if you really want to see them, they will visit you. I have had several experiences, all very strange. But I do believe I saw a UFO that day.

"I've dreamt about aliens for years, but what I saw that day from my nan's kitchen makes me think there is much more to it than dreams."

The Flying Triangle

EAST Kent is the latest centre of interest for the so-called Flying Triangle — and hot on its trail is Chris Rolfe, assistant co-ordinator of a group called UFOMEK (UFO Monitors East Kent).

Mr Rolfe used to be in the Air Training Corps, and has a natural curiosity about anything that flies. Yet, he was not particularly surprised by stories in early 1997 in a Folkestone weekly newspaper about a triangular-shaped craft seen in the area. Mr Rolfe, who lives in Folkestone, said flying triangles had been spotted all over the country and Kent reports dated back to the early 1970s when some schoolboys claimed they saw one in the skies above Dover.

Chris Rolfe, right, seen here with UFOMEK colleague Jerry Anderson, has the Flying Triangle in his sights.

The latest sighting was made by a woman driver around 3am on Saturday, 8 March. It was hovering over a field near to Donkey Street, between Burmarsh and Dymchurch and she was reported as saying it had 'a large dome at one end and a lot of bright lights around the sides'. It shot off 'after a few seconds' but then stopped again suddenly about 500 metres away.

After repeating the exercise three more times, it flew away into the distance. The newspaper also reported that two people in Donkey Street saw a 'weird floating object' in a field.

Two other sightings of a silver-grey object, not reported in the paper, later came to light — one over Lydd around 3am and another at Aldington at 3.30am.

"I interviewed the woman driver and she said the size of the triangle was about that of two jumbo jets or the same as the field," said Mr Rolfe. "What she perhaps did not realise was that the size of that particular field was enormous, much bigger than the average field. However, what concerned me most was the position of the UFO.

"It was only about a mile from the home of MP and former Home Secretary Michael Howard and I felt that there was a security risk, as it has never been known for such an incident to happen near a senior minister's residence."

He said he rang Mr Howard's agent and asked if anything unusual around the house had been noticed during the weekend. "Without being prompted, the man said, 'What, like a UFO?'"

Mr Rolfe said he was preparing reports to send to Kent Police, the MoD and MP Roger Gale. He wanted questions asked in the House of Commons about the incident.

The Flying Triangle case is just one of many investigated by UFOMEK, which was formed in 1994. UFO reports and data from Kent and South London are compiled and interviews conducted in strict confidence, said Mr Rolfe, who is assisted in his work by the group's leader, Jerry Anderson.

"The work of the group has allowed us to gain an insight into the magnitude of the UFO phenomenon, not just on a county level, but on an international scale. Our members [totalling around 50] attend bi-monthly meetings and are encouraged to play an active part. We endeavour to approach this fascinating subject with professionalism and take care to investigate thoroughly," he added.

The Flying Triangle has an echo in the following story which took place in 1993.

Ivan Parris, a bookbinder with a printing firm in Aylesford, finished work at 8pm. He drove home across Penenden Heath to his semi in Grove Green. The moon was up but it disappeared now and again behind low clouds drifting across the October night sky. He swung into his drive and parked the car outside the garage door.

As he prepared to join wife Christine indoors, he decided to take one last look at the sky. It was a fascination of his. He loved observing the stars and more recently, in the spring of 1997, enjoyed a nightly peek at the impressive Hale-Bopp comet which dominated the north-west sky.

Four years earlier, however, his thoughts were on the Plough and other constellations in the northern hemisphere.

Ivan could see the stars twinkling during breaks in the cloud. And as he gazed south-westwards across a neighbour's rooftop, he saw something that has mystified him ever since.

"I was looking up at the stars when I saw this white light. It was like a searchlight. There was no sound. The light came from a triangular, delta-shaped object, a bit like a Vulcan bomber.

"I've been to airshows and know the Vulcan makes a loud noise that, if it had been that low, everybody in the neighbourhood would have been out to look at it. I can understand why no one else saw it. It was just at the moment I looked up that it appeared out of a cloud.

"I've seen a Vulcan a mile away and the noise is horrendous. This happened in 1993 when I think there was only one Vulcan flying.

"The beam of light came straight down as though a door or something had opened and the light was shining out very brightly through it. It could not have been much higher than 1,000 feet. It was a dark silhouette. It just came out of the clouds which were very low. Anything that low would normally have made a noise.

"I'd say it was as big as a Vulcan bomber but it was covered in coloured lights, red, yellow and green. I've always studied aircraft. I know the American Stealth bomber, I've seen that. I know the Vulcan and have seen that. But I've never seen anything like this before or since.

"It wasn't as though I'd driven for a long time and was tired. It's only 15 minutes from my work to home, and my seven-hour shift had been

Ivan Parris said the object he saw was delta-shaped, like a Vulcan bomber, but there was no sound.

no busier than normal. I've never told anybody about this. It's something I can't explain but I think about it a lot.

"It still comes back to me how eerie it was that there was just silence. This all took place in a matter of five minutes. It came slowly over the house, then suddenly disappeared behind cloud above the North Downs. It was even stranger because I have never seen aircraft fly over the house from south-west to north-east. Most planes come from north to south or east to west, and they've never been that low."

With the passing years, the father of two grown-up children remains as baffled as ever. Now his thoughts tend to turn more to Amy, his little granddaughter, than weird objects in the sky, but that large delta-shaped image at about 1,000 feet continues to haunt his memory.

He remains an aircraft fan and a keen modeller, keeping his model of a Vulcan bomber in the garage. But he is convinced that what he saw that night was no real Vulcan, one of the most distinctive, stunning and noisiest aircraft in British aviation history.

Aviation had been Ivan's hobby since his boyhood, when his father Leslie thrilled him with tales of bravery and heroism by young fighter pilots over the fields of Kent during the Battle of Britain. Leslie worked at the Rochester factory of Short Brothers, where the Sunderland flying boats were made. But UFOs were never part of his son's education.

The nearest Maidstone-born Ivan got to a paranormal experience was when a psychic accurately told his daughter that her surname had French connections.

"I have never read science fiction. My head's not full of space and aliens. I think 99.9 per cent of mysterious things can be explained in some way. It's that tiny bit that defies explanation. I believe in life on other planets, although not little green men.

"What happened that night is something I can't explain. I wish someone would give me a reason why. Even if they told me it was just an experimental plane, I wouldn't mind.

"But never to know is the most frustrating thing of all."

Maidstone's X-Philes

THE *X Files* TV series is now a serious topic for conversation among devotees in Maidstone.

They have been meeting since June 1996, each Wednesday evening from 7pm onwards, at the Muggleton Inn in the High Street, to discuss the latest twists in the show's storylines.

A *Kent Messenger* reporter visited the group's inaugural meeting where warehouse operative Sean Jones, from Maidstone, said he was the man responsible for the advertisement which invited fans to go to the pub and meet like-minded people who shared their obsession.

"Mondays were out because that's when the repeats are on BBC1 and Tuesdays on Sky One are the new series so I picked Wednesday night because there's nothing on," Sean explained over a pint.

"Except *Star Trek*," someone muttered.

Sean Jones seen with fellow members of the Maidstone X-Philes group which meets weekly.

Sean was quick to explain it isn't a club or even a formal group as such but simply an opportunity for fans of the show to meet and chat without fear of ridicule from friends and colleagues.

Someone in the group asks if anyone has ever seen a UFO and a few hands go up, sparking an exchange of stories while over in the corner a splinter group discusses *Red Dwarf* and life on other planets.

Sean sums up what he thinks is the attraction of the show, apart from the good looks of its two stars David (Mulder) Duchovny and Gillian (Scully) Anderson, and what spurred him into issuing a general invitation to other 'X-Philes'.

He said, "It's not just about UFOs, although they do feature pretty strongly, and life on other planets, but all kinds of bizarre things for which there are no real explanations.

"The programme manages to offer possible explanations without pretending to have all the answers and treats its subjects intelligently. Unfortunately, if you're interested in these things people assume you're either completely sad or a bit of a nutter."

Mark Price, who works at Maidstone Hospital, is one of the few genuine X-Philes in that he regularly logs on to the Internet to chat to other fans.

He says that after the show is aired in America, the network is lit up for a good hour and a half as fans dissect every nuance of every line of dialogue in the latest episode.

Claire Hamlet, a nursery school nurse from Rochester, 'accidentally' tuned in one night and liked it so much she just kept watching. Friend and colleague Shelley Hook, from the Isle of Grain, says she is generally interested in the paranormal and the unexplained and started watching the programme after her mum told her about it.

Kelly Smith, from Gillingham, is studying law. She was one of the few people at the meeting who admitted to watching the series from the start.

"I definitely think these sort of things are going on and the Government has been covering it up for years, so it's good to see the subject taken seriously."

Abductions or Hallucinations?

NUMEROUS people across Britain claim they have been abducted by alien entities, taken aboard their ships and examined, often with the aid of medical implements. Can they all be deluding themselves, experiencing some kind of hallucination or are they having real close encounters?

Maria Ward does not claim to know who or what took her from her house. But she knows that she was fully awake and conscious during the entire episode. If true, and taken at face value, then her experience raises some terrifying questions about who we are and why something is taking an extraordinary interest in us.

On 21 November 1990, Maria woke up in her house at Greenhithe, near Dartford, at 3.15am and lit a cigarette. She had a strong urge to go to the window.

"It was unusual because I am a deep sleeper and never just wake up in the middle of the night," she said.

When she looked out of the window she saw an object in the sky like a cartwheel which was spinning. "I had a strong feeling that it was coming here.

"Obviously, I wanted to know what it was."

Maria's husband was away from home working at the time and her son was asleep in her bed. He slept through the whole thing.

She went out of the room on to the landing where she was confronted by a ball of intense white light. "A voice told me to follow the light." Maria followed the light down the stairs to where white light was streaming in under the bottom of the front door.

The voice told her to pick up the ball of light and she bent down. "As soon as my hands were round it, I was pulled upwards right through the front door. I could tell you exactly what the insides of the door were like, the joins, the cobwebs, everything.

"Outside I was lifted upwards. I looked down and could see a tennis ball stuck in the guttering. I continued up and then there was something solid under my feet."

At this point Maria could not see anything but could hear a shuffling sound 'like children in a gym'.

Maria Ward said a taller 'off-white' coloured being joined the small browny-grey creatures in the room where she was examined.

As her eyes became accustomed to her surroundings Maria started to see shadows and then what appeared to be people.

"There were three of them and a very strong smell like rotting leaves or mushrooms."

The three creatures were three and a half to four feet tall and browny-grey in colour. As with many encounters, the beings had large bald heads and large black eyes. "They looked like little kids," said Maria.

The beings put their hands under Maria's elbows and led her along a corridor into a small room which had a low shelf right the way around it. The two small entities left Maria there. In the middle of the room was a silver rectangular platform. Maria sat on the edge of it. Unable to rationalise what was going on, she was terrified. "I thought I was going to die. I did not believe in UFOs — in fact I was anti the whole thing."

Another being came into the room. Maria described it 'as about 5ft 6ins tall, with larger eyes'. She said, "It was an off-white colour."

She was made to lie down on the platform and was examined. Maria claims that something was inserted into her head behind her ear and hair was taken from the back of her head. Something was also stuck into her finger.

Maria grabbed the creature's arm. "It stared at me and all of the pain I was feeling went away. I felt completely calm."

During her examination Maria said she got a strong vision of a dusty world with two suns. "Everything was browny orange and there was what looked like mud huts on the landscape. There was something very familiar about it."

She says she was also made to see a vision of the Earth with what looked like yellow bruises over the North and South Poles. Then the Earth was rocked by explosions and it 'imploded'.

Maria said, "Other abductees have seen the same thing."

Suddenly she found herself back at home, walking up the stairs. She entered her room, climbed back into the bed and wrapped herself in the duvet.

The power was off but her battery-operated clock showed that she had been away for exactly 45 minutes. "My feet were filthy and my nightshirt was the wrong way round. I went to sleep."

Maria slept until 8.15am. In the morning she found blood on her pillow, a mark behind her ear and a bald spot on the back of her head. Her nostrils were also caked with dried blood. Downstairs the cigarette she had lit the night before was standing butt end down on a table next to the front door.

Since that night in 1990, Maria has had other experiences including being shown, along with a group of other people, images of disasters on Earth which include a vision of a terrorist attack on a French nuclear power station.

She has since met one of the people who was in the group with her. "We instantly recognised each other," she said.

She says she has also started to remember strange experiences as a child including one when she was 'put into a plastic bubble' by something.

Maria has also taken pictures of objects hovering over her house, a huge bright object stationary over the nearby Bluewater Park development and pictures of a bright egg-shaped object which hovered over her car. She has been plagued by electrical problems in the house, balls of light and strange noises on her stereo and television.

Maria also says she has been visited by strange men claiming to be from 'the Government'. During one visit the men tried to force their way into her house and demanded to know if she was given any 'artefacts' or technical information by her abductors. She also says that her house has been broken into, her phone tapped and mail opened and interfered with.

Her experiences are similar to those of other abductees but, unlike others, she does not assume that the creatures who examined her were from other planets or galaxies. "In truth, I have no idea what they were, so I cannot jump to the most convenient conclusion."

A fierce debate has raged for decades over alleged alien abductions. Thousands of abductees claim to have been subjected to medical examination by aliens. Some female victims even say that the 'Greys', as the entities have become known, have taken unborn foetuses from their wombs.

Such claims are met with disbelief and derision by the medical establishment and all talk of implants, bizarre operations and womb robbing by the Greys are dismissed completely.

Dr Susan Blackmore, a professor in psychology at Manchester University, suggests that many alleged abductees have experienced 'temporal lobe liability'. This, she says, is when a person hallucinates what appears to be a real experience because of the effects of electromagnetism on the temporal lobes in the brain.

But such arguments do not sway people like Maria Ward. She remains utterly convinced that her experiences are real and involve real creatures. And there are many researchers in Britain and the United States who believe the experiences to be real and involve some form of extraterrestrial race.

Despite their conviction and a number of interesting cases where apparent abductions and missing time have been witnessed by other people, there has never been any concrete evidence presented that the human race is being subjected to scrutiny by beings from outer space or other dimensions.

No evidence has been found of stolen foetuses and nobody has yet been able to present the scientific community with the implants many abductees claim to have had inserted into them. Nevertheless, Maria Ward's story is compelling and highly believable. Most reasonable people would describe her as an average person and not one who is particularly interested in New Age philosophies or apt to automatically believe every paranormal story she hears.

Quite clearly she is convinced that in November 1990 she was taken from her house by some form of intelligence she does not understand. It would appear that she has nothing to gain from publicity and has never sought it. In fact, it could be argued that she has much to lose — including her credibility.

Maria Ward has been counselling a teenage boy from the Sevenoaks area whose experiences sound just like her own.

Carl, whose parents William and Joan were for years unable to comprehend what was going on, was referred to child psychologists. The boy has suffered strange experiences since he was a baby.

Joan said, "At first we thought it was just ghosts. We used to live in an old house near Dartford. Objects were being moved and we could hear things." But in 1994 Carl started to describe frightening experiences of little men with large eyes performing what sounded like medical experiments on him.

He talked of needles and examinations and a hospital the men took him to. At the same time Carl would go missing from his room at night and in the morning would be found with strange marks and nose bleeds.

Carl, whose father worked shifts late into the night, slept in his mother's bed. But even that didn't stop the visits by the little men and their bright lights and humming noises. Alarmingly, Carl would disappear from the house for hours on end even though all the windows and doors were locked.

At around the same time a herd of cattle the family owned on a calf-rearing unit close to Ministry of Defence woodland fell sick and, one by one, the cattle died. William called a vet and shortly afterwards several vans carrying men in protective clothing and gas masks arrived to examine the carcasses. William says that they told him the animals had a dangerous form of salmonella and the remaining four were destroyed.

He was advised that, for the next 12 months, he would not be able to put animals on the land. After this time a certificate of good health would be sent to him. A year later, having heard nothing, he contacted the Ministry of Agriculture who told him that they had no knowledge of the strange 'spacesuited' visitors.

The couple have also noticed men dressed in dark clothing who appeared to be watching them from the edge of the MoD woodland.

Carl, according to his parents, continues to be taken at night by the little men. They have heard strange noises as if people are walking around in their house, suffered electrical problems and seen strange lights around the house and while out in their car.

Joan says that she, too, has experience of the little men and believes that her father and her grandfather were also victims. "It's possible they target a particular family and continue to monitor subsequent generations."

She added, "It just goes on and on. There is nothing we can do; we are just trying to come to terms with it."

X marks the spot for a young north Kent woman who says she may have been abducted from her bed by strange beings 'six or seven times' over a three-week period. On the first occasion, she thought it might have been a bad dream, but now she is inclined to believe it was something more sinister.

Twenty-year-old Sally Walker and her husband, Colin, both appear sincere and level-headed, with no reason to hold themselves up to ridicule by inventing their story.

Sally believes a small bump on the back of her head may be the result of an operation carried out by aliens and that, beneath the skin, a type of bar code has been inserted... bearing some numbers preceded by the letter X.

Does this mean that, if there are aliens, they have records of human beings on file — their own X-files, indeed?

At the time of her experience in March 1996, Sally — unlike Colin — was a confirmed UFO sceptic, which proved to be an intriguing aspect of a conversation she believes she had with her captors.

She says the implant was carried out on the 'second or third' abduction and she suffered severe headaches afterwards, "I knew something was wrong with my head and one day I just sat down and drew pictures of everything I could remember. I drew the typical Grey face, slightly different in shape, but with the same big eyes and I also drew what looked like a bar code with X179 written on it.

"Colin and I believe that was my code number and we think the bar code's in my head because I have a scar."

The mark is a small, white circular lump, now covered by hair, but, immediately after the scar was discovered, Colin said 'something grey' could be seen under the skin and Sally is now considering consulting a doctor to have it examined, "We've only just decided to bring this out in the open. We have been living with it since last March and we haven't really told anyone else about it."

When Sally woke in her bedroom after the 'operation' experience, she said that in her 'dream record' she could see the bar code. She said, "What I see is this bar code thing and what is in my dream is what is in my head."

During the following three months, on a number of occasions when she saw programmes on the television about UFOs or visitors from outer space, she passed out. Colin said, "She would wake up with an intense headache exactly at the point of the little lump."

The couple, who, in 1997, launched PUFORT — the Paranormal & UFO Research Team (North Kent) — recalled the night it all began, shortly after they had moved into their new home (we have agreed not to publish their address):

"I remember waking up in bed and seeing a really bright, white light," said Sally. "I didn't notice the time on the clock, but the next thing is I'm walking down a corridor and there's a queue of people, humans. Then I'm in a big, circular room. It looks like aluminium or steel and white... a room with lights all over."

She found herself lying down, but did not appear to be supported by anything.

"I've got the feeling that I am going to be hurt, but I am not particularly scared about the idea. I know it's going to involve pain, but I am not worried. The next thing, I can hear this in my head and I say,

'Why are you taking me?

"Why not take Colin, because he wants to know about it; Colin would love to be abducted?'

"And he [the being] says to me 'We take sceptics. You don't believe, we'll take you.' "

She said she remembered the being leaning over her in the room and also standing by her bed at home. The people she saw in the corridor wore everyday clothes, not night clothes and they were not talking, just standing in a line and looking forward as if waiting to go into a room. There were men, women and children.

"I was at the front of the queue," said Sally. "I was walking past people to be taken somewhere. I knew I wasn't at home and I knew something had been done to me." She said she felt pain during the 'operation'.

Meanwhile, back in the bedroom, Colin was literally paralysed. He said he could not move — it was as if an electric current were passing through his body.

"I know I was awake although I couldn't open my eyes. It was about half-four in the morning. My brain was full of strange images and I could sort of see an eye in my mind. I had this really intense feeling of helplessness, not being able to do anything, not being able to move to see if Sally was OK.

"I can remember physically screaming inside but not making a noise. Then I came out of it just as Sally said, 'Are you OK? I've just had a strange dream.'"

Sally said she had several similar 'dreams' and added, "Being a sceptic, I thought I was going crazy. I was taken several times all within the space of three weeks. I think I was taken about six or seven times and tests were done on me."

Thankfully, nothing unusual has happened since those alarming three weeks, but Sally has decided to develop her psychic abilities by opening an advice clinic on the paranormal. She says she was regressed when she was younger to what may have been a previous life (or death) in mediaeval Maidstone.

"I remember seeing myself wearing a frilly milk cap and a pinafore. There were animals around and hay. Apparently I was hanged for adultery by the riverside, near to where the Ferryman Tavern is now. Perhaps it explains why I don't like my neck being touched and why I used to absolutely hate Maidstone!"

They May Be Here Already

NEXT time a group of government politicians and their aides appear on your TV screens, peer a little closer — and look for an alien intelligence.

Not that you're likely to recognise one easily, because they will look like us, dress like us and, no doubt, speak like us.

This is the disturbing scenario painted by author and former aerobatic pilot Derek Sheffield, now enjoying retirement in a beamed cottage overlooking the village cricket ground in sleepy Rolvenden. Derek believes that entities could be here already, helping to influence decisions at the highest level in the corridors of power.

Indeed, he thinks they may have infiltrated many aspects of our way of life, working and living among us (yes, that could mean Kent, too) for whatever their grand plan might be.

"I feel quite strongly that there could be intelligent beings living and working among us," he said. "I think they are on this planet now. I have no example in my daily life; I can only go on what seems to be happening in the world.

"I think they are penetrating our system. Some of the people we see on television, who look like we do, around key politicians, might be extraterrestrials — that is how far they have penetrated. But what I find disconcerting is the fact that, if their intentions are open and honest, why do they go about things the way they have ...and why the cover-up?"

Derek, who was chairman of the 600 (City of London) Squadron at Biggin Hill for 13 years, is finalising the manuscript for a book which he says will lift the lid on an alleged conspiracy of concealment by governments about UFOs. He reached his conclusion about an extraterrestrial infiltration while researching his earlier controversial book on philosophy called A Question of Reason.

Derek Sheffield believes extraterrestrials are already living and working among us.

It questioned the theory of evolution, taking readers through steps in the development of the universe — from the formation of galaxies to the appearance of Man on Earth. He used powerful reasoning to propound alternative hypotheses concerning such phenomena as standing stones in Europe, the immense desert drawings of Nazca in Peru and the stone heads on Easter Island.

"I was impressed by the statements of two of the greatest astrophysicists of our time, Professor Carl Sagan and Professor Bernard Lovell," he said. "Sagan used an extremely complex formula to calculate the amount of planets in our galaxy capable of supporting life and evolving intelligent extraterrestrial civilisations. Lovell quoted the odds against us evolving by chance as 130 to the power of 10. Ten to the power of 75 would cover every single hydrogen atom in the observable universe, so, in effect, the chances of us developing by chance were nil.

"Therefore, we must have come from somewhere else. This is the logical answer and this was the conclusion in the book."

Derek, who has a MENSA IQ rating of 155 — an intelligence classification which puts him in the top one per cent of the population — said our evolution took place elsewhere over a far longer period of time. "That being so and the fact that we have now explored every planet and satellite in our solar system and found none capable of supporting life, then our origins must have been in the stars.

"The evidence of existing ancient artefacts that would have been beyond the capability of prehistoric man to construct is proof of an earlier visit by an intelligent extraterrestrial entity which could, indeed, have been our predecessor.

"In chapter six of the *Book of Genesis*, it refers to the sons of God seeing that the daughters of men were fair and breeding with them and producing children. In South America Indian folklore there is an almost identical story. Who were the sons of God? I think they could have been our predecessors who came back again at that time and perhaps taught people how to farm and gave them skills. If these extraterrestrials are of our species — they must have been if they went with the daughters of man and produced offspring — they would look like you or I.

"Everything fits in so well. They look like us, so we would not recognise them. How could they be penetrating our system the way they are if they didn't look like us?"

In the last chapter of *A Question of Reason*, Derek postulated that, if our origins were in the stars, there must be a case for the existence of the UFO and he reasoned that radar evidence would establish the physical evidence of such objects.

"I received letters from three airline pilots who read my book and said that if I wanted to find out more about the radar detections of these objects, I should contact the Belgian Air Force — and that's when the fun started," he said. "I discovered something happened above Belgium that, officially, we didn't know about here, but which we *must* have known about."

He investigated three UFO cases, including one in which he says five NATO radar sites detected an object which was later described as 'hostile' by scrambled Belgian fighter pilots who chased it virtually the length of the country.

"Lots of people said it got within six miles of Dover; it didn't — it got within six *minutes* of Dover. It was flying at speeds in excess of 1,000 miles an hour so, at this speed, it was within 100 miles of Dover. It wouldn't have been sighted from Kent."

Despite official denials from the Belgian Air Force, the evidence seemed to prove that unknown objects of some kind had been in evidence above Belgium in 1989-90, but if it were such a major incident, why was it not reported in the British press?

Derek is convinced that, at senior levels of the media and government, there is an unwritten pact which says that anything contentious should be debunked: "That's exactly what has happened for the last three years on every television programme I've seen about UFOs. Every major UFO factor has been fictionalised.

"The Ministry of Defence have evaded the issue even though a chain of events links London with the Belgian incident. A 40-page report which I submitted directly to the President of the European Parliament did produce results — my application for an enquiry was referred to the Committee on Research, Technological Development and Energy for their consid- eration.

"However, it soon became apparent by their attitude that a hostility existed among various members involved and nothing was heard for two years. Last year I wrote again and stated that the same concerns applied as before, that my application should be reintroduced. The wheels are again in motion — we must wait for the outcome."

But why the earlier inaction?

"I suspect the European institutions have been penetrated by this intelligence along with so many other organisations," he said.

Derek is determined to press for more open disclosure of the facts, but, in the meantime, is concerned about the question of infiltration: "It's happened and I don't think I can do anything. I don't think any of us can do anything about it.

"Their purpose is to penetrate our whole system in a covert way. If you're talking about a race who looks the same as we do, but are as much as a million years in advance of us, you don't know how their minds are going to work.

"The people who came here all those years ago were of a different mind and intellect to the present visitors. They have changed.

"I think we have been conditioned to the point that we almost accept they are here and the situation now is the same as Mexico City — if continuous waves of these objects flew over central London, no one would turn a hair."

Really? But, if the same thing happened above Rolvenden, as happened above Belgium... wouldn't that be a story?

"I have to agree with that. It would be worth covering and no doubt the *Kent Messenger* would be there," he smiled.

Dawning of a New Age?

THE Age of Cosmic Awareness is almost upon us. That is what the calendar of the ancient Mayans forecasts, claims David Quickenden, founder member of the Margate-based group, Astrasearch — and that is what he believes.

"The Mayans have been very precise with their predictions throughout history and they predict the Age of Cosmic Awareness will start in 2012," he says. "At this time all knowledge about extraterrestrials will become universal. It will also herald our total awareness about what we call 'flying saucers'.

"I look forward to the next 15 years. I think it will be tremendous; there will be earth changes as we go through climatic adjustments, but human conciousness will prevail."

Ufology has occupied a big part of David's day since he became redundant, although he still finds time for his other great interest as second tenor in the Thanet Male Voice Choir.

The Age of Cosmic Awareness is nigh, says Astrasearch founder member David Quickenden, left, seen here with wife Freda and Mervyn Newells (East Kent UFO Research Unit) at the UFO Kent '97 conference.

"People are keen to know about ufology because they want to know the truth," he says. "There is a lot of misinformation. Knowledge is power and has been the subject of manipulation and deceit by the controlling bodies as far back as you wish to go.

"There are two sides to the coin. On the one hand, there is suppressed technology, with governments testing craft far beyond known capabilities, particularly in the United States. On the other side, more and more people are saying they have worked at secret bases, such as Area 51 (scene of the famous Roswell incident), where ETs, both dead and alive, have been seen. It is alleged that liaison has taken place between aliens and the American government."

He is not alarmed at the thought of alien visitors; in fact, he intimates that the human race could have been artificially introduced to this planet: "Where did we come from? There is a missing link in Homo Sapiens evolution — it has never been satisfactorily explained by science. There is also compelling evidence that our planet has been visited in our ancient past."

David and his wife, Freda, formed Astrasearch in 1994 to study UFOs and related phenomena. The group meets fortnightly at the Wig and Pen function room in the Market Place, Margate, and activities include an annual visit for members to the Barge Inn, Wiltshire, where members spend time with other groups from across the world on 'sky watches'.

Freda — who is a psychic ("When I was 17, I knew my father was going to die before Christmas of that year, even though he was not ill") — and her husband, together with the East Kent UFO Research Unit, staged the UFOKENT '97 conference at The Lido, Margate, in April of that year. It was the first time an event of such magnitude had been held in the county and speakers put over their views on a range of diverse subjects, from crop circles to alien abductions.

"We are very pleased with the interest shown in Kent and both groups are working hard together to make it an annual occasion," says David.

Chapter Two

MYSTERIES

Nightmare at Dream Cottage

THE claims of a man that he may have been 'zapped' with some form of microwave weapon in the woods behind his Weald house make up one of Kent's greatest mysteries of modern times.

Antony Verney eventually abandoned his cottage in Biddenden, saying he had been driven out by the military. Mr Verney stood by his claims right up to his death in his eighties in 1996.

Mr Verney and his wife, Doreen, bought Ivy Cottage, Biddenden, in 1969. The couple, who worked for Mrs Verney's textile company, H.A. Percheron in London, at first used the house as a holiday cottage for 14 years.

In the summer of 1983 they both retired, selling their flat in Bloomsbury, London, and moving down to Biddenden full time. The cottage was their dream home — set in an isolated position in a thickly wooded area. The woodland, consisting of Shorts Wood and Sandpit Wood, is a small nature reserve.

Mr and Mrs Verney spent the first few months making improvements to the cottage. Mr Verney, a writer and an inspector for the *Good Food Guide* and who had served in RAF Fighter Command during World War Two, said, "The weather was good and the weeks passed most pleasurably."

On 1 October, Mr Verney claimed, their dream came to an end. A visitor to the house noticed a strange humming over the area behind the cottage. Mr Verney said, "The humming occurred over the next four days and nights."

Five days later the Verneys went on holiday, returning on 25 October. They were greeted by the humming noise which was now much louder and extended around the cottage, at times sounding as if it came from within. In the small hours of the morning the woods would start throbbing and vibrating. The woodland to the north-east was lit by yellow and pink lights.

At the beginning of November the humming stopped, only to be replaced by a loud throbbing noise, accompanied by vibrations. The noise was at its worst in the small hours. Mr Verney claimed the noise became progressively worse during November and he became concerned that the disturbance was affecting his wife's health.

One night, Mr and Mrs Verney set out to track down the source of the problem. They met two police officers in a patrol car.

Mr Verney said, "The two policemen heard the noise, which was very loud. They thought it was coming from Shorts Wood to the north-east of the cottage. They said that they would put the matter on report and would contact us if they could locate the source."

On 26 November, Mr Verney went into Tenterden Police Station where he spoke to the station sergeant. He said, "The matter had not been put on report and I made a formal complaint in the desk book. It was not a matter for the police but the responsibility of the local environmental health department." On 28 November, Mr Verney phoned Ashford council's environmental health department. He explained the nature of the problem and left his phone number asking that somebody call him back urgently. "Nobody called me back," he said.

Mr and Mrs Verney went away on 1 December for five days. "When we came back we left further messages with the council; none were returned. The whole operation continued to worsen, life was rapidly becoming intolerable inside the house."

Then, over the weekend of 17 and 18 December, the Verneys experienced problems with their electricity supply. Mr Verney complained to Seeboard. On 20 December, Seeboard engineers worked in the woods, telling Mr Verney that they were 'putting more power into the lines'.

The supply was improved but the vibration continued and the Verneys contacted a firm of acoustic engineers in Maidstone. Mr Verney said that a representative from the firm visited him and obtained a strong reading on his instruments.

The following afternoon an environmental health officer phoned My Verney. After two conversations, Mr Verney said, the officer promised to get back in touch after Christmas.

Becoming increasingly concerned about the effect this was having on their health, the Verneys went to London to see if they could hire some equipment to measure the vibrations. In one electronics shop in Tottenham Court Road, Mr Verney explained his problem. The owner of the shop said that he thought the couple might be having trouble with the Ministry of Defence.

They were put in touch with an electronic scientist, John Dyus, who offered to come down to Biddenden after Christmas.

Mr Verney said, "I had not considered the Ministry of Defence. It would explain the reluctance of the police. The MoD would not be subject to the Control of Pollution Act or any other civil law."

The Verney's Christmas was wrecked by the vibrations which continued all day and night. Mr Verney said, "The nights were awful with lots of activity from lights."

On Boxing Day, Mr Verney witnessed a startling new phenomenon: three unidentified flying objects. He described them as horseshoe-shaped. "They were lit up, like flying 'tiaras'. They disappeared, losing height over Shorts Wood."

After Christmas the Verneys went away to a motel in Sussex and started to look for a new house. They were becoming convinced they would have to leave Biddenden. They found a house after only a few days and made a firm offer on it.

Mr Verney said, "The noise continued unabated when we returned to the cottage, complete with pink lights and the flying tiaras."

The vibrations, humming and screaming sounds continued 24 hours a day into the new year until on 5 January Mr Verney claims that he and his wife were 'zapped' by some kind of 'electromagnetic beam'. He said, "It made no noise but caused excruciating pain in the top of the head and temples, like some kind of electric drill."

They were zapped again the following night and then, on 6 January, an environmental health officer came to see the Verneys.

Mr Verney claims, "He was most unhelpful and wouldn't take any action on our behalf, claiming that he couldn't hear anything. He went, having spent less than ten minutes with us."

Meanwhile, the noises and zapping continued.

On 18 January, the scientist, Mr Dyus, came to visit. Mr Verney took him out to lunch at the Three Chimneys pub in Biddenden. "While we were there my car was broken into and a cheque book and bank statement were stolen," said Mr Verney.

When the two got to the cottage they were met by the environmental health officer who, Mr Verney claims, immediately recognised Mr Dyus. After he left, Mr Dyus made recordings of the vibrations. Mr Dyus left at 10pm and said he would analyse the recordings he had made.

The nights of pain continued. The Verneys continued to speak to the council who, during one conversation, told them that members of the public had reported sightings of UFOs over the area.

They spent much of late January and February away from Biddenden and put the house on the market on 21 March. A buyer was found and the house was sold on 2 April for completion on 24 May.

On 6 April, while the Verneys were in London, the house was broken into, although nothing was stolen except some of Mr Verney's financial papers and a bar of chocolate.

Mr Verney's diary entry for 20 May is the last he made while in Biddenden: 'About 1.30am, all hell was let loose. The noise at the highest level ever was heard, vibrations tearing through the ground of the woods towards the house at a frightening velocity, The zapper was deployed once again. The whole operation went on non-stop until 7am.'

The following week, Mr and Mrs Verney moved to Sussex.

Antony Verney's wife died in February 1996 following a stroke. Doreen Verney, having been given a clean bill of health in June 1983, suffered severe health problems in the months that followed whatever happened in Biddenden.

On 31 August 1984, she was admitted to the Fitzroy Nuffield Hospital in London where five and a half pints of fluid were drawn off her chest. She was diagnosed as suffering from lymphatic leukaemia and given only a ten per cent chance of survival. She pulled through the operation and was given two months of chemotherapy.

Mr Verney's health had suffered, too, and he had lost most of his teeth and hair during the months of problems in Biddenden. Subsequent X-rays revealed permanent damage to his spine.

Mr Verney claimed to have been subjected to repeated break-ins and thefts of personal papers even after he left Biddenden. He also claimed to have been harassed by police officers, had his phone tapped and mail interfered with.

His allegations were rejected by the Ministry of Defence, Kent Police and senior ministers including Lady Thatcher while Prime Minister. The Government blamed what he suffered on 'criminal elements' and not the 'legitimate activities of agents of the Crown'.

Over the years, Mr Verney's bizarre story has featured in a number of fringe interest magazines. Some of these magazines are well researched and make a convincing effort to get to the bottom of some of life's stranger happenings. However, others on the extreme outer fringes are less concerned with serious investigation and philosophies and act as little more than platforms for wild and sometimes highly paranoid theories, with little or no basis in fact.

During the course of the Kent Messenger Group investigation, reporters encountered a number of people who either worked for such publications or who pursued a personal interest in investigating mysterious cases.

Indeed, later owners of Ivy Cottage said the only strange occurrences they had experienced since they moved there in the late 1980s, was the unwanted — and sometimes downright frightening — attentions of 'researchers' into the Verney case. Few of the researchers, it would seem, have been willing to actually knock on the couple's door. Instead, the new owners had to endure people creeping around in the woods near their home.

Some of the fanatics of the strange and paranormal regularly get together at informal meetings to swap theories. At one such meeting at a house in Folkestone, the Verney case was retold and theories about possible causes expounded.

One gentleman, who had travelled down from Scotland for the occasion, suggested that a 6,400 mile-long underground antenna — which was, he claimed, used by the Government for 'mind control' — was responsible for the Verney's problems.

Far fetched? Possibly — he also believed that senior members of the British Establishment were 'reptoid aliens' from another galaxy and that M15 put an implant in his head when he was a baby because he was 'too intelligent'.

Going Round in Crop Circles

A LIGHT aircraft flies low over the Kent countryside. Inside, grandmother Joyce Galley focuses on the fields of wheat and barley below.

Like a safari photographer hunting leopard or rhino, she is on the lookout for another rare species... the crop circle. However, unlike some endangered species, crop circles are becoming more evident in the fields of the world.

Yet they are a fairly recent phenomenon, with a much shorter recorded history than ghosts and UFOs. Though universally known as the crop circle, 'circle' is something of a misnomer. Many are complex patterns, conforming to geometric law with a precision that baffles science. Most remain unexplained despite intensive research.

Joyce Galley, convener for the Kent branch of The Centre For Crop Circles Studies, displays some of the literature on the subject.

While Joyce is in the plane, fellow-enthusiast Andrew King, of Chatham, might be up in his microlight peering at the land below. Joyce and Andrew are in the frontline of the quest for truth, seekers after these most mysterious of formations.

Both are prominent members of the Kent branch of The Centre for Crop Circle Studies. The Centre, which calls these patterns beautiful and baffling, sums up the dilemma: "Are they a message from another reality or place, some extraordinary natural phenomenon, or part of a gigantic conspir- acy?"

Joyce is no oddball. She is a one-time nurse and retired medical journalist. She is married to a former farmer and she recalls how she became interested in crop circles.

"I saw my first pictogram on television in 1989. I'd read about them and was intrigued. I also saw something in the newspaper. I cut the piece out which is very unusual for me. I don't save newspaper cuttings as a rule.

"It was a Sunday. I left my husband and went off to Wiltshire. I thought I'd go and look round and it had the most peculiar effect on me. I hadn't seen anything quite like it before.

"It had an emotional effect which is quite unusual because I'm a bit sceptical. I thought 'what's going on?' I've never looked back since then."

She admits her husband is a practical type who remains sceptical. "He's still waiting for definite proof. Until I see something that I can connect with the circles, I have an open mind."

Sightings anywhere in the country will prompt her to take off on a journey to see them for herself. Kent has reported fewer crop formations than many other places. Joyce puts this down to the shortage of people reporting them rather than the fact that they are rarer in Kent than elsewhere. She firmly believes there are many out there in the Garden of England.

Joyce Galley, centre, and her team investigate a crop circle at Wye in 1991.

A few years ago, a sighting was reported at Wye College, the world-beating farming and horticulture campus of the University of London, near Ashford. Two crop circles had been spotted. But was it a hoax? It was claimed to have been done by two out-of-work students.

"But I haven't closed my mind to the possibility that it was something else. I've always had moments of doubt because hoaxers have been very convincing with their claims.

"Nobody has actually caught anybody in the process of making one, apart from a schoolboy who was found messing about in the corn and got roundly ticked off by the farmer."

Why are some 'circles' so intricate? "I don't discount new technology. There may be things we ordinary people don't know about, but I can't see why on earth somebody would use it to make patterns in a field. And it's such a worldwide phenomenon.

"They started as simple circles, then they got a bit more complicated. Now they are really quite intricate. People have found all sorts of geometrical proportions and ratios."

She recalls the famous formation at Barbary Castle, Wiltshire: "They were so intricate, so complex that the geometry was quite mind-boggling. I defy anybody to have done it overnight. A friend said it would have taken 20 men three weeks to have executed it.

"We haven't had many in Kent. But the problem with Kent is we have only just organised ourselves as a branch and we haven't had enough people to report sightings."

She has this plea to UFO buffs who scan the skies: "Keep your eyes on the ground as well."

While Kentish crop circles may be rare, some splendid specimens have been discovered. They have been spotted in Ashford, Maidstone and Romney Marsh. There was a fine circle in a wheat field at Seddington, near Ashford, and, in August 1996, the most intricate ever seen in Kent appeared at Thanington Without, near Canterbury.

A diagram in the winter 1996 issue of the centre's magazine, *The Circular*, shows five circles, two of which are 47 feet in diameter. Two smaller ones are 25 feet across, with the smallest 18 feet.

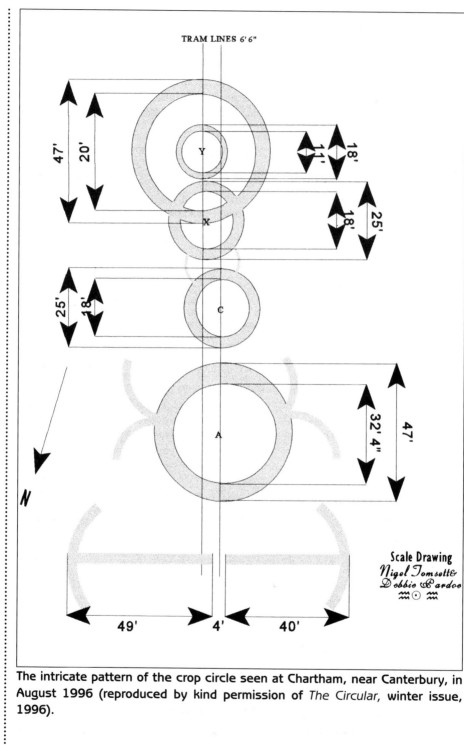

The intricate pattern of the crop circle seen at Chartham, near Canterbury, in August 1996 (reproduced by kind permission of *The Circular*, winter issue, 1996).

"There was a lot of energy in the top part of the circle," says Joyce. "One of our members went to Canterbury to speak to a local archaeologist who confirmed that this site was unique."

All sorts of reasons have been given for crop circles. Psychical, biopsychical and other scientific disciplines have been deployed in the quest for answers. An expert recently claimed that crops inside circles had different natural characteristics to those outside. An American biophysicist found that plant samples revealed several unusual findings.

A researcher reported these findings to *The Circular*: "The seed heads in the formation plants looked normal on the outside, but inside they were completely devoid of seeds, a highly unusual finding in a crop planted for commercial harvest...

"Another important discovery was the fact that something was clearly altering the normal growth and development of seeds taken from within the formations.

"Seeds germinated and followed in the laboratory for up to 14 days exhibited clear alterations in germination and growth patterns when compared to their controls sampled outside the formations."

Joyce admits that her two sons think mum is a bit weird. "But I don't think I am. You can't have weird nurses. I've never seen a ghost, but I'm longing to see one."

How does she account for crop circles? "Some say they herald the next coming of the Messiah but I'm not so sure. One thing I do know is that, since I've been involved, I've met people from all over the world. There is something in crop circles that binds everyone together. It's a nice feeling."

The Centre is anxious to attract new members to a fascinating area of the paranormal world that cannot be lightly dismissed.

A recruitment leaflet said, "We invite you to consider the evidence and make up your own mind — or, like so many already, remain open-minded, bewildered but enthralled."

The Circular puts it like this: "There are feelings of comfort, peace and well-being when sitting in a circle.

"It's a stronger feeling than the contemplation of its origin. Some people have experienced physiological effects, more have probably enjoyed these relaxing feelings simply by being in the middle of a cornfield on a summer's day in delightful countryside.

"Perhaps it is the recollection of mother/child comfort — some might say Earth Mother — in the bed of laid-down crop surrounded by a protective expanse of standing crop; a return to early childhood or cradle comfort.

"But it is also the feeling of something relatively new. Before crop circles, nobody walked into the middle of a cornfield, unless ramblers were following public rights of way which are sometimes left if they pass through crop fields.

"But nobody stopped. It was merely to walk to the other side of the field. The feelings are compounded within an intricate pictogram by corners, nooks, crannies, pathways and little alcoves …such felicity.

"Then, if you're lucky, there's the experience of the graceful waving of the immense sweep of the barley field as a light, warm breeze passes over the landscape, and perhaps the sound of the lark high overhead.

"This is the positive element to that furtive, elusive, nocturnal activity, whatever its origin and reason.

"Enjoy crop circles while we have them."

Joyce does not quibble with that.

Big Cats on the Prowl

TALES of big cats living in parts of Kent date back to the turn of the century and have long been dismissed as urban myth. But a string of sightings this decade have convinced many people that a puma or panther-like creature is on the loose in the county.

Paw prints, savaged livestock and filmed evidence have all added to the mystery and even sparked Government interest. With the growing number of reported sightings, can so many people really be mistaken?

Sightings of mysterious big cats prowling woods, gardens and streets have escalated enormously in Kent over the last six years. Conclusive evidence remains sketchy, but witnesses are convinced they have seen more than just a large domestic cat or dog and sightings have been investigated by police and Ministry of Agriculture officials.

Descriptions from the dozens of reports since 1991 have varied, but in most cases the animal is described as black and standing about three feet high.

Several possible explanations have been offered for big cats being on the loose, including escapes from zoos and cross-breeding of other wild animals. It is thought most likely that any big cats in Kent could have been released from private collections in the mid-1970s.

The highest concentration of sightings have been in the Maidstone and West Malling area and in east Kent, mainly Dover, Deal and Sandwich. A pattern has been established running through the middle of the county, creating a vague corridor along the North Downs.

Big cats were also linked to the killing of sheep in Canterbury two years ago, a possibility which was not ruled out by a vet who attended the scene.

Opinion has been divided over the filmed evidence, the most recent of which was a big cat strolling the grounds of Aylesford Priory, captured on a camcorder by holidaymaker Eddie Dedman in June 1995.

Animal welfare worker Dave Riches, from Studdal, near Deal, set up traps in a bid to catch one of the beasts. He has carried out investigations in partnership with a local police officer and believes there are at least three adult big cats living in east Kent.

Mr Riches, who runs a wildlife refuge, said, "I am more than certain that a few big cats are out there. They have been breeding and establishing their own territory — they may have been here for two or three generations. In a few years people will be seeing them all the time. So many people believe it already."

In January 1997, a Bilting farmer made a video of fresh paw prints left by an animal he had seen close to where he lives. The prints are four inches across and four inches long and the film shows the animal to have a 57-inch stride.

The farmer, who is well-known in the area, but does not want to be identified, said, "I had half been expecting to see deer tracks because of the snow, then I drove up the track and saw huge footprints. I looked up the tracks and saw this black cat, the same as I have seen previously. It was slightly smaller than an Alsatian dog."

In 1996, Mersham farmer Tom Tyrell lost nine of his flock of 22 sheep to what he believed to be a big cat. The farmer, who has spent his whole life on the land, has seen big cats on three occasions, and, in February 1992, had five sheep killed. "They were completely stripped, there was nothing left," he said.

He sees the disappearance of deer from his part of the wood as further evidence of predators.

Another farmer had casts made of prints — later confirmed as being those of a puma — found on his farm and 15 years ago a snow leopard was shot in the area.

In answer to the cynics, the Bilting farmer said, "There is absolutely no question of the prints being fakes. I am not some crank who goes out looking for big cats, I am a farmer and gamekeeper. But you get a feel for them.

"I think there are quite a few of them, not just one or two. But I do not think they would hurt anyone and the only people who have cause for alarm are owners of livestock."

He also says he has heard the animals at night: "When you do hear them it makes the hairs on the back of your neck stand on end."

Sightings seem to have become more frequent since the 1976 Dangerous Wild Animals Act. The Act tightened controls on the keeping of wild animals and it is believed some big cats may have been released by owners who could not afford to comply.

The biggest difficulty for people who have spotted big cats is trying to convince others of what they have seen. Financial advisor Grant Miles, who saw a tiger-shaped animal in Marden in August 1996, said he had had a mixed reaction.

He said, "A lot of people wind you up and think it's a big joke, but a majority have said they believe it."

Malcolm Dudding, managing director of the Big Cat Foundation in Smarden, has helped investigate several sightings. He says he remains open-minded but has never seen paw prints or droppings to suggest a big cat was living wild in the county. Many sightings have probably been large domestic cats, he claims.

"What people have been seeing is not likely to be a lion or a tiger and the sightings of something like a puma would have been more frequent," he said. "It is also unlikely that these animals would be breeding."

Parts of Kent, with dense forest would provide a suitable habitat for big cats, he added.

A spokeswoman for the Ministry of Agriculture said many sightings had been investigated in Kent but no conclusive evidence found. She said, "Reports are taken seriously, particularly in cases where farmers have had livestock killed. We will continue to investigate these incidents."

List of sightings

May 1991 — A string of sightings in the Mid-Kent area:

9 May– A nurse at Leybourne Grange Hospital, near West Malling, spots an animal which she claims could have been a leopard.

10 May — PC Ian Harvey reports a puma-like beast crossing the road in front of his patrol car along the Pilgrims' Way, Trottiscliffe.

22 May — A startled man rings police to report a puma in his back garden at Maidstone Road, Marden. Officers can find no trace of the animal.

26 May — A man reports a big cat in his garden in Snodland. He claims the beast made a hole in a hedge.

June 1991 — A rodent's remains are found in a garden at Plowenders Close, Addington. Home owner claims to have seen a big cat walking across his lawn the same weekend. A week earlier, a motorist had reported seeing a big cat cross the road on the A20 at Addington, near West Malling Golf Club.

July 1991 — Staff at a home for the elderly in Southfleet, near Gravesend, report several sightings of a black panther in their garden. Police are alerted.

August 1991 — Winifred Moss, 72, claims to have seen a big cat prowling her garden at Allington.

May 1992 — Computer analyst Maureen Tulloch reports a puma roaming in woods near Paddock Wood. Sighting is reported to police.

September 1992 — A puma is blamed for the mauling of a ginger tom in Paddock Wood. Eileen Akehurst, 56, claims to have seen a big cat near her home several days earlier.

January 1993 — Joyce Ridden reports seeing a 'lynx-like' creature at the bottom of her garden in Wigmore, near Rainham.

May 1994 — Pensioner Edith Bryant is startled by a big cat while walking near her home in Snodland.

May 1994 — Staff at a kitchen and bathroom suppliers H.M. Potts, East Malling, lay sand on their showroom car park after spotting a cat-like beast. A large footprint is found several weeks later.

June 1994 — Wildlife enthusiast Dave Riches chases but loses a big cat in the Ashley area of Dover. After more reported sightings, a police investigation begins and Mr Riches sets up big cat traps.

September 1994 — Sightings continue in the east Kent area. Plaster-casts of an animal's footprints are taken in a field near Ribble during continued investigations by Mr Riches and PC Ian Woodland. The pair claim there may be up to three big cats roaming the area.

September 1994 — Large cat spotted by motorist Graham Theobald at Upper Hardres, near Canterbury. He reported seeing the creature emerge from woodland as he drove home from a night shift.

October 1994 — A panther-type cat is spotted by several farm workers in Boughton, near Canterbury. A sighting of a similar animal is reported several weeks later near Bysing Wood lakes, Faversham.

October 1994 — Four sheep are savaged at a field in Bridge, near Canterbury, only days after a black puma-type animal is spotted in the area. Vet Patricia Cornwell says the injuries could have been caused by a feral dog or a large cat-like animal.

June 1995 — Retired BBC television worker Eddie Dedman films a big cat on his camcorder while walking at Aylesford Priory. He is convinced it is either a puma or a panther.

– Solicitor Henry Moorhead, 39, spots a leopard-like creature while walking his dogs near his home in Smeeth, near Ashford.

August 1995 — Former police dog handler Damon Hadlow, 26, claims to have seen a black panther in Bearsted. Sighting is backed up by

Andrea Chambers, who claims to have spotted a big cat in fields in the village.

September 1995 — A couple claim to have seen a big cat 'four times the size of a retriever' while walking in Shipbourne, near Tonbridge.

October 1995 — An anonymous motorist reports seeing a puma in his headlights as he drives between Cliftonville and Kingsgate, near Margate.

April 1996 — Financial advisor Grant Miles, 29, claims to have spotted a big cat walking across a horse training area in Marden. He said, "I definitely saw a big cat — I'm not a nutter and wouldn't make something like this up."

January 1997 — Farmer reports seeing big cat, slightly smaller than an Alsatian dog, in Bilting area.

A Burning Question

CAN a living person be reduced to ashes by spontaneous human combustion (SHC) — a killer blaze emanating from the body? Although Government scientists reject such a phenomenon, the number of claimed SHC cases is growing. Let us look at the file on Barry Soudain.

The harrowing scene that greeted Reg Gower in 1987 was to haunt him for the rest of his life. In the kitchen behind his Folkestone bakery lay the body of a man so badly burned his upper body was almost entirely a charred black mass. Only the dead man's training shoes and the remains of his corduroy trousers gave any indication of his identity. The shock of the gruesome sight is said to have hastened Mr Gower's own early death some years later.

What was extraordinary was that, apart from the charred body, only a plastic air vent in a wall showed any signs of fire damage. A nearby tea towel showed no sign of scorching and a plastic dustpan and brush lying inches from the body were undamaged by heat. Could the dead man have been the victim of spontaneous human combustion?

The post-mortem examination report by pathologist Dr Michael Heath mentioned the products of fire in the larynx and upper part of the remaining trachea. A former police officer claimed the findings suggested Mr Soudain had inhaled the products before his death. He also argued that Mr Soudain, who was Mr Gower's tenant, burned upwards and not down- wards 'like a candle' as stated at his inquest.

The medical and forensic establishments, however, are not convinced of arguments for the existence of SHC, despite other claimed cases worldwide.

Kent Police Sergeant Nigel Cruttenden, the scenes of crime detective who dealt with Mr Soudain's death, is among those who are sceptical. Sergeant Cruttenden, whose 11 years as a SOCO included three at the Home Office forensic laboratories at Aldermaston as a police liaison officer, was nevertheless surprised at the unusual circumstances.

"I haven't seen anything like it since," he said. "But I feel there is a rational explanation."

Nearly ten years on, Sergeant Cruttenden has not forgotten the bizarre scene which confronted him on 28 December 1987.

"When you went into the kitchen it was quite small," he recalled. "The room wouldn't have been more than seven feet wide with the sink on one side and a kitchen unit on the other. There was a gap of 3ft 2ins between the two.

"At the far end was the body of a male lying there. He had been fully dressed and his head was towards the rear wall. The upper body had suffered severe fire damage; the face was unidentifiable, the rib cage had burned away but the legs were not so badly burned."

The extensive burns meant Mr Soudain had to be identified by the training shoes he had bought from Mr Gower's stepson. Tests revealed Mr Soudain, a former Army man, had the equivalent of 17 single measures of spirits in his bloodstream. He was an alcoholic. The blood sample was also found to be ten per cent saturated with carbon monoxide. This is a level associated with a heavy smoker.

The forensic science laboratory's report concluded neither levels were sufficiently high to have killed him. Despite tests, due to the severity of the injuries the pathologist was unable to give the inquest a cause of death.

Having ruled out murder and suicide, Sergeant Cruttenden suggested it was likely Mr Soudain had died of a natural cause, such as a heart attack and caught himself alight on the hob. There were, however, he admits no pieces of clothing on the stove to corroborate this.

Sergeant Cruttenden added, "I considered SHC but, theoretically, it is impossible. After speaking to the pathologist and a Home Office scientist we dismissed it because there is no scientific evidence."

Coroner Brian Smith, who recorded an open verdict at the inquest, said the case was particularly perplexing although he did not accept there was any scientific evidence for such a phenomenon.

He said, "Had there been an ignition and something of a blaze in the kitchen and Mr Soudain had expired from carbon monoxide inhalation, I might have taken the view that it was accidental death."

The coroner was also mystified as to how a kettle on a gas ring, which was still alight, had not boiled dry despite the fact Mr Soudain's body had lain for some time before being discovered.

"One would have expected the flame to go out because you can't have a flame without oxygen to feed it." Mr Smith said. "This is one of the major puzzles."

Numerous cases of spontaneous human combustion have been claimed all over the world throughout history. One of the earliest cases recorded is that of the Countess Cornelia de Bandi in Italy in 1731.

Her sparse remains, a pile of ashes next to her bed, were found by her maid one morning. The case was meticulously investigated by Giuseppe Bianchini, a prebendary of Verona, in the same year.

The novelist Charles Dickens was one of many over the years fascinated by the topic. In *Bleak House* he famously described the death of Mr Krook, an eccentric marine store dealer, through spontaneous human combustion.

The description and propagation of the phenomenon was to upset his friend George Lewes and several letters passed between them.

In a later preface Dickens defended his description and denied wilfully or negligently misleading his readers. He said, "Before I wrote that description, I took pains to investigate the subject."

Return to Ancient Rome

WHEN the dolphin flipped over to signal the last lap and Charlton Heston finally threw off the manic challenge from baddie Stephen Boyd, the crowd roared — and *Ben Hur* entered into film history.

Jack Pleasant, like all those now in middle age, sat through the most exciting race ever seen on the silver screen and still remembers every turn on the circuit and every skirmish among the charioteers.

The big difference between Jack and the rest of us, however, is that he thinks he was actually there …or rather that he was in ancient Rome when such races were held and was himself a charioteer.

It is an extraordinary belief to hold for this long-time Kent investigative journalist and writer who admits: "I've always been sceptical about the various cases I've covered." Yet, Jack, who has recently moved over the border to live in Peasmarsh, East Sussex, is as convinced as anyone could be that he took part in chariot races — and was pretty good at it, too.

He found out about his colourful past when he went to Croydon to interview representatives of the Foundation for Global Unity for a women's magazine three years ago.

"They insisted they take people both forward and backward in time," said Jack. "They do not use hypnosis, but most of the people they see have had previous lives and, just as I was leaving after doing the interview, they asked if I would like to experience it myself."

Despite some initial reticence, Jack decided to have a go.

"So, these two ladies sat there, directing, as they put it, spiritual energy at me through the palms of their hands. They did not put their hands on me; they sat at a distance.

"And, much to my amazement, within a minute I was pouring out all this material. I was a charioteer in ancient Rome! My name was Flavius and my wife was Arcadia. I had two little kids, both boys and both fair.

"I can still envisage it now and immediately bring to mind what my wife looked like. She was a little, plump woman …dark hair, brown dress, sandals, very flimsy sandals, with coloured straps on them.

"We lived in a villa with pillars and I remember the coloured mosaic floor.

Journalist Jack Pleasant remembers being a charioteer in ancient Rome.

"I must have been in my early 30s or late 20s and I can recall the actual racing with one brown horse and one white one, which is a bit strange, having two differently coloured horses; you would have thought they would have been both the same if you had been making it up.

"I remember the excitement of racing through clouds of dust around the arena to the cheers of the crowd."

Unlike the popular image of olive-skinned Mediterranean people, Jack, curiously, was fair, with blond curly hair. He must have cut a fine figure as he steered his steeds towards the starting line wearing what he described as 'a sort of tunic with edging'.

An interesting aspect was that he remembers being poured some wine after a race by a servant girl. "She had this ornamental jug — I can see the neck and handle now — which had a big dent in the side. You think to yourself, if you're fantasising, do you dream up a dent in a metal jug? Wouldn't it have been perfect?

"I seem to have been quite good as a charioteer, something of a favourite."

Jack was obviously well regarded among the Roman hierarchy because he was entrusted with taking a package of important documents all the way to Amiens in France as part of an entourage. He recalls riding on horseback and remembers the wheels of the wagons 'being solid, with a big wooden spindle going through them'.

It was a long journey, but, eventually, tired and dusty, the caravan arrived at Amiens — only to be met with French disdain.

"They were not too pleased to see me for some reason or other and not very charitable about giving us any food. I said, 'We've come all this way from Rome and you're not happy to give us anything to eat.' I was a bit annoyed."

The story moves on to modern times when, a few months after his regression, Jack went on a press trip to France. He was in a tour coach and 'dozing away' when the guide brought him to his senses by declaring, "We are now on the road to Amiens and up there, on the left, are the remains of a Roman fort."

Was this the fort Jack and his entourage had trekked to many hundreds of years ago?

"Who knows? But it was a bit of a coincidence," he said. "It does make you wonder if you've seen *Ben Hur* too many times, because people do fantasise. I can't explain it, but I have clear memories of it."

Aside from his own extraordinary case, Jack has a file of strange incidents gathered over many years in his capacity as an investigator into the paranormal. Among the most unusual is the story of Deirdre Morris, a widow from Tunbridge Wells, about whom he has written articles on two separate subjects.

In the first instance, he visited her shortly after her husband, David, died because she was experiencing poltergeist-type phenomena at home, including the mysterious movement of pieces on a chessboard.

The pieces on the chess board move mysteriously at Deirdre Morris's home. She believes it is the work of her late husband.

After the death of her husband, Deirdre left the board set up for the next game he never played. And yet, regularly in the mornings when she got up, the black and white pieces had been moved.

Deirdre and David used to play chess together and she is certain his spirit is responsible for arranging the pieces on the board. She lives alone and nobody else could be moving them. "She believes he is moving the chessmen to let her know he is still around," said Jack.

David was very keen on roses and Deirdre claims she once found her sink full of rose petals. On another occasion, there was a flower next to the plate she had set out the previous night for breakfast.

"David hated leaving a gap in the curtains downstairs in case people looked in from the outside," said Jack. "So, Deirdre would throw the curtains together in a casual fashion and go off to the supermarket, but when she came home, the curtains had been pulled together tightly, as if to say, 'That's not good enough, I'll just straighten them up'. She might even leave them open and she'd find them pulled together."

Some time later, Jack went to see Deirdre about another odd incident. "She always had an interest in Japan and, in fact, the house was full of Japanese figures and paintings. She told me she had been meditating in the garden and had had a mental picture of an ancient Japanese monk in a gown. Suddenly, her mind was full of poetry and she felt this overwhelming need to rush indoors and write it all down."

Among the pieces she wrote were the following:

'In our lives, strangers are often friends and friends strangers.

'Why complain about the coldness of a snowflake on the cheek when such beauty is held in a single drop of water?

'Spring is like a young woman setting forth to meet her lover, soon her beauty will fade as the blossoms and the veil of autumn will come upon all.

'It is better for one eye to see clearly than two eyes to see nothing'.

After her revelation in the garden, Deirdre got in touch with an expert on Japanese literature in Tokyo and was told the work was similar to that of a monk called Ryokan who died in 1831.

Jack said, "He wrote things like this:

'Watching children happily playing, soon my eyes fill with tears.

'I came to admire the pink blossoms, but light spring snow has fallen, the cherry trees are wearing white coats.

'He is only a straw hat and a torn coat, but the scarecrow is good at his job'.

"As you can see, it's a very similar style."

A local medium told Jack that he believed Deirdre was being inspired by Ryokan. He said spirits seemed to find it easier to communicate to people who had interests similar to their own when they were alive. It was significant that she had always been fond of poetry and Japan; this had drawn the monk Ryokan towards her.

Jack added, "This is a fascinating case. She's a very sincere woman and there is no reason why she should make up these things."

In another case, also in Kent, Jack went to see a man who had uncovered, in his garden, a slab with curious properties.

"The garden was overgrown and he found the slab when he was clearing things up. When he moved it, he found a shaft. He didn't know what it was, whether it was a well or whatever, but he got a rope and started going down.

"He got a little way, but found it very eerie so came back up again. He went into the house and told his wife about it, but she interrupted before he could finish and said, 'Yes, some funny things have been going on in here, too. All the clocks and watches in the house stopped at once!'"

The couple tried to restart the timepieces, but without success. Two days after the slab had been raised, the clocks were still silent.

"The chap thought he'd better put the slab back before anyone fell down the hole and, would you believe, as soon as the slab was in position, all the clocks and watches started again!

"Now, that is inexplicable. That can't be coincidence, can it?"

With the typical cynicism of a respected, hard-nosed journalist of many years' standing, Jack retains his healthy inclination to question the truth of claims of fact, but now admits, "I've come to the conclusion that when you die some sort of essence is left behind."

He is not sure if it is reincarnation or just the act of tapping into this 'essence' of a previous life, perhaps left by someone else.

"Children and animals seem to be tuned into these things, but you lose it as you get older," he said.

"I have sat in on regressions and I don't know what it is — whether you are tapping into something or not — but you have to accept the fact that people do come out with these things.

"For instance, there's a lady in Liverpool who thinks she went down on the *Titanic* in a previous life. She had an inexplicable fear of water so she asked a hypnotherapist to see if there was something in her life that might have given her this fear.

"He took her back and went past this life, apparently, to when she said her name was Lucy Latimer, a young girl living in an obscure village called St Kew Highway in Cornwall. She seems to have fallen in love with a local farm worker, they eloped and it appears as if she went down on the *Titanic* because she remembers screaming, 'The ship's sinking, the ship's sinking!'

"I had never heard of this Cornish village, but the interesting point is she found that it did exist and she went there.

"She said she had lived in a house called Lanarth and when she went to the village, sure enough, she found a house called Lanarth, which is now the Lanarth Hotel."

When 'Lucy' asked the owner to take her around, she said she felt there should be a pond in the garden. The owner said there used to be one, but they had filled it in two years previously.

Jack remembers one particular case with fondness. It concerned a couple who ran a lawnmower business in Cardiff and were amazed to be showered with money out of thin air.

"As you might expect, after they had got over the shock, they were quite pleased; they would get a fiver fall out of nowhere and also pound coins. They had £70 in a fortnight," said Jack. "They called the poltergeist Pete."

The coins were always hot (there are reports of such items, called 'apports', which suddenly materialise, having been transported from one place to another).

Eventually, the couple moved because the lease was increased so much they could not afford to stay there …even with Pete's generous handouts.

Jack added, "The couple did some research and found that a 12-year-old boy had been killed on a nearby bridge. The wife's brother claims he was in the shop once when he felt someone looking down at him. He turned around and there was a boy, dressed just like Richmal Compton's 'William', with a cap and socks and everything, sitting on a shelf. He thought he was Pete.

"It was a strange story, but a nice one, because they were pleased to have him. They still wonder if he's piling up the money for somebody else."

Chapter Three

GHOSTS

A Policeman's View

WHEN you have been investigating ghosts for more than 30 years, you are entitled to a high degree of respect in the world of the unexplained.

And so it is with Dennis Chambers, a long-time member of the Society for Psychic Research, author of *Haunted Pluckley*, lecturer on psychic matters and ghost tour organiser. Dennis, who lives in Loose, near Maidstone, has another attribute — he is a retired police officer.

It is this background, the analytical observation, the training to recognise the salient features of an incident, which lends considerable credence to the evidence of the paranornmal which he has compiled over the years.

The story begins in 1966. While his fellow police colleagues were fighting crime on the streets around Manchester, Dennis had an even more chilling struggle on his hands at home. His father had died unexpectedly, although it had been predicted by a local clairvoyant, and the experience had led him and his wife to experiment with a ouija board.

What began as an occasional evening's entertainment with friends and family became something of an embarrassment when one of the 'spirits' revealed himself to be a former tennis club member known to

Dennis Chambers, a former police officer, has been studying ghosts for more than 30 years.

one of the sitters. His messages and jokes were personal and in bad taste, said Dennis, and he became a nuisance at a number of subsequent sittings.

"When we threatened to end one session, the glass spelled out an apology and a plea to my wife, 'Sonia, Sonia, please!' Did he need help? The only way we could think of assisting was to offer a prayer and so we did. That was the last time he communicated through the glass," said Dennis.

However, later that night Sonia, who was wide awake in bed, suddenly saw an apparition just a few feet from her bed. It was the face of a man, suspended in mid-air between the carpet and ceiling. He seemed to be in his early 30s and he had light brown hair, with bushy eyebrows. The eyes were bright blue and the face appeared to be lit from within, like a colour transparency held up to the light.

Sonia said that, as she turned away, the forename of the man who had caused trouble at the sitting came into her mind. When she dared to look again, the face had gone. Later, when she sketched the face, the sitter who knew him said it resembled the man at the tennis club.

This scary incident was nothing to what followed.

"Getting involved in the ouija board threw up problems for us," said Dennis. "I think it provided an invitation to things that were not there before. We had all kinds of experiences, including bright flashes of light. We were having noises around the house, really evil smells that couldn't be traced back to anything normal.

"I was a police dog handler at the time and had a highly-trained animal. We were champions and I never had any trouble with my dog, but he became disobedient and seemed to be responding to orders that I hadn't given."

Obviously deeply concerned at what was happening, Dennis made contact with the local branch of the National Spiritualists' Union for help and guidance.

"A group came and held a clearance seance. It took two or three sessions. The house became clear, the smells changed from quite offensive to something like beautiful flowers, the noises subsided along with the activity around us."

From that point on, Dennis joined the spiritualist association and began to develop his psychic skills. "I was still a police officer and this was one of the difficulties. There was a lot of press interest and I had to be very cautious about what was said. Being in that profession at that time, you didn't talk about such matters unless you were sure. It can cause all kinds of problems if you do."

Shortly after the house noise problems, Dennis sought a transfer and moved to Kent where he linked up with a number of people who had shown an interest in his ghostly investigations in the North. "One was Jack Hallam, who was picture editor of the *Sunday Times* and also an author on the subject. Unfortunately, Jack has since passed away, but he had written a paperback, which provided a guided ghost tour of an area in Kent and when I came to the county I decided to establish a ghost tour of my own."

The tours have now been going for more than 20 years and centre on the Maidstone area, particularly Pluckley, which has the reputation of being the most haunted village in England, a claim Dennis says is a sound one.

"The general idea of the tours is not to take people along with the promise of seeing anything, but to enlighten them about what is said to have happened at the various places ...to give them a period of entertainment at the same time as being informative. Everything I do on the tour is from belief; I either believe it 100 per cent or it's a story I pass on as I have received it."

The ghosts of Pluckley number 12 in total, according to local claims.

"They are the characters you would expect to find as part of normal village life — for instance, a schoolteacher, the bride of the lord of the manor (known as the Red Lady), the miller, a coach and horses, a highwayman," said Dennis.

"There are two routes for the coach and horses. One route runs along the Charing to Smarden road, passing an old forge en route and the other is reported to be along a stretch of old Roman road behind property near to the Pinnock Bridge on the Pluckley to Egerton road.

"I don't know of anyone who has seen the Charing Road coach and horses, but in 1977 a man claimed he saw a two-wheeled carriage pulled by one horse cross the lane on the Bethersden road. It came from Pond House, along the drive of what was an old rectory following an old road which was closed off with an iron gate. Its passage would have been impeded, but it went straight across and through."

The Black Horse, at Pluckley, is reputed to be haunted, along with several other places in the village.

The ghost of Dickie Buss, the miller, no longer appears. He was also the village baker and his bakery was just across the road from the Black Horse pub which has its own ghost.

After Mr Buss's death, the mill fell into disrepair, but it was said that the miller could be seen walking around the parapet of the building. Eventually, the mill was struck by lightning and was demolished; bungalows are now on the ground where it once stood. But there is a lane, called Dickie Buss's Lane, where it is reported that a schoolteacher hanged himself in a tree about 150 years ago.

"When I was researching for my book, back in 1984, I spoke to an elderly gentleman in the village who, as a schoolboy, recalls seeing the schoolmaster being cut down from the branches of a tree and put on an old gate and carried off," said Dennis. "So, here we leap from one version saying it was 150 years ago to another within the span of a person's lifetime."

Of all the ghosts in Pluckley, Dennis has two favourites — the highwayman and the Watercress Woman. "The highwayman is not to be confused with the typical type, with a tricorn hat, pistols in his hand and

The Gambling family, Gerry, Laura and daughter Joanne, who run the Black Horse. Laura heard ghostly noises on her first night at the pub.

riding a horse. He is more of a footpad and he used to hide himself in the hollow of a tree at Fright Corner, on the road from Pluckley to Smarden where a right fork takes you towards Egerton.

"The corner is very near to two woods, one of which was called Screaming Woods and the other called Fright Woods. Today it's known as Frith Woods.

"The highwayman would wait for people to go past and then would sneak out behind, sword in hand, and demand whatever they were carrying. His reputation spread far and wide and one particular traveller decided not to get caught by this ploy. He pretended to walk past the tree, but when he got alongside, he drew out his own sword and thrust the blade into the hollow.

"There was a scream, the blade came out bloody and the highwayman was no longer, in the physical sense, able to pester anyone

— but he remained in spirit form. Around the area, it is said you could hear the piercing scream, groans and then silence."

The Watercress Woman was reputed to sit on a bridge above a stream called Pinnock's Stream on the road towards Egerton.

Quite an odd character, she would gather watercress from the stream and then sell it to the nearby households. One of her traits was to smoke a pipe and she, apparently, also liked a drop of gin.

One day, while enjoying a puff after a day's labours, a spark from the pipe ignited her gin-sodden shawl and she went up in a ball of flame. Soon after, there were sightings at the bridge of an image of a woman surrounded by fire, which gradually diminished to an outline and then disappeared. However, no such sightings have been reported in recent years.

In addition to his expertise on Pluckley, Dennis is often asked on his tours about the famous Blue Bell Hill ghosts. "This tragic story goes back to 19 November 1965, when three young girls had a fatal accident by the Lower Bell public house," said Dennis. "One of the girls was due to marry that weekend."

It would be easy to imagine spectral visitors in the mist-shrouded churchyard at Pluckley.

The Red Lady is reputed to haunt the area between the village church at Pluckley and the Black Horse pub.

(Copies of Haunted Pluckley, by Dennis Chambers are available from the Black Horse, priced £1).

Dennis has serious doubts about the various reports by drivers who claim to have picked up ghostly girls on or around the hill.

"One story is that a girl gets in the car, chatters away and asks to be taken to Maidstone. She then disappears when the car reaches the County Hall area. The other young lady is much quieter. She wants to go to an address which she gives near to Rochester airport.

"Having been driven most of the distance, but before reaching the estate where she lived, the driver is said to have become aware of a change of atmosphere in the car, that he is alone — it is not the silence that brings attention, but the change of atmosphere.

"When you look at it, there are so many loopholes in these stories. For instance, why has it only happened to a single individual driver and the girl has always got into the back seat?

"If someone sat alongside you in the passenger seat you would be physically aware of her disappearance. Always it's the back seat, but, more often than not, if you are giving a person a lift, you have them sit next to you. You open the passenger door, you don't say, 'Jump in the back'.

"I dispute that those drivers who, in recent times, claimed experiences on Blue Bell Hill (assuming that they travelled the main road) have met the original ghosts of the 1965 tragedy. A couple of years after that incident, the route was diverted from the old road, which passed in front of the Lower Bell public house to make use of the newly-created dual carriageway which has since carried the bulk of the traffic.

"Very little traffic now travels along the stretch of road on which the accident happened.

"Recent reports have included collisions with young girls, an old 'hag', etc. As well as ghosts not being likely to change the locations of their hauntings, they are also not likely to change their age.

"The young ladies who perished in that fatal accident were around the 20 years-of-age mark. I do not dispute the possibility that the people who have reported these incidents have had an experience of a similar nature, but I do say that they should not be automatically linked to the 1965 event — which is what the media seems to like to rush to do.

"In general terms, those who report giving lifts to the victims of accidents like the Blue Bell Hill one are experiencing the phenomena known as the 'Phantom Hitch-hiker' which is common throughout the world, although there might be variations to the way it presents itself.

"It is the type of incident you expect to find at the scene of an accident — one of the victims flagging down someone for a lift to continue the journey."

In all his years of research, Dennis believes he has seen only one ghost. That was in the early days, around the time of the noisy house near Manchester. He and his wife were in the lounge one evening when they sensed something in the room. Their youngest child's pram was under the front window and, to their surprise, it began to rock.

"Suddenly this little face appeared around the edge of the hood and looked at us. It was a child's face, but it was not our child," said Dennis.

"We went out later to a psychic session and when we arrived, before we had spoken to anyone, one of the regular sitters, whose spirit guide was a very young child, said in this childish voice, 'I was in your place tonight!'"

Dennis says the subject of ghosts does not keep him awake at night, even though he has had some strange experiences.

"If you examine the possibilities, you have to ask yourself what are these ghosts? What we are really talking about are deceased relatives, friends, people with whom we have worked, people with whom we have socialised. It is purely the fact that their state is the state of the unknown.

"Some of these people don't know they are dead. That's why I am against the rush to exorcism because, to me, it is like taking a sledgehammer to crack a walnut. The service of exorcism is about driving out evil spirits and I think before you take any remedial action, you have got to diagnose first and be sure there is something to get rid of — and you've got to be sure that whatever's there is evil.

"To be regarded as evil just because the state of your presence doesn't fit with the general picture of 'normality' would not be easy to accept and would likely prove greatly distressing to say the least.

"When people ask me what I think ghosts are, I say that the truth is in each and every one of us — that we have a far broader life than we acknowledge at a conscious level. The gap between Nature and normality to us may be just another plane, another state of existence. I see nothing wrong with the theory that worlds can be intertwined."

The above interview was conducted at the Black Horse public house. As it was taking place, the landlady revealed that, on her first night at the pub, she heard unexplained noises while she was upstairs.

Laura Gambling, from Folkestone, now runs the Black Horse with her husband Gerry and daughter Joanne. She said, "I could hear lots of running about which I assumed was downstairs, but the running seemed to approach the door of the room where I was and I imagined somebody would come through it at any time.

"I was most surprised when I went down and asked my husband if he had been upstairs and he said 'No'. It was about nine o'clock.

"There were people downstairs in the bar, but no customer would normally come upstairs because it's private. I had heard about the pub's reputation for ghosts but they do not worry me. There is a room upstairs in which there is a strange atmosphere and this room could have been our bedroom, but I chose not to go in. Generally, though, the atmosphere is lovely, so if there is something around, it's got to be friendly."

Jackie Oliver, the cleaner at the pub, said she had also experienced a ghostly presence at the Black Horse. "It was in the fireplace where I was cleaning the brass horse on the wall. Someone came up to me and touched my shoulder from behind. It was just a pat, but when I looked round, there was no one there. I think it was trying to attract my attention and ask me something."

Ghost Rider: The Movie

IT WAS early evening in the summer of 1985 and a slight chill had fallen over Cobham Manor riding school near Maidstone. The riders were making another circuit of the paddock. The fading sun sent long grey shadows across the sand ring. The trees and scrub to one side of the ring darkened as the sun dipped lower in the west.

This remarkable photograph appears to show a ghostly Quaker-like figure in the centre. It is taken from Martin Emmott's original videotape, itself recorded by a 1980s Canon video camera.

Barry Hollis, the Kent Messenger Group's picture editor, explained how he took the picture from the tape: "The moving image was frozen on a Sony video player using the still frame mode. I used a Nikon 801 35mm camera with an 80mm F1.8 Nikon lens to focus on the Sony Trinitron television screen. The exposure was 1/15 sec at f4 using Fuji 400 ISO daylight negative film."

Trevor Sturgess writes: 'Although not perfect, this photographic image, or videograb, is close to the quality captured on Mr Emmott's video. I was originally sceptical over claims that ghosts had been faithfully captured on film without the intervention of any technical wizardry. But that mysterious figure, so lifelike, has made me think again. Seeing it for the first time in Mr and Mrs Emmott's home gave me an eerie feeling.

"A lot of highly rational, technical people have examined the image. But no one has yet come up with any explanation other than a supernatural being...'

There was no road or pathway beyond the scrub. But it was not far from the ancient Pilgrim's Way hewn out of downland chalk and fringed by trees.

Down the centuries, the ancient track known to millions through Chaucer's *Canterbury Tales* had been trodden by the feet of rich and poor alike.

Many had journeyed from Winchester to Canterbury to see the last resting place of murdered Archbishop St Thomas A'Becket in Britain's most famous cathedral.

But it was no ordinary riding lesson that Sunday in August. For Janet Emmott, it was the first time on horseback since her teenage years.

"It was my first lesson after 20 years of not riding," she recalls. "You ride as a teenager and then give up. My daughter started riding so I decided to join her that day."

Up at Cobham Manor, beautifully situated close to the North Downs, she and Kirsten, then aged ten, circled their mounts. Outside the ring, Janet's husband Martin was pressing the record button on his camcorder. He did not normally video 'everything that moved', but he wanted to capture Janet's return to the saddle, so he panned the riders as they made several circuits, proudly watching his wife and daughter through the viewfinder.

It should have been just another home movie. But it became a movie like no other, provoking debate and controversy and triggering one of the biggest paranormal mysteries ever known in Kent.

As the sun disappeared over the horizon, the lesson ended and the family went home. The following day, with Martin out of the county on work, Janet settled down at home in Weavering, near Bearsted, to watch the video and relive those exciting moments on horseback. What she saw was not what she expected.

"There it was, clear as clear," she recalls. "Martin rang me and I said jokingly, 'Did you realise there's a ghost on the video?'"

What she had seen was one of the few instances of an unexplained presence captured on film — and it remains a mystery to this day. Looking very much like a Pilgrim Father, or a 17th-century preacher, or perhaps a Quaker, the white-haired figure with starch-white cravat stands at the edge of the scrub.

It is no trick of the light. Every avenue of technology has been explored to dash the theory, but nothing has yet explained away the figure in black. Martin took the video to experts at the television studios in Vinters Park, Maidstone. "They put it on their enhancing equipment and said, 'Yes, it's definitely a figure'.

"And they added, 'Did you realise that the previous time you panned past that spot, there's what appears to be its head coming out of the ground?'"

Janet, a policeman's daughter very much accustomed to evidence in black and white, thinks back to that day: "I can guarantee there was nothing there at the time. I know that. It's such a puzzle.

"I felt really creepy when I saw it. I'm still not a believer in ghosts but I can't explain what's on that video. But if something was there, why didn't the horses react? They are normally spooked by strange things.

"I can't imagine what it is. It isn't a trick of the light. It's too clear. It actually has form but I can't explain it. I'm a very rational person and I like cut and dried explanations for everything. This isn't rational."

Janet and Martin Emmott return to Cobham Manor Riding Centre. The video 'ghost' appeared close to where the horses are in the background.

Martin has delved into books for the answer, but so far the clue to the figure's identity remains elusive. He is a practical man, but the video ghost is not his only brush with the equestrian paranormal. Years ago, he recalls, a rider tried to get his horse to jump a gate at the point where Weavering Street meets Ware Street, Bearsted, but the rider fell, broke his neck and died. It was said that the tragic incident could be seen and heard years after.

"We used to stable a horse in that area," Martin recalls. "One winter's morning, I took it up to the fields. It was about half-past four in the morning. There was no moon. I got to the crossroads and stopped to make sure there was no traffic.

"A voice called out, 'Are you real?' I said, 'Yes.' It was a neighbour, Barry King, from up the road.

"He then said, 'It wasn't you who frightened old Charlie the other morning, was it? He could hear this horse breathing and clip-clopping but he couldn't see a thing. He thought it was that ghost.'"

Martin has also felt touched by the spirit of the dead during visits to the Somme battlefield in Northern France and the tombs of ancient Egypt. Others have felt the same. But he is still perplexed by his video ghost.

"If anybody took the thing apart frame by frame and said it wasn't a ghost but a reflection of the light off a tree, or a hologram, I wouldn't mind. It would just be nice to have an explanation. But I don't suppose that will happen because it doesn't fit in with any known or read-about situation. The animals went straight past, and animals are supposed to be sensitive to ghosts. We saw nothing at the time.

"It doesn't fit in with normal accepted ghost appearances. It's a bit of a puzzle. We've never seen sight nor sound of it since, even though we've been back to the riding school many times."

The Emmotts are quite proud of their ghost. It frequently crops up in dinner conversation. Said Janet, "You forget about it for a while then someone will mention ghosts and you say, 'Oh, we've got a ghost.' Neither of us are ghost freaks or into the paranormal."

But they have to admit that something very strange happened that summer Sunday.

Haunted Pubs, Theatres and Stores

THE Ghost Club was founded in 1862 and is the oldest body of its kind in the country. Its aim is to research the inexplicable — particularly psychic phenomena. Crop circles, UFOs, the Loch Ness Monster and poltergeists are other subjects of interest.

Past members include Charles Dickens, Sir Arthur Conan Doyle, Air Chief Marshall Lord Dowding, Sir Julian Huxley, Professor C.E.M. Joad, Beverly Nichols and W.B. Yeats. Among present members is the explorer Colonel Blashford Snell. Membership is by invitation only and sceptics are as welcome as believers in the paranormal.

One dark Friday night, acting on information received, members descended upon Shepherd Neame's Faversham brewery. A *Kent Messenger* reporter joined them and compiled the following:

We are in the corridor by the office of the chairman of Shepherd Neame, Britain's oldest brewery. It is 4.45am and we are holding a seance. It is a last, tired attempt to establish contact with any ghost that may haunt the old building.

We have blundered our way through the twisting, snagging corridors to the bar in search of a wine glass, we have found a small polished table and have written out the letters of the alphabet and the numbers 1 through 10 on strips of Post-it notes.

Steve and Yvonne sit down, a finger each on the glass. Norman stands over them, illuminating the table in the spill of light from his torch. Ruth asks the questions. Michael is standing back and Cliff, who is none-too-keen on seances, holds a notepad, ready to record any answers.

Outside, the early morning traffic is just beginning. Inside there is a feeling that time is running out; that soon, cleaners and early risers will be slipping in, turning on the lights, banging doors, powering up vacuum cleaners and computers — shattering the silence. This is a last gasp call.

"Is anybody there?"

"Is anybody there who would like to talk to us?"

The glass is motionless.

"We are your friends."

"Did you work here?"

"Are you attracted to this place?"

"Is there anybody there?"

The only movement comes from the light in Norman's hand.

Norman and Yvonne take over the table.

"Is there anybody there?"

"Is there anybody there? Would you like us to go to the boardroom?"

"You can talk to us."

Then Norman and Trevor:

"Is there anybody there?"

"We are your friends. We want to help you."

"Are you trapped?"

"You know we are here. Surely you would like to talk to us?"

Ruth and Yvonne:

"Is there anybody there?"

Was that a movement? No one is sure.

"Is anybody there?"

"We are your friends and want to help you."

Nothing. Stillness crushes down on tired eyes.

This is when the decision is taken to pick up the table, complete with Post-It letters and numbers around its edge, and carry it along the corridor, down the stairs, and into the boardroom.

A night watchman studies our passage without comment. All night the security guards have quietly and respectfully allowed the club to rummage where they will.

Now Trevor and Yvonne are at the table, with Ruth asking the questions. Perhaps, because of the furniture-moving shuffle, the mood has changed.

"Is there anybody there who would like to talk to us?"

Nothing.

"I think that's a resounding No," says Trevor.

Norman joins Trevor and Yvonne:

"Is there anybody there who would like to talk to us?"

Ruth joins the circle:

"Is there anybody there?"

"We are your friends. Did you used to work here?"

"Do you know Eustace?"

Did they feel a pull there? No one is sure.

"Do you mind us being here?"

"Do you like frightening the secretaries?"

"Is your name Eustace?"

Yvonne feels a pull on the glass, but no one else looks convinced.

"Are you another Neame?"

The glass is drawn around the table to 'show' it the letters and numbers.

"Is there anybody there?"

"Do you like it here?"

"Do you want to speak to anyone here?"

Norman and Yvonne:

"What about trying to make it angry?' Trevor suggests.

It is not a concept that meets with the slightest enthusiasm.

The table is moved into the corner where a ghost has been seen.

Norman, Trevor, Ruth:

"Do you want to speak to Trevor?"

"Come on, speak up," Trevor urges in his best, brisk schoolmasterly voice.

The mood has gone, the team is tired, it is 5.10am and another night has ended inconclusively.

Most have to return to London, one to Reading, and it is a long journey ahead of them as the night begins to pale outside.

"Ninety-nine times out of a hundred we find nothing more in our investigations," says the Ghost Club's Trevor Smith.

If a cynic can be described as a disappointed romantic, someone who wants to believe in true love but finds the truth is an unfaithful lover, rows and a messy divorce, then Trevor Smith makes a good cynic. He wants to believe in ghosts, but has found so many scams that he looks for scientific proof before giving his heart to any new claims. Thus, the rigour with which he pursues his ghost hunts.

First, those using the building are asked for any accounts they may have of hauntings. These are kept confidential and not shared with the team members. The building is searched for likely sites on the night. Sudden temperature changes, unexplained cold spots, are good signs. Psychic members also give their impressions.

The investigation team is equipped with tape recorders, digital thermometers, torches and cameras. Trigger objects, some out-of-keeping objects that might attract the interest of any ghost, are placed in the room.

Watches are synchronised and check sheets given out. These record names, locations, exact time — for later cross reference purposes — lighting and background sound conditions, temperature fluctuations and details of any movement of the trigger object.

You may not believe in ghosts or take seriously those who hunt them.

But you have to have respect for people who will drive themselves so at the end of a working week when they know, even by their own records, the chances of finding anything are roughly one in a hundred on such nights.

Research into company records shows that William Eustace Neame worked as head clerk in the bottling department from 1906 until at least the end of World War Two. He was known to all as Eustace.

Female members of Shepherd Neame's staff report an uncomfortable sense of being watched. The boardroom is particularly unsettling and some say they will only enter in pairs, and even then will prop the door open.

One woman reports seeing the figure of a small man dressed in a dark suit entering the boardroom. But when she followed him in, there was no one there.

Another woman reported seeing a man in his late 50s, wearing a faded work jacket and trousers, crouching down in the stores. She could see every detail of his face and remembers how unnaturally grey it seemed.

One man said he had seen a pair of legs go up the stairs in the brew-house. A woman reported seeing a man in black walk into the chairman's office. She waited for him to return but he never did.

The Wheatsheaf Beefeater restaurant and pub at Cliftonville, near Margate, is reputed by staff to have a very spooky atmosphere. There have been several incidents which they have been unable to explain.

William Stephens, the manager, claims to have heard someone call his name one night at closing time. However, he was the only person there, since all the staff had gone home. He says a lot of activity is centred around the cellars: "We have members of staff who refuse to go into the cellar because they find doors mysteriously closing behind them when they are alone."

And two contractors were disturbed one night while steam-cleaning the carpet in the bar. One of them claimed to have seen a 'grey' woman. He turned away and then looked back to discover she had gone. The contractors decided to leave their work until the morning.

A medium who has eaten at the pub before says, "There are actually three ghosts at the Wheatsheaf — a grey woman, an old man and a very troubled younger spirit who seems to have drowned in a well that used to be in the garden of the old Wheatsheaf." In the extended pub, the well is under the modern reception area.

Like pubs, theatres thrive on ghostly tales and the spectral activities reputed to occur at Kent's two Theatre Royals — one in Chatham, the other in Margate — give stage fright a new meaning.

Richard Parker, chairman of the Friends of the Theatre Royal, at Chatham, believes there could be as many as six ghosts haunting its dark recesses. He says, "It would not be unreasonable to claim that it is Britain's most haunted theatre."

This Grade II listed building, once the premier theatre in the Medway Towns but closed for more than 40 years, is now a rather sad sight. Its welcoming façade hides an interior in dank disrepair after years of neglect, so the work of Mr Parker's volunteer group to try to restore the theatre to its former glory deserves support from all local quarters.

Up to £10 million is required — hopefully including money from the National Lottery — and the plan is to re-open as close as possible to 1999, a century after its original completion.

"We formed the 'Friends' in 1995 to assist the Theatre Royal Trust," said Mr Parker. "The current fund-raising campaign is a community project and our aim is to re-open as a full working theatre, very much with the fabric and feel of the original Theatre Royal."

When the curtain went up in 1899, safety regulations were not what they are today and the theatre could pack in 3,000 people. The size of the audience in the newly-restored Theatre Royal will be nearer half that number, which will still make it the biggest in the South East.

And, perhaps, among those enjoying the proceedings will be 'Humphrey', regarded as the ghostly guardian of the theatre, having protected it through two world wars, its closure in 1955, and recent town centre development.

It is believed there may be as many as six ghosts at the Theatre Royal, Chatham.

Richard Parker shows the door which Humphrey the ghost is supposed to bang when he is displeased.

"Humphrey is our main ghost," said Mr Parker. "He is a friendly ghost, although not necessarily one you would see. Stories about him date back to early 1920s and there are several thoughts about who he was when alive. One is that he was an acrobat who gave a performance in front of some important people, but made serious mistakes and became so depressed afterwards that he was found hanging from the gallery the next morning.

"The other story is that he was a former employee who used to count the takings in the manager's office upstairs."

There is anecdotal evidence from former employees who say Humphrey has appeared on the stage, in the dress circle or in the 'gods' walking through locked doors. A former dancer claims she has seen him watching performances; if he did not like what he saw, he would walk off, slamming a door behind him.

Volunteer workers say tools have been moved and electrical equipment turned off; during a psychic investigation, a tape recorder picked up high-pitched musical notes in a descending scale. Although the investigators themselves did not hear anything, they said they did feel unseen hands touching them.

Apart from Humphrey, there are reports of the 'Green Ghost' who is said to shimmer in one of the boxes and 'Charlie', supposedly the noisy ghost of Charlie Monks, a former member of the theatre staff.

"Humphrey is the ghost who you can feel but can't see, the Green Ghost is the ghost you can see but can't hear and Charlie's the ghost you can hear but can't see," said Mr Parker.

Other spirits haunt two of the ladies' lavatories. One is a poltergeist who moves chairs around in the old washroom outside the cubicles upstairs and the other, active in a toilet on a lower level, is a quieter soul who causes no disturbance.

Mr Parker, who helps organise fund-raising ghost tours, said that research indicated the poltergeist was a young girl who lived in or around the Theatre Royal at the turn of the century and died in an institution, while the quieter spirit was that of an old lady who died in the toilet in 1911.

"We had policemen here one night on a stakeout and they went into the room where the poltergeist had been detected. Chairs fell over, doors slammed and they felt hands on their shoulders — they were completely freaked out," said Mr Parker. "They refused to go back and we got their colleagues to go in, but didn't tell them what had happened — and the same thing happened to them."

The sixth ghost, and the most recent, could be called the 'Pipe Smoker'. The aroma of old tobacco has been detected in the foyer and the auditorium since the summer of 1996 — even though no smoking is allowed on the premises.

"This is one I have experienced myself," said Mr Parker. "It's a very sweet smelling pipe tobacco which people tell me dates back to the early part of the century. One lady I took on a tour said she smelled tobacco in the auditorium. Another said that, as she walked down a passageway, she felt somebody tap on her shoulder and blow on the back of her neck. When she turned round, she saw a lady in Victorian garb asking, 'Where's the major?'"

Nipped off for an interval smoke, perhaps...

Britain's second-oldest theatre is reputed to be a favourite haunt of one of the most notable characters ever to grace its stage. Often sighted at Margate's Georgian Theatre Royal is the actress and manager Sarah Thorne, who was involved with the venue on and off for 45 years.

Miss Thorne's father, Richard Thorne, had taken over the lease of the theatre in 1855. As a child, and alongside some of her ten siblings, she acted in her father's resident company at the Royal. When he decided to retire in 1866, she took over as manager, having spent much of her early life establishing herself as a tour de force of the acting profession.

Her first appearance at Margate had been around the age of 20 when she played Pauline in Lord Lytton's drama, *The Lady of Lyons*. She then went on to build up a starry reputation for her performances in theatres throughout Britain. One of her most popular roles, and one oft to be seen in Margate, was as Lady Teazle in Sheridan's play, *School for Scandal*.

Miss Thorne also began making a name for herself by giving lectures after performances. At the Royal, after taking over as manager and redecorating the building, she celebrated her new role by appearing as Meg in H.T.Craven's play, *Meg's Diversion*. In one of her famous addresses to the audience she described herself as 'the captain of a ship that had left the harbour and was spreading her sail in the breeze!'

Her first reign at the Royal lasted until 1873 and she took over the venue again in 1879, remaining in the director's chair until 1899 when she died aged just 62. Her ghost has been seen as she was in her latter years, in full majesty parading up and down the aisles of the old theatre, ascending the stage, only to disappear.

Several actors report sightings of her, and claim she watched them go through their paces in a performance. Her favourite seat was in the middle box of the three to the left of the stage.

In 1990, when a production of Susan Hill's ghost drama, *A Woman in*

Black, was being staged at the Royal, actor Derek Waring said he saw a figure of a woman in the haunted stage box, which has been out of bounds and unused for some years now, and the door slammed with an almighty bang. As the redoubtable Miss Thorne always watched her company perform from that very same box, she could well have been watching the actor that night.

Miss Thorne, who lived at 5 Hawley Square, which is on the corner of Addington Street, right next door to the theatre, has also been spotted by one of the volunteers who works at the theatre. He said that, whenever he has seen her, the house lights mysteriously go on and off, and the voice of a woman is heard, although the theatre is empty.

During her lifetime Miss Thorne also ran a successful theatre school in Margate which was the *alma mater* of many Victorian and Edwardian stars of the stage. Those of her 'pupes', as they became known, who went on to help shape the story of British theatre, included Violet and Irene Vanbrugh, Edward Gordon Craig (son of Dame Ellen Terry and an actor who later became world renowned for his work as a stage designer) and Harley Granville Barker, who first produced the plays of George Bernard Shaw.

During her reign as manager of the theatre, Miss Thorne encouraged Londoners to visit 'Merry Margate' and enjoy its fresh air.

However, life was not so merry for another spirit reputed to visit the theatre on rare occasions. This is the ghost of an actor who threw himself into the orchestra pit from the top box, stage left, after he failed to get the part for which he had auditioned. He landed on his head and died instantly.

In 1996, a psychic society called 'Sightings' stayed overnight at the theatre to record any mysterious sights or sounds. With a video camera, members captured a ball of light which has been reported as hovering centre stage when the lights are out.

Michael Wheatley Ward, who is development director at the theatre, said, "Funny things have happened with the clocks, too. My watch has stopped at a certain hour when I have been working in the theatre and other people have experienced similar incidents."

International clairvoyant, Peter Walker, visited the old Royal a few weeks before appearing on stage in his own show in March 1997. He encountered several ghosts.

Mr Walker told Mr Wheatley Ward, who has felt a curious link with the theatre ever since his childhood, that among these spirits was the ghost of one of the first owners, Thomas Robson, who was urging him to continue his campaigning work for the theatre.

Mr Wheatley Ward said, "Ever since I was a boy I have always felt I have known the old Royal. I met my wife at the venue and when I got more involved, it all felt so right. Mr Walker the clairvoyant confirmed that it was the spirit of Thomas Robson who is behind me in my endeavours."

Robson, a retired singer from Covent Garden, and Charles Mate, a sea captain with a passion for the theatre, were named as first proprietors in 1787. They also received funding aid from the owner of a successful Margate brewery named Francis Cobb and it was, apparently, the influence of Cobb which Mr Walker detected when he walked around the upper circle bar area in the theatre.

He claimed no knowledge of the venue's early history and connection with brewery money. Indeed, Mr Walker's visit to the theatre meant the list of ghosts at the theatre grew. For the first time, a sighting of Charles Dickens was recorded in March 1997. Mr Walker said he walked into the 'haunted' box stage left and immediately felt Dickens push past him.

"Dickens was in his late 40s and was certainly not very happy," he said. "He was also fairly portly. He was sitting with another man and was fairly arrogant in his demeanour. He had his eyes fixed on a performance on the stage and I detected a great sadness about him."

This is an interesting piece of information as Dickens did, indeed, visit Margate Theatre Royal. In 1842, an actor named Henry Betty was appearing in a play called *The Athenian Captive*. The play, a tragedy, had been written by Dickens' close friend, Thomas Noon Talfourd. Was this performance the one the ghost of Dickens was purported to have seen? Was the other man with him his friend, Talfourd?

Dickens, summering at Broadstairs, confided to another friend,

Samuel Rogers, that he intended to walk eight miles to Margate to see the play and, knowing his friend the author would be in the theatre, 'detect him ensconced' within.

Of course, as many know, Dickens had always been interested in all things theatrical. He had briefly acted himself and was involved romantically with the actress Ellen Ternan. Dickens died in 1870 and by 1876 Miss Ternan had moved to Margate with her husband, George Robinson, who became headmaster at the local school. They lived in Hawley Square — not far from Sarah Thorne — and Miss Ternan gave classes in Shakespeare.

The Theatre Royal is a smaller version of the Old Vic in London. It is second only in age to its Georgian relative in Richmond.

If it is haunted, it is understandable. It is a place of acting and a place of energy, of consciousness known and unknown. The Royal is a theatre visited by those who often believe and applaud the enigmatic mysteries of dramatic art. Is it any surprise that its old friends see fit to drift in and out now and then?

When it was announced that a Co-op store was to close in Sheerness, there was an unearthly protest. *Kent Today* reported, in September 1996, that an apparition 'lurking' in the Wheatsheaf Hall — part of the main Co-op building in Sheerness High Street — had appeared following the closure announcement.

Staff in the furniture and glassware section would not go up into the adjacent Unity and Wellington Halls, which were used as stockrooms.

A woman dressed in black had been seen in the dressing room of Wheatsheaf Hall and, in conversation with a medium, had pleaded that she be left in peace to roam the three halls. The woman, who called herself Mary, said that many years ago she fell down in the Wheatsheaf Hall and was locked in. She managed to crawl into a dressing room, where she suffered a heart attack and died.

There is evidence that a woman was found dead in the room and had suffered a heart attack. But nobody knows for sure whether she was a staff member, customer, or one of the many players who used to perform on the Wheatsheaf stage.

Warehouseman Ian Belsom said, "There are so many things that are unexplained since the announcement that the stores would close. The first noises I heard were like someone in torment. Then there were sounds of footsteps, lights coming on and off, showers of new nails and nuts being hurled around and smashed mirror glass in a place where there was never a mirror."

Mr Belsom said that none of the dancers who used the Wheatsheaf Hall regularly reported any strange goings-on.

"But now there are sounds from all three halls. We hear footsteps and in Unity Hall we were astonished to see the head of a mannequin go flying across the room. Then, for no reason, an old brass light-fitting crashed to the floor, from a ceiling where there are only strip lights. We've also ducked a well aimed ashtray."

Mr Belsom, who is the keyholder, was called out by police when the alarm sounded in the hall. "It was strange to be in the place after dark, but not particularly eerie," he said. "After the police had gone, I had to call them back when I heard footsteps and doors banging. They searched and found nothing. But the engineer checked the alarm system and agreed that something had set it off."

Mr Belsom, who adopts a down-to-earth approach to the happenings, admitted, "There are times when the hair stands up on the back of my neck — there is a presence."

A Metropolitan police officer says he has twice felt the ghostly touch of the Co-op spectre in Sheerness. PC Tony Stubley, 31, worked in the haunted warehouse above the Co-op furniture store before joining the Met. He said, "I actually saw the figure of an old lady dressed in black and twice felt her hand on my shoulder."

Tony is a member of the Association of Scientific Studies for Anomalous Phenomena.

He added, "I worked at the furniture store as a warehouseman between 1986 and 1988. I was first made aware in the November of my first year at the store. The date was significant, because the being is always more restless in winter when the afternoons are dark. I believe it is the anniversary of the time a woman was actually found dead in the building."

Tony, who now lives in Bexleyheath, said, "When I read the article I had to support the story told to *Kent Today* by Co-op staff."

A ghostly woman is reputed to haunt Oxney Court, a country mansion ruin off the Deal-Dover road. It stands in an isolated position amid a dense wood and about half the original walls are still intact, although there is no longer a roof.

The *East Kent Mercury* reports that, apart from the 'Grey Lady', who is believed to be the ghost of a woman killed by a horse and cart, Oxney Bottom also has a phantom coach, with its horses galloping at full tilt out of the long-vanished driveway of the house.

A masked horseman, also seen riding along the road, is reputed to be the son of a Deal innkeeper hanged as a highwayman on a gibbet at the side of the road.

Is Pocahontas There?

Prologue

THE life of American Indian princess Matoaka ended in the Kent Thames-side town of Gravesend. She is better known as Pocahontas, a nickname given her by her father Powhatan, a powerful tribal chief. It means 'the playful or mischievous one'.

Although the story of Pocahontas has long been well-known, millions of filmgoers now know of her from the successful Walt Disney cartoon feature film. She has been debated in columns of newsprint and on television. Her name even features in the lyrics of the Peggy Lee hit song *Fever*.

Thousands visit Gravesend every year to see the place where she died, still only a young woman, in 1617, either from plague or tuberculosis. But the visitors seek her final resting in vain. Despite extensive searches, her burial place remains a mystery.

But why was she in Gravesend at all?

The story goes back to 1607 when a European settler, Captain John Smith, was captured on American Indian territory. The early 1600s were trying times for the tribes. They had seen their land infiltrated by settlers in their quest for gold and new colonies. The young Pocahontas, born in 1595, grew up in this changing world.

After his capture, Captain Smith was taken before Powhatan for a trial almost certain to lead to his execution — but Pocahontas, still only 12, pleaded for the captain's life.

When that strategy failed, the courageous young woman threw herself between the captain and the men who were about to kill him. That heroic gesture saved John Smith's life, with Powhatan unable to go against his beloved daughter's wishes.

Captain Smith went on to found Jamestown, the first settlement in Virginia. Meanwhile, settlers and Indians continued to raid each other's camps, but Pocahontas was fascinated by the newcomers.

In April 1613, she, too, was captured and the white settlers demanded a ransom for her release.

During her year-long captivity, she took to English ways, learning manners and religion from 28-year-old widower John Rolfe. She is believed to be the first Native American to be baptised and she became known as Rebecca or Rebekah.

She had fallen in love with Rolfe, the recorder of Virginia, and married him in 1614. They lived on a tobacco plantation and had a son Thomas.

In 1616, the family set sail for England with an escort of 12 American Indians. In London, she was taken to the court of King James I and almost certainly met the royal family. News of her good looks had spread far and wide. She was called 'the beautiful savage'.

Still young, she no doubt had an impish sense of fun which enchanted the court, but it was snuffed out far too early by the sad sequence of events that was to forever link her name with Gravesend.

In March 1617, after a year in England, she became homesick for Virginia and prepared for the voyage home. It is believed she travelled to Gravesend to catch the boat, but, shortly after boarding, was taken seriously ill.

She was taken back to shore and possibly given succour in The Three Daws pub. However, within hours, the princess was dead. She was just 22 years of age.

After a short funeral, her body was buried in St George's Church. The entry in the parish register reads, '1617, March 21st. Rebecca Wrolfe,

Wyffe of Thomas Wrolfe, Gent. A Virginia Ladye borne, was buried in ye Chancell.' Any memorial must have been destroyed when fire gutted the church in 1727.

Although the location of her exact last resting place is now lost, Pocahontas is commemorated in stained glass windows in the present church. And, in the church garden, stands the handsome bronze statue of Pocahontas unveiled by the Governor of Virginia in 1958. It is now a magnet for pilgrims, historians and tourists from all over the world, and a potent symbol of friendship between the peoples of Gravesend and the United States.

Now Read On...

BUSINESS writer Anne Pass looked at her computer screen in amazement and surprise. She could not understand why several letter Ms had suddenly appeared. She had certainly not keyed them in and no one else in the publishing office where she worked had been near her computer.

But there on the screen were two lower-case characters, followed by two capital Ms and another two small ms. At the end of the six letters was a question-mark. It was 13 August 1996. M is the 13th letter of the alphabet. Pocahontas was born Matoaka.

These were not the first curious goings-on in the 18th-century Heritage House. Standing in splendid isolation at the lower end of Gravesend, the elegant four-storey building is but a few yards from the River Thames and The Three Daws, reputed to be the oldest pub in Kent.

Heritage House is a reminder of Gravesend's fascinating history, so intertwined as it has been, and is still, with Britain's greatest river.

The Hole in the Wall Alley where poverty-stricken men would pick up rags for a pittance from the nearby paper-making mill ran just behind the building.

A few yards to the south-west, on slightly higher ground, stands the old church of St George with its distinctive white spire and gilded clock. It seems to look down benevolently on the old house and still provides a

Does Pocahontas haunt Heritage House? Business trio, Margaret Goulding, left, Tony Tompkins and Anne Pass, believe she may be up to her mischievous tricks.

famous landmark to the seamen, cruise passengers and river pilots passing by.

The well-tended weatherboard building — painted pastel green rather than traditional white — is now a business centre and is a far cry from a modern-but-anonymous serviced office, yet it offers a pleasant working environment for small businesses with a taste for quaint surroundings.

On another floor, Tony Tompkins and Margaret Goulding are busy developing their growing wholesale greetings card business. One day, they noticed the computer screen had an altered date setting for no apparent reason.

"Then the characters changed," recalls Tony. "There were circles and triangles that were not even on the keyboard. It was most weird. Some time later, we spoke to Anne and she said she had had a similar experience. We had never spoken about these things to each other.. She didn't know we had experienced strange things. We didn't know she had."

As a journalist, Anne Pass is accustomed to rational explanations to a whole range of questions. Yet she is convinced that a spirit is a regular visitor to Heritage House.

If the twin computer experiences are not conclusive evidence on their own, there is more. Anne first became aware of something strange in the building when she was on her own one Saturday morning.

"I heard sounds and thought there were other people in the building. I went upstairs and found I was totally alone," she said. "Then, one night, a colleague and I were the last people in the building. There was a company that used to work quite late but we were sure they had gone home.

"All the 'in/out' signs downstairs except ours had been switched to the 'out' position. We thought it was perhaps a mistake but it wasn't.

"There was no doubt that we heard sounds from that office. It sounded as though someone was typing with an electric typewriter, you know, the sort that uses a golf ball. But there was no one.

"Some time later, we moved offices. In the process of putting up the shelves, we experienced cold spaces on the stairs. Yet, it was a really hot day. It was like going into a deep freeze or the coldest fridge you can imagine.

"On other occasions, objects get moved around inexplicably. We had a cheque which appeared under a pile of leaves outside in the garden leading to the old Hole in the Wall Alley, yet it was fresh and undamaged. And then there is the case of the electric kettle. We sometimes hear it go on and off even though no one wants to boil the water.

"We used to joke that the presence, whatever it was, would make us a cup of tea. One day, we were in the kitchen and the kettle came on, but it wasn't plugged into the wall."

A mystery persists about the office shelves. The carpenter who came to put them up asked, "Is there something strange in this building? Every time I turn my back, the dowel pins come out as though someone is pushing them out."

Sometimes a smell of bacon cooking wafts through the office. "If you put your arm against the wall, it feels as though there is a fire there," said Margaret. The smell of baking bread has also been detected on the landing. In the kitchen sometimes there is a cold, eerie feeling. Then it disappears.

"We say it's our friendly ghost, our lucky ghost," says Margaret who was brought up in East London close to the Thames but spent much of her life near the River Medway. She said she found it comforting.

She and Tony started business from nothing. Both had been made redundant, both were down on their luck. But they're still going.

"As soon as I came here in 1993 I felt at home," said Margaret. "I believe it was fate that we ended up here. I feel she is on our side."

She?

"It's like a mischievous ghost who likes playing little tricks. We think it could be Pocahontas. She was very young, so she could be mischievous. She did not have much childhood and may be living a mischievous part of her life that she didn't have when she was alive."

In a separate room, without collusion or prompting, Anne echoed Margaret's words: "It's playful, not nasty. The day I saw the Ms on the

St George's Church, Gravesend, towers above the statue of Pocahontas.

computer screen, I did feel something but it didn't frighten me. It was a presence and you can feel as though somebody is in the room."

Anne said there had been business people who have moved into the building and moved out again very quickly. They felt uncomfortable. One woman was quite panicky.

"If it were a malevolent presence like a poltergeist throwing things, I wouldn't feel so good about it, but I think our spirit is playful with perhaps a little edge. We call her Pocahontas. We say, 'Oh, there's Pocahontas again,' whenever something odd happens."

Anne is a Christian and believes in an afterlife. She sometimes wonders whether, with all the things happening in the building, there should be an exorcism there.

She has spoken to a friar about it. He was very practical and down-to-earth when told about the computer screen. He asked whether the Ms might have been caused by a computer virus.

"This spirit is good company," said Anne. "It was very much in her nature. She was on her way to Virginia. Maybe she has an unfulfilled need to get back there.

"Although she was a Christian, there is speculation that, because of the plague raging at the time, she may have been buried quickly. Maybe she didn't get the kind of burial she wanted. Or perhaps her deep cultural roots remained with the American Indian tribe from where she came and she wanted an Indian burial, not a Christian one.

"I keep an open mind. I try to be a rational journalist, but too much has happened here to too many people to just write it off as a figment of the imagination."

And Anne, a painter as well as a writer, has spotted another unusual thing — the engraver of the stained glass window in St George's Church depicting the American Indian princess is called de Pass.

Are the tales of Anne, Tony and Margaret — three level-headed business people — coincidence, imagination... or manifestations of a vital young woman cut down before her time in a Kent port far from home, yet playful and mischievous for eternity?

Those Who Care For Us

WE HEAR a lot these days about stress. Worries and the illnesses that sometimes follow are bugbears of the life we lead. It can happen at any age, whether you are at work or at school. So, it is nice to know someone is looking out for you when things get rough — even if it is a ghost.

Take the case of Joanna Robinson, just nine years old when she met the man she described as 'like the one on the packet of Quaker Oats'.

Joanna was living with her parents, Carol and Tony Robinson, who run the delightful 'olde worlde' grocer's shop, Lurcock's, in the square at Lenham. When you walk inside you are transported back more than 500 years. The beamed building dates to 1480 and the shop has provided groceries for villagers since 1821, being owned by the Lurcock family for several generations.

When the incident happened, Joanna was feeling under the weather. Her mother takes up the story: "She was off school with tonsillitis. It was lunchtime, about one o'clock, and it was a bright day. Her father was in the garden burning some rubbish.

"The old door in the room used to have a brass handle. She heard the handle go and thought it was one of the staff. She said she was aware that someone was in the room. When she turned around, this person was standing there. It was a man, wearing a tall Quaker's hat and a black cloak."

Joanna could not distinguish the features — she called it an 'outline ' — but the strangest thing about it was that she could not see his feet. "They were in the ground," said Carol.

The apparition was there for only a short while. Probably just as well, although Joanna said she was not frightened.

"Joanna showed me a packet of Quaker oats on the shelf and said that was how the man looked, although his hat was taller," said Carol. "She has not seen him since, although my son, Chris, has felt something — he does not like being on his own in the house now."

Joanna's experience occurred in 1975, about two years after the family moved into the shop.

"When we came, we were a very young family," said Tony. "It was probably the first time in hundreds of years that children had been in the building. I think he was probably just looking us over as newcomers."

Carol had another view: "I understand from people I've spoken to that he appears only when someone is ill, so the fact that we haven't seen him again is good, because it means we must be healthy!"

Tony Robinson, above, and his wife, Carol, think a friendly Quaker spirit may be resident in their 15th-century shop.

However, their Quaker friend may still be around because in the room where he was seen by Joanna, the Robinsons' cat Fifi, often sits on a chair looking up the stairs. "It's as if something is going on above," added Carol.

The belief that the Quaker shows up when people are below par is supported by neighbour Joan Walls, who runs the Tudor Room hair salon in a similarly aged building across the road from the grocery shop.

About 25 years ago, Joan used to live in a flat next door to the Robinsons when the building was a single property (it was divided in 1969). She was a young hairdresser in those days and worked in the shop below.

"One day, I was bending down, putting on some slippers, when I pulled a muscle really badly in my back. It was so painful, I couldn't work," she said. "We had a couple who used to visit and he was a medium and healer. He told me I had been working too hard and I would now have to take it easy because of the injury.

"He said, 'The Quaker thinks you're doing too much as well. He says you must slow down.' I was a bit taken aback. 'Who are you talking about?' I said, and he said, 'Didn't you know about him? He's here now, standing by your bed!'

"Well you can imagine …I said, 'Get him out of here.' But the man just stood there, talking to him."

So, here was young Joan, hardly able to move, having this bizarre conversation with a visitor who, apparently, was also chatting away to a ghost.

"I said, 'What's happening?' and he said, 'He's laughing'.

"I just couldn't believe it, but it seems the Quaker had turned up because I was unwell. I was told that he had had three daughters while he was alive and they had lived in the house. But he did not believe in letting the girls have parties or enjoy themselves …he thought the way to heaven was through hard work.

"But when he died, he said he felt very sorry that he had not given the girls their freedom and his penance was to come back whenever he thought people were in need of his help. He was a good man."

Joan said she never actually saw the Quaker, but added, "Downstairs, near the loo, my cat would often turn his head as if he was following someone walking by."

She stayed in the flat for three years and said it was a 'very calm, lovely' house. She added, "I was never afraid."

There is a sequel to the story. About two years ago, Joan met a girl who asked if there had been 'anyone else' there when she had stayed in the flat.

"I said, 'No,' because I didn't want to upset her, but I don't think she believed me. She said, 'He comes, you know.' The girl was going through a stressful period at the time. It seems he still appears when there's a problem — he's a very caring person."

During the interview with Joan in her salon, a client under the drier showed a lot of interest in the ghostly tale she was relating …because she, too, had a story to tell.

Dora Gregory, who lives in Harrietsham, recalled an occasion in World War Two when bombs were dropped near to her uncle's house where she was staying with her sister. Her uncle said the girls would have to get out and stay the night up the hill at the nearby Boughton Malherbe Rectory. Dora was then 14 and to her, no doubt, like most teenagers, the event was probably more of a lark than a drama. She and her sister spent a peaceful night and the following morning they slipped out of their room, ready for a hearty breakfast downstairs.

"As we walked along the corridor, we saw an open room. Curiosity got the better of us and we looked inside. There, at the foot of a four-poster bed, was a young girl with a long, white nightdress. She had very long hair and was platting it," said Dora.

"Over breakfast, we enquired about the girl and were told the vicar's daughter was away. There was nobody who fitted the young girl's description.

"My aunt later let on that the rectory was haunted and what we had seen was a ghost. I also know a couple who had a flat there and they said it was horrible some nights, so unnerving. They felt these presences. They said there was something particularly nasty in the powder closet."

Glyn Hickey, who is a night sister at Acacia House, a nursing home in Tenterden, believes she has a benevolent spirit who watches over her family in times of difficulty.

What makes her ghostly guest unusual, however, is that he follows her around … even when she moves house.

The story starts more than 20 years ago, shortly after the birth of her first child, Alex. It had been a difficult pregnancy, resulting in an emergency Caesarean section. The baby was premature and Glyn says he was 'rather poorly' in his first few weeks of life.

"I gradually became aware of a presence by my bed," she said. "I couldn't see it, but I knew it was a man dressed in black and later it occurred to me that he had started visiting us only after we had put Alex into his room at night."

One day, when Alex was about nine months old, friends came to stay with Glyn and her late husband Dick. They had a son of similar age called Tim and he had fallen ill on the train. Tim had been taken to Bart's Hospital where he was kept in overnight.

His parents, Maggie and Eric, collected him the following morning, but not before Maggie asked Glyn if she was aware that her house was haunted. Apparently she had felt a figure by her bed during the night and thought she had seen it going into one of the bathrooms.

"Dick and I had never discussed this matter with anyone else, but thought the time had come when perhaps we should," said Glyn. "We spoke to my mother who had many useful contacts in that sphere. She said she would mention it to her healer whose wife was a medium. An appointment was made and the medium arrived with her husband and a young man who acted as the 'devil's disciple' looking for explanations of any phenomena such as causes of draughts etc."

They all sat in the drawing room, chatting while Alex played on the floor. When the lights started flashing on and off, Glyn explained that was a fairly recent occurrence and that they had had no electrical work done to the house since it had been rewired while being converted into three self-contained flats three years earlier.

What Glyn did not know was that she was in the presence of more than restless spirits — the medium was none other than the one and only Doris Stokes. "This was in the days before she became famous and I have always felt privileged to have had her help and advice," says Glyn.

"Mrs Stokes suggested a tour of the house, especially to the places where I felt the presence strongest. It was a large Victorian house. We were planning to move to Kent and, as tenants left, they were not replaced, so that it would be easier to sell the flats. Fortunately, this gave us the run of the whole house without disturbing anybody."

In Alex's room, Mrs Stokes found what she called 'the cold spot'. Her assistant immediately started looking for open windows. When Mrs Stokes was convinced that it was the genuine article, she invited Dick and Glyn to stand on the spot.

"It was the most peculiar sensation," said Glyn. "Starting at the heels, a biting cold sensation worked its way up the back of our legs.

Mrs Stokes then announced that, having found the cold spot, we would go downstairs and discover who was causing it."

During the next two hours, Dick and Glyn were given a lot of information about themselves, their families, their past, present and future — things that they did not know but were later confirmed by their parents. It transpired that their 'visitor' was Dick's grandfather, Thomas Buckingham, born in the early 1880s who had died in the 1960s, leaving two daughters, each of whom had a son.

Alex was Old Tom's only great grandchild. Dick had known his grandfather well; he had been an electrician by trade, had adored children and had always carried a pocketful of sweets to give out in the days when it was safe to do so.

"Therefore, Alex had a guardian angel who came and stood by my bed if the baby was uncovered, hungry, wet or just needing me. He was also very distressed when Maggie and Eric had brought Tim after he had been ill on the train."

Tom always announced his presence by flashing the lights. Dick and Glyn went out for dinner one evening taking Alex with them ...and also Tom.

"The lights started flashing in our friend's house and we had to explain what it was. A few weeks later these same friends baby-sat for us. They had a daughter the same age as Alex, so we took him to their house for the evening, plus Tom, of course. This time our friends were prepared for the electrical disturbances!

"Tom even came away with us for the weekend. We went to stay, again with friends who were used to Tom at our house, but who were surprised to find that we had brought him with us. On the Monday evening I received a phone call from our friends to say that they thought we had left Tom behind.

"Apparently, not only were the lights flashing but they were getting a lot of banging on the pipes. I thought the poor old boy must be quite frantic — he must think that he had lost us. I said that if the disturbance carried on, to just say, 'It's all right, Tom, they've gone home.' This worked, which was just as well as the neighbours were complaining about the noise from the pipes — it was a modern semi, with rather thin walls."

When Glyn and Dick moved to Kent, Tom moved, too.

"By this time I had another son who we named after him," said Glyn. "As the years went by, Old Tom's visits became less frequent. The boys were obviously doing well and perhaps didn't need so much looking after."

In 1987, Dick died and Glyn moved to her present home in Woodchurch. For several years she could sense Old Tom in the hall of the new house, just keeping an eye on things.

But he has not been around for about five years. "I expect he's safe in the knowledge that the boys and I are happy and settled and perhaps he has gone on to further things."

Glyn never knew Tom in his life, but she says he was always a welcome guest in her family.

Not so welcome, however, were uninvited 'guests' in the bedrooms of a flat in Sturry, on the outskirts of Canterbury, occupied by three girls. But, for Enid Billings and her friends, that was what appeared to happen in 1961.

Enid, who still lives in Canterbury, says the flat was in a big house, standing in its own grounds.

"We had a bedroom each; I had the large room with twin beds. My window looked into the garden and down the hill to Sturry. The house had been divided into flats by the owner who lived with his wife and Alsatian dog on the ground floor. There were probably three or four flats including the landlord's," she said.

"I remember in one of the flats there were three young men who worked in a bank in Canterbury and there was a couple; I think one was in insurance.

"While we were talking one day, someone mentioned that they could have sworn something was trying to pull their bedclothes off during the night."

This was not the only ghostly experience. One evening returning home late, the girls had a real scare. The garages were some way away from the house and these were the days before security lighting. When the landlord went to bed he would turn off the light by the steps, at the corner of the house. At the bottom of the steps stood a row of dustbins, on the other side of the pathway.

"With the aid of the moon and a cigarette lighter, we managed to get almost to the bottom of the steps, when, one after the other, the dustbin lids took off. I can see them now — almost the same as dominoes going down," said Enid.

"We didn't stop, we just ran to the front door, a big oak door which had a Yale lock fitted. As we approached the door, it flew open. We thought it was the landlord, but it wasn't, and our front door, just inside the hall, then also flew open. I don't think any of us slept that night."

The flying dustbin lids and self-opening doors became the major topic of conversation with the tenants for a few weeks, then, like the previous experiences, it was forgotten. Enid continues, "One evening, I was awakened from my sleep by the bedclothes being pulled. I saw a kind of fog, rather like a cloud of cigarette smoke. It was by my bed, not too tall, and I could make out curls in the hair in the cloud of smoke."

Some time later, a Dr Mcintosh, who had lived in Sturry for a number of years, visited the house and asked if the girls had ever met the ghost.

"It would appear someone who had owned the house previously had had an invalid wife," said Enid. "There had been a 'live-in' nurse to care for the lady. The nurse's small daughter had fallen from my bedroom window and had been killed. Was this our ghost?"

Enid and her friends stayed in the flat for just a year. The house changed hands a couple of times and it is now a retirement home.

She ponders, "I wonder if the residents get any 'visits' as we used to?"

The Dunkirk Spirit

RICHARD Card had just finished work after another hard shift as a bouncer. Moments earlier, he had been standing, as usual, outside Nero's nightclub on Ramsgate seafront.

He turned the ignition key of his car and the engine exploded into life. He headed for home just as he had done dozens of times before, but this journey was unlike anything he had ever known before.

Heading towards the Lord of the Manor traffic lights, his nostrils filled with a smell that had never before filled his car — the distinctive aroma of hair oil, the Brilliantine or Brylcreem that was the hallmark of the fashionable man in the 1930s and 1940s.

Jars of the stuff were used in France and wherever British servicemen fought the Nazis in World War Two. The smell was familiar to a generation already qualifying for their pension in the 1970s and 1980s when Nero's was enjoying its heyday. But on the day Richard's car filled with the smell, hair oil like that had gone long out of fashion.

Richard did not use the stuff. Yet, there it was in his car, pungent, overwhelming, unexplained. And it was mingled with another aroma which reminded the former soldier and policeman of lint dressings.

Richard momentarily took his eyes off the road to check if he had anything inside the car remotely linked to hair oil, but there was nothing. He recalls, "I couldn't believe it. It stayed in the car for two or three minutes while I was in the Lord of the Manor area.

"It made my hair bristle, I can tell you. I smelled the hair cream definitely. I smelled the antiseptic smells in my car, which made my buttocks play sixpences and half crowns for a couple of minutes."

As he drove away form the Lord of the Manor, the smell faded.

Richard's experience had strong links to strange happenings at Nero's itself. Bouncers are a burly down-to-earth bunch, not given to pondering psychic phenomena or the life beyond. Theirs is a practical, macho world where keeping troublemakers and undesirables out — and keeping themselves from harm — are the name of the game. But Nero's bouncers had good cause to shed their no-nonsense attitude. The Club End had emerged as the most notorious way of entering the lively nightspot. Even the alsatian dog owned by the club manager Fred Wynn would refuse to go through the Club End door when the disco was empty.

Richard takes up the story: "The Club End was opened on Tuesdays for Country and Western nights. On Wednesdays, it was out of use.

Richard Card stands among the rubble which was once Nero's nightclub at Ramsgate, where the spirit of a World War Two soldier may have appeared.

"We had to get to the cash till without the lights on, to bring the takings to the other entrance. None of the bouncers liked going down there. When you went on your own, you'd get a smell of hair oil or lint dressings. You'd come out with your hair prickling.

"The smell in the car was the same as the one you used to get down the Club End. The story emerged that bouncers over many years had experienced unusual things at Nero's."

One night in the 1970s, something happened that would be the talk of bouncers for years to come. It was a routine evening. Most clubbers were well-behaved. There was the usual crop of high spirits hell-bent on a bit of mischief and some were a little worse for drink when they turned up at the Club End.

"A bouncer saw a man in khaki uniform on the disco balcony. Now, in those days, you didn't let in people in uniform. So, when he saw someone in khaki, he assumed he must have been let in by the emergency fire exit.

"He went behind a pillar but when he came out the other side, the guy had gone. That same day, a manager had seen the man drawing on a little rolled-up cigarette in the empty club when only admin staff were in."

Who was the man in khaki? The story would take a long time to unravel.

A few years later, Richard was on duty with a fellow bouncer Brian Southern.

"As usual, he went up to the balcony for his tea-break. A few minutes later, he came down as white as a ghost. He said he had seen the whole building clearing in front of his eyes. He could tell me what colours the building was painted and how the beds were spread out."

Beds? What Brian had seen was explained and confirmed by subsequent investigations. During one of Britain's darkest moments in World War Two, the building served, not as a happy dance hall, but as a grim staging post for wounded soldiers. These were the men who escaped the beach hell of Dunkirk.

Ramsgate had been the welcome face of Blighty after their evacuation by an amazing convoy of little boats crewed by plucky civilians. It was the classic case of snatching survival from the jaws of defeat which gave us the phrase 'Dunkirk Spirit'. What later became Nero's had then been used as a hospital. So, who might have been that mysterious figure in khaki who haunted the club?

John Williams, curator of Margate Museum, has little doubt: "I am sure he was a 19-year-old squaddie and just one of 47,000 men who went through that hospital. I think he was badly wounded at Dunkirk and evacuated as soon as possible to Ramsgate which had this temporary hospital facility. It is almost certain that he died there.

"Nero's was used during the Dunkirk evacuation as were so many buildings in Thanet at that time. The Winter Gardens and Dreamland at

Margate were also used as first-aid stations.

"People in the club perhaps did see something. Over the past years, there may have been a bit of elaboration, but the pith of the thing could really be true."

Richard says the Nero's ghost had a remarkable effect on the bouncers, seeming to make them more reflective and giving them a sense of mission and purpose.

"They pursued excellence which reduced the sum total of human misery because we stopped fights and prevented conflict effectively. Had our ghost had a gut-full of violence and man's inhumanity at Dunkirk? Did that create an ambience which made even bouncers reflect on how to do their job?"

Nero's phantom squaddie was dealt a blow in 1997 when the building was demolished. Has he been demobbed from ghostly duty? Or perhaps he continues to stroll along Ramsgate seafront, a Woodbine in his mouth, hair oil slicking down his locks, gently reminding new generations of the sacrifice he and so many others made in the original Dunkirk spirit.

From little boats of the evacuation to the motorised bathtub in which Alan Witt tried to cross the Channel. Alan, who admits to several odd experiences in his life, said, "It was a real bath, a pressed-steel bath, but it had to be modified to be seaworthy." That little escapade occurred early in the Swinging Sixties when Alan was press officer for the Students' Union in Brighton. Needless to say, he did not complete the voyage — it turned stormy halfway across and they had to abandon ship.

It is doubtful whether all this prepared him for the strange incident a few years later, in 1964, when he was staying in digs at Farningham while working at Dartford.

Now industrial sales manager for Whatman International Ltd., of Maidstone, and living in Charing, Alan was then in his mid-20s and unmarried. He called into the local pub, The Chequers, at Farningham, to ask if they knew anyone who had digs to offer.

"They gave me the name of a Mrs Colver at Parsonage House, just down the road. It was right next to the church, so it was probably the old vicarage," said Alan.

The house was something of an oddity that recalled days gone by. When Alan first moved in the property had no electricity and even when he moved out, there was only one electric light bulb — in the sitting room.

"Mrs Colver told me she had had 64 foster children, many of whom were still around the place, and there were also lots of animals," he said. "It was like a Dickens play — there was no hot water and she used to bring me up a jug and a bowl of water in the morning. I had a paraffin lamp to take to bed at night."

He said there were a variety of 'inmates' at Parsonage House, all of whom could have been characters invented by Dickens.

"There was Jack the sewage man. He used to grow the most delicious vegetables, although I don't quite know where. And there was an Irishman called Ted who was a navvy, and then there was old Mr Colver who had been injured in World War One and, obviously suffering from that, he was seriously ill.

"At night, he used to moan. It was a very distinctive moan," said Alan, making a brave attempt to mimic the sound, "as though he was in pain. He often used to tell a particular story. It was something like the song of the Battle of the Somme: 'In 1916, I led 3,000 men across the Somme and only came back with six'."

Mrs Colver, among other things, did the cleaning for the church and she was also the local layer-out.

One Sunday evening, Alan came back from his usual weekend at home in Brighton to find old Mr Colver laid out in a coffin in the dining room. He expressed his sympathy and expected that to be the end of the story. However…

"I can't remember how long afterwards, probably a couple of months, but I woke up one night and heard this moaning. I am a light sleeper and I thought I could have dreamt it. But now I was fully awake — and I heard it again.

"I thought, quite honestly, someone was playing a joke — you know,

Ted the sewage man or Jack the navvy — and I waited to hear the sounds of laughing or someone scuttling away. I waited and waited and there was nothing ...no noise, not a sound.

"The moan was the same as Mr Colver's. I stuck a chair under the handle of the door because, by now, I was feeling nervous. I don't get nervous very easily, but that certainly wasn't normal."

After a fitful sleep, Alan went down to breakfast in the morning and pondered on the night's events.

"Mrs Colver said to me, 'Did you sleep all right last night, Alan?' I said 'Well, as a matter of fact, I didn't.' She said, 'Don't worry, that was dad coming back to see us.'"

Alan insists he did not tell Mrs Colver about the moaning he'd heard. "She just knew what I was saying..."

Alan believes he may have had one other supernatural experience, although he confesses it could have been a childish fantasy or dream. His family moved to Surrey during World War Two after being 'bombed out' in London. Alan was about five years of age when he had a strange visitor in his bedroom.

"I had a little electric night-light and I saw — at least, I think I saw — on a long wall in the room a silhouette of what I could only describe as a German soldier with a tin hat, floating across the wall.

"I remember screaming for my parents. They came in and said, 'Don't be silly'."

Hills From Hell

CARS seem out of place among the narrow roads and undulating countryside around Elmsted, a tiny settlement near Wye. After turning off the A228, you reach it by following your nose and asking (and dodging) the occasional walker. Eventually you spy, high on the horizon, Elchin Hill where Jennifer Denny lives with her husband, pet spaniel and lovelorn goose (since his mate died, he has befriended the garden wheelbarrow for company).

Jenny's lovely home is called, appropriately, High Lodge and, with its panoramic views, it is easy to see why it is so popular with her bed and breakfast guests. Nothing untoward has ever happened at High Lodge — "It's totally benign," she says.

However, just down the road, 200 yards away, is a notorious hairpin bend where all manner of mysterious events have taken place. Years ago, Elchin Hill was called Hell Chine Hill — and with some reason. Its snake-like bends must have been hellish for the horse and carriage driver and, even today, you need to keep your foot firmly on the brake as you descend. Not that brakes seem to work too well here...

Jenny recalls an accident at the hairpin bend: "The brakes apparently failed and the car went straight down the hill, through a gate and crashed into a field. Fortunately, the person was uninjured, but when they recovered the car, there was nothing wrong with it — the brakes had not failed after all."

A horse trailer and a normally reliable Volvo broke down at the spot, blocking the road. When the AA came along to tow them away, no fault could be found.

Bikes, too, have their problems. "My daughter ended up in hospital when her cycle brakes seemed to lock at the bend, but we could not find any fault. The same happened to her friend on a brand new cycle. They both went over the handlebars and we couldn't find anything wrong with either bike."

About four years ago, a cycling club rider died of a heart attack near the bend. "All the riders were quite young and they were cycling from Faversham to Folkestone," said Jenny. "Admittedly, it's a steep hill, but the rider who died hadn't complained of anything at all. He was cycling up the hill and, just above the bend, had a heart attack."

The bend has a darker reputation: the daughter of a respected local resident was attacked by a man who laid in wait on the corner and, some 20 years ago, a young woman committed suicide with a shotgun. Is it purely coincidence that so many strange incidents have taken place on the old Hell Chine Hill bend, or is there some other explanation?

One clue could be a strange story related to Jenny by her husband. "Years ago, when he was 15, my husband was shooting rabbits on a sunny Sunday morning in a field on the hairpin bend. When he looked up, he saw a coach and horses, with the driver sort of hunched on the box over the reins, coming down the hill towards him.. He thought, 'Oh how exciting,' and he stopped to break the gun, ran towards the road to see the coach …but there was nothing there at all.

"He said it looked solid to him. He doesn't like to talk about it, but he is insistent that he saw it.

"And then, years later, I was in a pub at Stelling Minnis and there was this old man who spoke to me about Hell Chine Hill. He said his driver knew of the Honeywoods coach that had gone out of control down the hill.

"It had whizzed round the corner pulled by two horses and the shaft went into an oak tree and one of the horses was killed. I never mentioned to him about my husband and the coach and horses that he'd seen. Whether that was it, I wouldn't know."

Jenny, who admits being 'a little psychic', said she had personally experienced only one odd occurrence on the hill: "About 14 years ago I had a very astute horse and I was starting up the hill towards home when I saw somebody riding down the hill. The horse saw it, too, pricked up his ears and quickened his step.

"But, suddenly, there was nothing there. I thought it might have been a trick of the sun, but the horse saw it — they always prick up their ears if they see another horse coming towards them. It was about a quarter of a mile up the hill, in the sun …a big dark horse with a figure on it wearing a large hat. It was not a riding hat, it was a three-cornered one, a tricorn hat."

The fact that it was sunny when Jenny saw her strange rider is interesting. "It's always on hot, sunny days that things happen with me," she said. "When I was a child, I was told to go and play when we visited a house with a friend of my mother's, but the whole place felt very depressed and weird.

"More recently, I was at Scotney Castle on a summer's day, by the lake with my husband, when I suddenly got this fearful feeling of oppression and depression pressing down on me. We made our way back to the car and went home. I did ask if they had any ghosts. There was nothing they knew of, but I believe somebody in the past had been murdered or drowned in the lake."

Jenny has an open mind on the subject of the paranormal — perhaps it is merely a part of a natural existence which 'we don't fully understand', she says.

For instance: "We had an eminent QC and his wife stay here for bed and breakfast and he'd come back especially to visit a house he used to go to when he was a child in Stelling Minnis. It was there that he saw an old man come downstairs and go through a wall dressed in a mackintosh and cap.

"When he visited the house again, the people there said, 'Oh yes, we see him. The old boy does come down the stairs and go through the wall — it's where the front door used to be.'"

As for the hairpin bend, Jenny claims all the stories do not worry her, although she says the local vicar told her to say a prayer when going past. And she admits that, once, in the middle of the night, while she was walking down looking for the dog, "I was saying the *Lord's Prayer*..."

Paul Harris who lives in Folkestone, writes about strange phenomena for several magazines and has also produced books about mysteries in Kent, including *Ghosts of the Coast* and *Ghosts of Shepway*.

One of his recent investigations concerns Sugar Loaf Hill, near Folkestone, a conical hill which has been 'a subject of rumour, speculation and mystery for many generations,' according to him.

"This striking 400 feet mound looks distinctly artificial, like a giant-sized version of the prehistoric man-made Silbury Hill in Wiltshire, which is known as Europe's largest 'pyramid'. In fact, Sugar Loaf was once believed to be something of the sort.

"Author 'Felix', in *Rambles Around Folkestone*, published in 1913, quotes another [unnamed] writer as saying, 'It [Sugar Loaf] is evidently not a hill of Nature's formation and was probably fashioned to its present shape, as a monumental remembrance of some eminent warrior, or as a trophy of some great warlike achievement."

A summary of one long-standing belief is to be found in an account of the annual meeting of the Kent Archaeological Society, held in Folkestone in 1874. The relevant passage reads, 'Sugar Loaf Hill is surmised by some to be the burial place of Prince Vortimer who it is said desired to be buried near the place where the Saxons used to land. Consequently, this funeral pile was erected, that future invaders in beholding such a gigantic memento mori should tremble.'

Paul, however, does not believe the hill is the burial place of Vortimer who was the son of Vortigern, King of southern Britain in the mid-fifth century; he says reports suggest that Vortimer is buried in either Lincoln or London.

Be that as it may, there is little doubt that burials of some kind have taken place on Sugar Loaf Hill. These may be from the Bronze Age when it is believed a village existed nearby, as revealed by Channel Tunnel excavations carried out by the Canterbury Archaeological Trust between 1988 and 1989.

The exact purpose of the hill is still open to debate, although Paul says local ghost stories may provide an entertaining solution.

In his booklet, *Sugar Loaf Hill — the Mystery Solved*, he writes:

There is a long standing tradition that in Sugar Loaf resides a spirit protecting the country from invasion. This probably originated from the tradition of Vortigern's burial here, a burial, as we have seen, that eventually took place elsewhere.

More tangibly, there have been recently described experiences of a terrifying nature in this locale. A shaking, pale-faced Channel Tunnel worker told staff at a local flower shop that he had just come from the 'Holywell site' near Sugar Loaf. They had been carrying out preliminary work in the area when suddenly he and his companions found themselves surrounded by a group of black robed 'monks' who looked quite three dimensional and warned them not to dig through the sacred Holywell area.

The figures vanished as quickly as they came, the workers then departed in a hurry. As it happens, the tunnel did not pass through Holywell, nor was it ever intended to. Was this someone's ploy to try and scare off the tunnel workers, a tall story, or a genuine ghostly experience?

Paul also said that, some years earlier, a biker on his way back from Folkestone to Canterbury had an incredible experience. Somewhat the worse for wear, he decided he could not continue his journey and camped down on the top of Sugar Loaf Hill.

After an hour or so he awoke to a terrible din and commotion — finding himself still on the hilltop, yet in the midst of a battle between 'Britons and Romans'.

"Needless to say, he made a quick escape from the scene of the phantom battle," said Paul. "I have heard similar stories to these and I know of no recorded battle on this site, but it's tempting to imagine that some grave robber of earlier times was frightened by such spectacular apparitions into dropping his ill-gotten gains all over the hilltop!"

Perhaps the most active of all the paranormal research groups is the Association of Scientific Study of Anomalous Phenomena, or ASSAP for short.

A registered charity, ASSAP was formed in 1981 and now has a worldwide membership of more than 400. Most of the organisation's officers are based in the South-East — including a number in Kent — and the late Sir Michael Bentine was its most recent president.

ASSAP describes itself as an association dedicated to discovering the scientific truth behind unexplained phenomena and its main activities are to conduct detailed research into reports of anomalous phenomena, to analyse it and publish the results. Among its literature is a twice-yearly publication called *Anomaly* and a quarterly newsletter.

David Thomas, who lives in Maidstone, is an accredited investigator with ASSAP and keen to found a local group. He would like open-minded people to contact him, but he stresses they must take the subject seriously.

"People would be free to come along and carry on their interest, whatever it may be — UFOs, ghosts or whatever," he said. "We've got experts we can call on for advice and we have an extensive library; the key point is that it is a serious, scientific investigation."

Mr Thomas, acting manager at the Royal Mail office in Maidstone, is affectionately known to his work colleagues as 'Spook' because of his

Ghosts and UFOs are just some of the paranormal incidents investigated by David Thomas, of the Association of Scientific Study of Anomalous Phenomena.

interest in the paranormal — and a ghostly encounter he experienced in his youth.

Now in his mid-40s, he said, "We have to go back to when I was about 13. I was living in south-east London and I was about halfway up the stairs when I just knew there was somebody behind me. I looked round and there, at the bottom of the stairs, was a man, in Edwardian-style clothes, with a top hat and tails and frighteningly white face. He looked in his 40s or early 50s.

"It was the classic case, really. He was there; he shouldn't have been there. I managed to get to the top of the stairs and ran round so I couldn't see him any more, then I screamed."

After that incident, Mr Thomas began to read about and research into the paranormal, but it was not until his late 20s that he became active in ASSAP.

"I decided to join as soon as I saw the members weren't cranks. They were down-to-earth people who wanted to know a bit more and look into the subject," he said. Since then, after a spell as media officer for the Association, during which time he was an adviser to several television programmes, Mr Thomas has concentrated on compiling evidence of strange phenomena — and developing his own theories.

He is not convinced there is an afterlife; he prefers the 'stone tape' explanation. This proposes that stones and the fabric of a building or location can soak up the emotions and pictures of a scene and play them back at a later date to a person with brain wave patterns similar to those of the past individuals.

As for UFOs, he says they remain unexplained: "If you talk to an American, UFOs are alien — alien technology. You speak to someone British and he'll say it's unidentified — unidentified lights in the sky, unidentified craft, but he's not saying they're alien.

"That shows a different culture and I think that, when you look at all this phenomena, you have also to look at the folklore, the culture, to see what's behind it."

UFOs have figured prominently twice in his research. On the first occasion, with a group of friends, he watched 'speechless' for 20 minutes as parts of the night sky seemed to move while 'a very large, dense black object' manoeuvred between the stars.

On the second occasion, this time in Cornwall, he saw what appeared to be a rocket with a 'golden glow' head straight down towards the ground, but when he checked around the area, there was no debris and no one had seen anything unusual.

Ghosts, however, remain his specialist topic and Kent has provided a rich hunting ground for such investigations, particularly Dover Castle. Ancient doors have been seen to move and heard to rattle and a couple of Mr Thomas's ASSAP colleagues had an unnerving experience when they thought a girl may have fallen off the top of the castle. They heard a piercing female scream, but when they ran up to the top of the Keep, the door was locked, so they knew no one could have been on the roof.

"It was very odd, but lots of odd things happen in Dover Castle," added Mr Thomas.

What Sharkey Saw...

IN OCTOBER 1957, Laurie Debona was a leading hand in the Royal Navy. Still only 23, he had already served five years in the Senior Service and undertaken several overseas tours. There was no doubt that the briny was in his blood. His Maltese father had run away to sea at the age of 12.

In the late 1950s, the Royal Navy remained a formidable fighting machine. The fleet had been built up again after the huge losses of World War Two. It was now 12 years since the end of hostilities and the swagger was back. The Navy offered a good career to back-street lads wanting security, reasonable pay, a bit of globetrotting and perhaps a girl in every port.

Laurie would speak later of the good memories pushing out the 'hell of a lot' of bad ones. "But I never regret it and would do it again."

In 1957, Laurie was in Kent. It was a long way from his Geordie roots but he was happy in his shore-based job in the then bustling Chatham Dockyard. It was unimaginable at that time that some 27 years later the decision would be made to close the dockyard — a decision that would have a significant effect on the local economy with the loss of thousands of jobs.

As assistant chef to the admiral superintendent, Laurie knew both meanings of scrambled egg. He was part of an elite team carefully chosen to make life run smoothly for the top brass and especially the man at the helm of dockyard life. It was down to Laurie and his colleagues to keep the senior officers happy.

Apart from Laurie, the admiral's team consisted of two chefs, a coxswain, the chief steward and a couple of ratings who did odd jobs like gardening, driving and stoking the boilers.

One was Sharkey Ward, a bluff, larger-than-life Midlander who was most definitely not known for his nervous disposition. But even he was reduced to a quivering wreck by the strange goings-on that October night.

Laurie, now a grandfather and living in Maidstone with wife Shirley, recalls how it was that Sharkey, a 'man's man' if ever there was one,

Laurie Debona retraces Sharkey Ward's steps outside the Commissioner's House at Chatham Historic Dockyard.

came to be so frightened that he could barely keep hold of a pint of beer.

"We lived in the annexe attached to the admiral superintendent's big house which was built in the mid-18th century. It is now known as Commissioner's House. The crew's quarters were above the kitchens.

"Sharkey Ward was a very large, affable sailor, a down-to-earth bloke. I think his name was John, but we all called him Sharkey. That's what you called anyone with the surname Ward. It's like Shiner Wright, Jumper Collins or Knocker White.

"His final task each evening was to stoke the boilers for the central heating in the basement of the house as well as the boiler which served the greenhouse heaters in the kitchen garden. He usually did this about 10pm, just before we all turned in at about 10.30 or 11pm. Some of us had to get up pretty early the next morning.

"This particular evening, he was doing his usual rounds. He'd done the house boiler and went outside to do the greenhouse boiler. He was stoking it up as usual when he heard voices.

"There was a ten-foot wall around the garden. Fearing that intruders had climbed over the wall and got into the grounds, he went out of the greenhouse and along the back of the house.

"The kitchen garden had a lawn which sloped up to the back of the house. As he went around the back, he heard these voices on the lawn. And there was an eerie glow as if it were lit by lamplight, but he knew there wasn't a lamp in the middle of the lawn.

"He started to walk up the lawn and then suddenly saw these two gentlemen. They were dressed like Cavaliers and arguing violently in the middle of the lawn. He thought they were about to come to blows.

"He was walking up to them, preparing to say, 'Who the hell are you?' when they suddenly vanished. Two minutes later, a deeply-shaken Sharkey appeared in the mess-room, white as a sheet. He had run back from the garden and sat down, quivering like a jelly in the corner of the room.

"This chap was six feet tall and almost as broad. It took us about half an hour to calm him down and get the story out of him. He was really terrified and yet there was nothing much that frightened Sharkey.

"There had been tales of a ghost in the house, an old lady dressed in black up in the attic. The stewards reckoned every time they went to get linen out of the cupboard, she was behind them. They could feel a cold presence.

"And we knew about the 17th-century drummer boy who was said to have hanged himself on St Mary's Island. Every November, he's supposed to walk the length of the barracks playing his drum. Nobody lived on the island then. Now it's a new housing estate.

"But we knew nothing about the ghosts outside the house. Sharkey was shaking. We didn't know what to do with him. Then one of the lads got him a beer and shoved it in his hand.

"He could hardly hold his beer, he was shaking so much. It took him a good half-hour to sort himself out and start to tell us what he had seen. He was genuinely shocked.

"We spoke about it on and off for two days, then everything went back to normal. But it's always stuck in my mind. I never found out any more about it and there was nobody we could get to delve into it and find out who those gentlemen might have been.

"I've never had any experiences of this sort of thing. I was pretty sceptical until I saw and heard Sharkey. I now believe in ghosts, even though I've never seen any. I often wonder whether the row the Cavalier gentlemen were having ended in murder and that is why the spirits returned.

"I believe Sharkey lived in Derbyshire. He got married and we were drafted to different ships and lost touch."

Laurie served another nine years. He saw out his career on the frigate *HMS Yarmouth*, eventually leaving the Royal Navy in 1966, and later joining paper manufacturer Kimberly-Clark where he worked on the tissue-making machine until his retirement.

In quiet moments, Laurie thinks back to the strange events that night in 1957, trying to make sense of them.

Apart from the terrified look on Sharkey's face, there is something else which still bothers Laurie: Why did the two dachshund dogs owned by the admiral's wife always avoid walking over the kitchen garden lawn?

"She used to let them out in the garden every day. But they never went on the lawn. They went around the flower beds. Do you know, I never saw those dogs ever cross that lawn..."

Chapter Four

BLACK MAGIC

What the Files Reveal

BLACK magic and witches — both black and white — make up a very large file at the Kent Messenger Group's central information unit. And reports of incidents go back more than 30 years.

Back on 28 February 1969, the *Kent Messenger* reported the gruesome discovery by a student at the University of Kent, Canterbury, of a kitten hanging by its tail from a tree. It had been killed and possibly tortured by black magic devotees near the bridge over the river at Fordwich. The report went on:

> Simon Kenny said he found the kitten at about 9pm along a turning off the road from Sturry to Fordwich. Said Mr Kenny, "There were signs that it had been beaten, burned and possibly tortured. It was scarred and singed. On the ground was a makeshift grate full of ashes.
>
> "The butts of two black candles were nearby with an empty tin of lighter fuel and an empty cigarette packet. It appeared that a black magic circle had been eating at the spot because a spit had been built over the grate."
>
> He said he did not believe it was the work of students because there were none in either of the public houses at Fordwich that evening.

Black magic appeared to rear its ugly head again the following year. *The Kent Messenger*, on 15 May, 1970:

An animal skull probably used in black magic ceremonies has been found in a chimney.

The sinister looking blackened skull, inset with two brass cups, came to light as Mr Alessandro Cornachia was fitting a new fire place at his home in Luton Road, Chatham.

It must have been hidden in the chimney for at least 20 years.

There was a difference of opinion about the mystery skull. Mr Cornachia's 13-year-old son, Enzo, took it to school where a teacher identified it as belonging to a wild boar.

But another expert at his sister's school thought it was a tiger. And at Rochester Museum they said firmly: "It is a bear, you can tell by the teeth."

The *Kent Messenger* said that museum staff did, however, believe that Mr Cornachia's 'find' was used in black magic rites.

Animal skulls are popular accessories among witchcraft devotees.

Rams are most widely used, but there would appear to be nothing in the rules against bear skulls.

A week later, on 22 May, the *Kent Messenger* said that a gang, believed to be devil worshippers, smashed their way into a churchyard vault and took out the skeleton of a woman. The skull was found on the headstone of another grave.

Black magic symbols and the words 'Lucifer', 'Raylin' and 'Pigs' were scratched on the grave. The then Rev Robert Mansfield-Williams, vicar of the 19th-century St Gregory the Great Church at Canterbury, was reported as saying, "This was done by a gang of Satanists or by equally undesirable lunatics hipped with drugs. What they did can only be explained by some sort of perversion."

The paper went on:

The grave-robbers used heavy steel scaffolding poles to smash a three-inch stone over the vault, which is ten feet deep. They

Numerous cases of black magic have been recorded in the Kent Messenger Group files over the years.

climbed in and removed a skeleton from the coffin of a woman who died more than 100 years ago. The bones were found scattered near the vault.

The vicar said, "The desecration was found by someone walking through the churchyard. It makes me sick in the stomach. The sooner I can forget about it the better."

A senior police officer at Canterbury said, "We are not sure whether this was black magic or just ordinary vandalism. We are making inquiries."

The theft of skulls from a grave at Margate was thought to be the work of devil worshippers. On 10 June 1975, the *Evening Post* carried a story about robbers smashing their way through a concrete covering to reach three skeletons buried in the town's public cemetery.

The grave, which dated from 1896, was used for further burials in 1921 and 1948. The dates were believed to have a secret significance for the robbers. Police were called after a member of the cemetery staff saw that the grave had been disturbed and parts of human skeletons were scattered about. *The Post* said:

There is a row of bungalows opposite the cemetery in Manston Road and residents had told police that they were wakened by a noise like hammering.

Said one: "The raiders appear to have used a lorry to take the heavy equipment they needed into the cemetery.

"They must have been determined to rob one particular grave for they ignored hundreds of others which would have been much easier to break in to."

Three months earlier, after a full moon, a courting couple had come across signs of black magic ceremonies in Cobham Woods, near Gravesend. They found a small doll daubed with red and with knife slashes on its body, a magic circle painted in red with the sacred hexagon of Solomon in the centre and a dead rabbit with an eye gouged out.

The *Evening Post* interviewed an occult expert, who was high priest of a white coven. He said the dead rabbit suggested the worshippers were using an image spell designed to do someone physical harm.

"The blood of the rabbit, or red paint, would have been used to symbolise human blood. The waning moon is used for spells to do people harm."

In its report of 3 March 1975 *The Post* added:

Another white witch, who calls himself Vic, said, "The two magical festivals at this time of year are Candlemas on 2 February and the spring equinox on 21 March.

"There was no special festival at the last full moon, although the belief is that maximum power can be obtained on the night of the full moon.

"Different cults use different symbols and practices."

Evidence is strong that the ancient lore of witchcraft is still practised in Kent. In 1983, police received a report that witchcraft activities might be taking place at Foxhole Lane, Matfield, in the Weald.

Cranbrook police investigated after receiving a telephone report that people dressed in unusual clothes had been seen dancing in a circle in the road. The *Kent Messenger* (28 October 1983) said the report followed the discovery three weeks earlier of stones thought to have been used for witchcraft practices at a nearby woodland clearing.

The *KM* stated:

Traces of candle wax had been left on four stones round a larger central stone at the clearing beside a footpath running from Foxhole Lane.

A police spokesman this week said an officer found nothing after a girl reported the latest incident at the junction of Foxhole Lane with Bramblereed Lane on Friday.

Village policeman Clive Bryant said he thought youngsters were responsible when the stones were found, but he consulted a witchcraft enthusiast who suggested the discovery was genuine.

The origins of witchcraft, in pre-Christian religion, were explained in the *Evening Post's* 'Discovering Kent' series (21 March 1980). As originally conceived, it had nothing to do with black magic or devil worship. It mostly earned its present reputation of evilness during the

16th and 17th centuries, following the Reformation. As a result, witchcraft was forced 'underground'.

Many practising witches still met, but in secret. The sacred rites and ceremonies of the old beliefs gradually degenerated until they eventually came to be regarded as evil. Across Europe and the New World, accusations and reprisals against 'witches' were widespread and as the true principles of witchcraft became lost, many stories were concocted to discredit practising witches.

Such stories abound all over the country, nowhere more so than in Kent. *The Post* related one, particularly grim a tale:

One wild, stormy night, three murderers decided to employ the forces of black magic to help them with a crime they were planning to commit.

They severed the hand of a corpse hanging from a gallows and plucked five locks of hair from his head.

They took them to an old witch who lived on Tappington Moor, near Lyminge Forest. She made them a charm.

The three murderers made off with their 'charm' to Tappington Hall where they killed the owner and stole his gold. Afterwards they went to the Crown Hotel, at Rochester, to celebrate.

A page had witnessed the murder, however, and in due course the three murderers were arrested and later hanged.

The old witch was thrown into a pond with the severed hand tied round her neck.

A feature, written in 1965 by Ruth Spencer, delved even deeper into the history of witchcraft:

From its very beginning — with the beginning of man — until the present century, the story of witchcraft presents a picture of cruelty, terror, persecution and pain. It was not so much a matter of agonies being dealt out by witches, but suffering which they went through at the hands of those who brought them to a so-called justice.

There may have always been free speech in this country, but it did not always pay to take advantage of it. In 1534, a strange dreamer known as the Holy Maid of Kent, talked of the land being unhappy until a certain tree, revealed to her in a vision, was destroyed. This was taken to be a veiled attack on King Henry and other notable men and when the maid went on to say she thought that if Henry disowned Queen Catherine he would be dead within seven months, she was arrested and executed.

In the 17th century the hunting of witches reached the height of mania and in 1645 three women were condemned to death and hanged at Faversham. In 1652, at Maidstone Assizes, six women of West Kent were indicted for murder by witchcraft.

One of the accused, Anne Ashley of Cranbrook, admitted associating with the devil, but the methods by which admissions were forced were so hideously cruel that it is little wonder at any statements made.

Later in 1678, at Maidstone, another woman was accused of witchcraft. Prosecution witnesses said she had bewitched a young maid. At the trial, a pint of blood was produced, full of nails and crooked pins in strange forms, and this was said to have been vomited by the unfortunate girl.

Part of the lore of witches says: "A witch cannot die until she has passed on her power to her successor." Obviously not every witch paid heed to this — otherwise the craft would be as active today as it was in the Middle ages. In the Victorian era, witchcraft almost died out.

But, in 1940, an incident is reported to have taken place near Sevenoaks, when a woman demonstrated her power over animals. She placed a piece of straw in the road in front of a horse and, in spite of all kinds of persuasion, the animal would not move — until the straw was taken away.

The Medway Merlin

IN JUNE 1982, the *Evening Post* took its readers inside the home of a Medway Merlin called Kevin, who revealed some secrets of the occult.

Kevin's top-floor flat was like any other tiny Medway bedsit. It had a sink, a cooker, wardrobe and a bed — and very little else. It was only when the eye wandered to the bookshelf, stacked with texts on the occult, magic, astrology and witchcraft, that you became aware that something was different.

Hanging from the walls were several brass talismans and on the dressing table a bell, book and candle. Kevin was a witch, although he did not broadcast the fact.

Reports in the Sunday newspapers that witchcraft involved nude romps through moonlit woodlands leading to orgies of carnal lust were laughed at by Kevin. Although he admitted some covens might meet 'skyclad' (without clothes), he said this was to lower the inhibitions and to make one feel closer to nature.

The word 'witch' is said to come from the old English word 'Wicce', meaning a wise person. Kevin explained, "Witchcraft is not a religion, it's a way of trying to live wisely. It is the craft of the wise."

It is as old as Pagan man but has survived to the present day despite the intervention of Christianity. He said, "There are several covens in Kent to my knowledge, although many witches now work alone.

"There is no way you can tell a witch just by looking, although witches can recognise each other by a kind of telepathy. We seem just like everyone else. We are human and we do have feelings. Witches don't have power themselves — just the ability to use knowledge."

They have their own marriage ceremony, based on an old Romany gypsy tradition, called Jumping the Broomstick.

Kevin's interest in witchcraft goes back to when he was eight, preferring to read books on science fiction and the supernatural rather than the usual cowboy stories. At school he developed an interest in physics and went on to study astronomy.

His first clash with orthodox religion came at 16. Kevin, at that point a member of the Church of England, heard a canon saying that God created man.

"I asked him straight, who created who?' said Kevin. From then on Kevin began seeking out answers for himself and while stationed in

The witches' great circle.

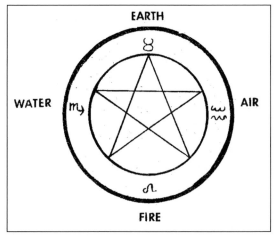

Warwickshire with the RAF, joined a group of witches who taught him all he knows.

"They didn't teach a religion — they taught a philosophy," he explained. "I found it very meaningful although the military took a dim view — I had to keep a low profile."

Witches believe in the force of nature. They also believe in reincarnation and Kevin said he was once told by a spiritualist that he was present when Joan of Arc was burned at the stake.

Kevin said witches used a circle for their rituals and aligned the rites with the phases of the moon, practising white (good) magic as it rose or waned. The circle is used to store and preserve powers and is usually nine feet in diameter and cast either in chalk drawn on the floor, salt sprinkled in the shape of a circle, or etched into the floor with a ceremonial black-handled knife called an Athame tied to a chord.

Inside is the altar which contains four candles, one for each point of the compass. An inner circle may also be cast in sulphur. These temporary circles are removed after the ritual is completed.

Permanent circles may be made up of stones outside or painted on a floor inside. Many modern witches now merely construct a salt circle on their floor then leave it hidden under the carpets, or simply seal a room at its edges with sea salt and mark pentacles on the wall with sacred water.

The main ceremonies are held at Candlemas (Easter)); Beltane (May Day); Lammas (1 August); Hallowmas or Halloween and Yuletide, the Druidic festival for calling up the sun.

Kevin added, "The witch can use his powers for self gain if so desired, but that is usually frowned upon. The witch is entitled to ask for things for the self, but only out of need."

He said that, all the while, witches work to the time-honoured code of "Do as thou wilt, as long as ye harm none."

A similar home visit, this time to that of a white witch in Rainham, was reported in the *Evening Post* edition of 9 February 1990. Tarot cards, crystals and books were spread on Jean Tighe's living room table — and there was a black cat walking around to complete the picture.

Jean said that the mere mention of the word 'witchcraft' had people throwing up their hands in horror. She found this odd when the main tenet of the Wiccan Way was merely respect for nature. Her speciality was that of psycho-therapeutic healing, but she was reluctant to differentiate between the various skills used in her work.

"Psychotherapy is healing by the mind. A tarot reading could turn into a counselling session, and end up as therapy," she told *The Post*.

Tarot, crystal healing, even — occasionally, and only for good — spells were all options.

"I learn from people all the time. When I give a reading it's a two-way thing." She found men were generally more sceptical than women. "They put a brick wall up. They want you to tell them what they had for breakfast before they believe anything."

Not that she was against healthy scepticism; she just wanted people to have an open mind.

A graduate of the White Lodge, the College of Psychotherapy at Tunbridge Wells, her main practice used crystal pendula to pinpoint imbalances in the body's six energy centres.

She asked the pendulum to show her 'positive' and 'negative'; without moving her hand, the pendulum swings slowly from side to side or back and forth.

Working from a point above the head down to below the navel, she said the energy centres were:

❏ The Crown — mental activity and spiritual energy.
❏ Pineal — eyesight and intuitive facilities; the mythical third eye.
❏ Throat — thyroid and emotional centre.

❏ Heart — again an emotional centre, but this time more retrospective, often dealing with family relationships.

❏ Solar plexus — digestion and the body's psychic centre.

❏ Procreative centre — sex organs and procreation; a still pendulum over this point could be symptomatic of a recent operation or pregnancy.

Jean said she used one extra point at the base of the spine, 'Kundalini', which was to do with physical energy. "You can sometimes pick up an ailment there that you missed in the other centres," she said.

White witch Kevin Carlyon, centre, with Sandi Jeffery and her daughter Rebecca, seen here in a cleansing ceremony at Little Kits Coty, Aylesford.

In 1996, *Kent Today* (23 August) reported a case of a paranormal investigator who performed a ceremony to protect an ancient stone circle site from vandals.

The *KT* said:

> White witch Kevin Carlyon is convinced Little Kits Coty at Aylesford could be hit by the same group who vandalised the stones at Avebury, in Wiltshire.
>
> He visited the remains of the Neolithic burial ground yesterday to conduct a 'cleansing' ceremony, which he claims will keep evil forces away.
>
> Mr Carlyon said, "It is like holding up garlic to a vampire. If good energy is placed into a site it cannot be used for evil."
>
> Eight stones at Avebury were daubed with black and white paint and covered with strange symbols, believed to be linked to black magic.

Mr Carlyon, describing himself as high priest of the Covenant of Earth Magic, had helped detectives in Wiltshire investigate the attack two months earlier.

The ritual at Little Kits Coty involved an altar, candles, incense burners and a ring of flour. He was joined by Sandi Jeffery and her daughter Rebecca, who helped 'invoke the spirits of nature'.

Little Kits Coty, also known as the Countless Stones, is the remains of a long-barrow and one of two Neolithic monuments in Aylesford.

The newspaper concluded:

A similar ceremony was performed at the site seven years ago by Mr Carlyon in a bid to stop the Channel Tunnel Rail Link affecting the stones.

Chapter Five

UNSOLVED MURDERS

Terror in Tunbridge Wells

MOST Kent murder cases are solved and the killers duly brought to justice. But some remain unresolved and perplexing. In this chapter, we open the files on a selection of cases of special interest.

In the run-in to Christmas 1987, the normally sedate spa town of Tunbridge Wells was being shaken out of its cosiness by an almost unthinkable terror.

A second woman living alone in the town had been brutally murdered. Like the first victim she had been subjected to a violent sexual attack before being killed. In addition to the brutal murders, another woman had been raped. Far from imbibing in the traditional Christmas spirit, the salubrious Kent town was transfixed with fear.

Was a sadistic killer stalking the streets for victims? Indeed, was any woman in the town safe? National tabloid papers fanned the flames with banner headlines such as 'Town of Terror' and 'Streets of Fear'.

Within six months, it seemed Tunbridge Wells might have more in common with Jack the Ripper's murky Victorian London than its traditional image as the home of irascible newspaper letter writers.

The growing horror had started back in June when Wendy Knell, a 26-year-old divorcee, was found dead in her Guildford Road bedsit. Wendy, the manageress of a photo-processing shop, had been sexually assaulted and battered to death.

In late November, there was further cause for alarm when Caroline Pierce, a 20-year-old single woman living in Grosvenor Park, was reported missing. Three weeks later her body was found 40 miles away in a dyke at a remote spot on desolate Romney Marsh. She, too, had been sexually assaulted and beaten to death.

Post-mortems revealed that both women showed signs of strangulation. The way in which both had been sexually attacked and killed were not the only similarities. Both were young women living alone in Tunbridge Wells bedsits, both had jobs in the same road and both were brunettes.

Those similarities were not lost on detectives; nor was a third terrifying incident in which a woman was raped in her town centre flat five days after Caroline Pierce disappeared. Police warned women not to leave Christmas parties alone as the hunt for the killer or killers was stepped up. It was grim advice.

Wendy's body had been discovered six months earlier after she failed to turn up for work at Supasnaps in Camden Road. Detective Inspector Greg Berry, then a detective sergeant, was the first police officer at the murder scene.

He said, "There were no clear signs of a forced entry and no one had heard anything from the flat at all. Wendy was lying naked on the bed with a head wound and was obviously dead."

A murder incident room was set up at Southborough Police Station as more than 50 detectives were called in. The investigation soon established that a diary and souvenir Austrian key ring had been taken by the killer.

The key ring had a small brass cow bell, a brass plate with Woman of the Year engraved on it and multi-coloured wool attached to a leather strap. It was similar to the one Wendy had brought back for her mother following an Austrian holiday. But why would the killer have taken those items?

Another important clue was a partial footprint in blood on a blouse belonging to the murdered woman. Checks with the British Shoe Index established that the killer was almost certainly wearing training shoes manufactured by Clarks. Officers became increasingly concerned that they might be dealing with a serial killer when it was reported that Caroline Pierce had gone missing. She was last seen at about midnight on 24 November when she was dropped off by taxi at her Grosvenor Park bedsit.

The situation, however, was confused by a number of reported sightings of Caroline either on Charing Cross station or on trains going there.

Five days after her disappearance, fears in the town were exacerbated when a 34-year-old woman, living alone in a town centre flat in Dudley Road, was brutally raped.

Then, on 15 December, just ten days before Christmas, the fate of Caroline Pierce was uncovered when farm worker John Minnis discovered a body in a water-filled dyke at St Mary in the Marsh on Romney Marsh. Caroline had worked as manageress of Buster Brown's burger bar and restaurant in Camden Road — just 400 yards from Wendy's workplace.

Because of the remarkable similarities between the murders, former Detective Chief Inspector Duncan Gibbins, then head of Kent CID, took the unusual step of deciding to personally take charge of the two murder inquiries. The joint inquiry was one of the biggest undertaken in Kent. More than 80 officers were used and a satellite incident room was set up at Lydd police station.

Like Wendy Knell, Caroline had also lost personal items. Among them were her passport and an Eastbourne Mutual Building Society passbook and cashcard. And, like Wendy, too, the items taken also included a bunch of keys that Caroline is believed to have had on her the night she went missing.

The bunch contained three tabs, one advertising Buster Brown's and another reading, 'Compulsive, neurotic, anti-social manic and paranoid, but basically happy.' The other poignantly stated 'Caroline's keys'.

Neighbours told police that they had heard alarming screams outside Caroline's home on the night she disappeared but had seen only a reversing car. Mr Gibbins, who is now retired, said, "I think she died then or very soon after. There were three screams. The first was loud and ter-rified and the last one was whimpering and trailing away."

The big puzzle for police was why the killer or killers had dumped her body where they did. Today it still remains a mystery. The murderer could have disposed of the body in a forest within a few miles of Tunbridge Wells. Why take the risk of a 40-mile journey when he could have easily been stopped?

Police painstakingly searched Caroline's bedsit and the graveyard backing on to her cul-de-sac but they could find no sign of her being attacked or of a weapon.

A man was sentenced to a lengthy prison sentence at Maidstone Crown Court in April 1988, for the rape in Dudley Road, but no one has ever been caught in connection with the murders.

Both murders were particularly violent. Mr Gibbins said, "The way these women met their deaths was absolutely brutal. Whoever did it treated them like lumps of meat. He didn't give a damn — he was a beast."

He also believes they may have been committed by a serial killer, such was the brutality. He said, "This type of person stalks his victims, doesn't take chances, and can actually eliminate the killing from his mind.

"Normally, he gets a memento of the victim over which he fantasises. The sexual motive is one of dominance. It doesn't have to be a single man — it could be a married man with two children." But if the murders were the work of a serial killer, the big unanswered question is why hasn't he yet struck again?

Despite the lack of a result to date, the investigation is very much a live inquiry. The current investigation is being led by Detective Chief Inspector Dave Stevens and Detective Inspector Greg Barry.

Detective Chief Inspector Stevens, the senior officer in charge of the case, said the police were still as determined as ever to catch the offender or offenders. He said, "We have to keep an open mind about whether they are linked because, whereas there are similarities, there are also dissimilarities.

"It could be that there was one person involved in the first offence and two or more in the second. There is also the outside possibility of a copycat murder."

Detective Inspector Barry said, "The biggest reason we would like to know is for the families. They are still grieving and they think about it all the time. The book is never closed for them and likewise for us."

Kent police called in a forensic psychologist for the first time ever to build up a portrait of the killer — or killers. Dr Gisli Gudjonsson's verdict: Detectives were dealing with a potential serial killer.

Dr Gudjonsson said, "I decided, on the basis of the information I had, that the two cases had a number of features in common which suggested the same assailant or assailants.

"I think it is likely that these women had been stalked and targeted by the offender and that they were selected because they were vulnerable."

The involvement of Dr Gudjonsson broke new ground in Kent police's approach to murder inquiries. Dr Gudjonsson, a consultant clinical psychologist who has been used by various police forces on numerous occasions, was called in shortly after the murder of Wendy Knell.

He suggested that the murderer was someone with a criminal history, including burglary, and was particularly interested in the efforts taken to tidy up the scene of the murder.

"The scene had been adjusted to make it look as though nothing had happened," he said. "It was as if the person had wanted to make it look like the beginning of the sequence rather than the end.

"The most likely explanation is that the person wanted to create a certain fantasy he had in his mind and that he wanted to remember the events in a certain way."

Dr Gudjonsson added, "I thought it was likely to happen again because it fell into a fantasy pattern."

When the second murder was committed six months later, police again called in the psychologist to help.

Dr Gudjonsson said, "I think it is highly likely, and nothing I have seen since convinces me otherwise, that the two murders were linked and likely to have been committed by the same man who, for some reason, stopped or was taken out of circulation."

The offender is thought by Dr Gudjonsson to be reserved, to have few friends and a tendency to walk the streets at night.

He added, "It is my view that the murderer knew the area very well, that he either lived or worked there at the time, and that people may still remember someone who said something that could help the police.

"When people commit these horrendous crimes, they sometimes give something away to indicate that they have done it. It may be there are people who can still assist the police."

Death In The Forest

BEWITCHING Bedgebury Forest is not in the mood for giving up its dark secrets. For, while the extensive pine forest, close to Goudhurst, continues to be a much visited beauty spot, it has also been the scene of two horrendous and, as yet, unsolved murders. Twice in a three-year period women were brutally slaughtered. And, in both cases, their killers are still at large.

The tranquillity of the forest idyll was rudely shattered for the first time in October 1979, as brilliant autumnal sunshine cast its own magic among the trees.

A young horsewoman from Bedgebury Riding School was among scores of people enjoying the forest when her horse shied and jumped into some bushes.

It quickly became apparent that her mount had reared at the scent of fresh blood, for below her lay the gruesome remains of a woman who had been battered to death. Police cordoned off the area and immediately launched a murder inquiry.

The dead woman was described as 5ft 1in with dark brown shoulder length hair, hazel eyes, a round face and a straight nose. Aged about 30 she was wearing a black and white floral smock, a pale green and yellow blouse, black polo neck jumper and brown tights. Mysteriously, there were no shoes at the scene, nor was there any sign of a handbag.

Bedgebury Forest, near Goudhurst, scene of a murder in 1979.

From the start, it was obvious that she had undergone the most violent death; half of her face had been virtually bludgeoned away.

The blood that had been splattered on the area convinced detectives that she had been murdered at the spot where she was found — a firebreak off a lane leading from the B2079 between Goudhurst and Flimwell. Detective Con Dave Holland, who was involved in the investigation from the start, said, "As far as we can gather, she had been taken there. It was a particularly frenzied attack. We found teeth knocked out by the blows."

More than 90 police officers were involved in the hunt for the killer but a fingertip search of the area and underwater search of the nearby lakes failed to reveal any immediate clues. However, detectives faced a far more fundamental obstacle in their inquiries. Who was the dead woman?

A skeletal X-ray revealed no deformity or injuries and there were no marks, scars or tattoos on the body to help the identification process. Home Office pathologist Dr Peter Vanezis did, however, discover at the post-mortem examination that the mystery woman was six weeks pregnant.

It was an ectopic pregnancy — the foetus being formed in the Fallopian tube — and the woman would have been suffering with considerable pain. Had she not sought medical help in the near future, it is very likely that she would have died as a result of her condition.

The pathologist was also of the opinion that she had previously given birth to a child. In addition, an orthodontic examination showed the dead woman had never received dental treatment and her teeth seemed to be self-cleaned by her natural diet.

Her lungs were also very clean, suggesting that she lived in the country rather than in a town. Police sent maggots found in the body to experts at Wye College for examination, with a view to establishing as near as possible the time of death, and came to the conclusion that it was likely to have been the Sunday prior to the discovery.

There was much to indicate that the dead woman was an itinerant worker who travelled around the country and abroad following fruit picking work. But again detectives faced another major hurdle: most itinerant workers had left Weald farms on the Saturday prior to the body being discovered. As a result, more than 700 farms were visited without a positive breakthrough.

An enormous publicity campaign to try to identify the mystery woman was also launched by police. Some 58,000 handbills and 2,500 posters appealing for help were distributed in Kent and East Sussex.

Inquiries were made with missing persons bureaux around the country, Interpol, the Salvation Army, schools, social services and other agencies but without success. In November, Kent police even contacted the Department of Medical Illustration at Manchester University to help them reconstruct how the battered woman would have looked.

Yet, despite extensive inquiries, both in this country and on the Continent, who she was has never been established.

Two months after she met her death, the mystery woman took the secret of her identity to the grave. Just six police officers mourned her at the lonely graveside funeral at Hawkenbury Cemetery, Tunbridge Wells.

Former Detective Chief Inspector Peter Spittles, who led the investigation, said, "One of the lads said it was very, very sad to think that someone could be murdered in this country and no one would miss them."

Certainly, it seems there must have been a child somewhere without its natural mother and, if they were still alive, a father and mother without a daughter. Clearly, too, her latest pregnancy seemed to suggest she knew someone fairly closely. Probably the nearest police ever got to establishing her identity came as a result of a BBC *Crimewatch* television programme broadcast five years after the murder.

A woman viewer in Stratford upon Avon rang to say she recognised the smock as one she had made for her mother and had later given to the Salvation Army following her mother's death.

Kent police sent a number of officers to the Vale of Evesham to follow up the lead but within several weeks all lines of inquiry had fizzled out.

Mr Spittles, who became a detective superintendent before retiring, said, "We always felt that identification was the key. If we had found out who she was, we would have been very close to finding out who had done it."

Less than three years after the first killing, the community was again shocked by the murder of another woman in Bedgebury Forest. Once again the dead woman was found off the same lane through the forest — about half a mile from the scene of the first murder.

But this time police quickly established the identity of the victim. She was Jean Brook, 46, a mother of three from Hastings. She, too, had been battered to death.

Mrs Brook was a driver for a Hastings-based agent for Ford and delivered parts and accessories to garages in the South.

She had left Hastings at 10.30am on Thursday, 10 June 1982. Travelling in a white Ford Transit van, she had called at the villages of Brede, Broad Oak, Northiam, Tenterden and Sissinghurst before arriving in Cranbrook at 12.45pm.

According to staff at a former farm shop in North Road, Goudhurst, it was her regular practice to drop off at the shop to buy fruit for lunch. The day of her murder was no exception.

Hours later, woodcutter Bill Greengrow, of White Limes Cottage, in Bedgebury Forest, raised the alarm. He had noticed that a white van parked off the lane since lunchtime was still there as darkness fell. Within an hour a police torchlit search had found Mrs Brook's body 50 yards from her van.

Detectives soon discovered that Mrs Brook had had a number of boyfriends in the Weald area over a two or three-year period. Mr Spittles, who also led this investigation, said, "We felt she was in the forest meeting a boyfriend, but we never found out who that person was.

"We think she may have wanted to finish a particular relationship and the other person didn't. Or it could have been a married man who wanted to finish and she had threatened to tell."

Whatever the likely motive, the second Bedgebury Forest murder, like the first, still remains unsolved.

Chronology

23 October 1979 — A young horsewoman comes across the body of a dead woman while riding in the forest. Police say the victim has been brutally beaten about the head.

24 October 1979 — A post-mortem examination reveals that the woman is six weeks' pregnant. Doctors say it is an ectopic pregnancy and she would have been in considerable pain.

2 November 1979 — The identity of the victim is still unknown. Detectives issue a picture of the smock worn by the woman in a bid to establish who she is.

18 December 1979 — The mystery woman is buried in an unmarked grave at Hawkebury Cemetery, Tunbridge Wells.

16 January 1980 — Detectives receive more than 25 calls after publishing a picture of how the woman may have looked, produced by the Department of Medical Illustration at Manchester University. However, the woman's identity remains a mystery.

25 January 1980 — Police close the murder incident room at Cranbrook Police Station.

10 June 1982 — The body of Jean Brook, 46, a mother of three and delivery van driver, is found in Bedgebury Forest. She has been battered to death. Police launch a second murder inquiry.

28 December 1984 — A BBC television *Crimewatch* viewer in Stratford upon Avon recognises the smock worn by the first murdered woman as one she made for her late mother. However, police inquiries in the area draw another blank.

Gruesome Find At Boxley

NESTLING cosily in the beautiful North Downs countryside, just off the Pilgrims Way, the picturesque village of Boxley had for centuries conjured up all that is splendid about rural England.

But, on the morning of Wednesday, 22 April 1987, the normally peaceful village, with its attractive mediaeval church and associations with the poet Tennyson, was to be rudely awakened.

Farm worker Graham Ling, who lived at Street Farm in the heart of the small community, had made a gruesome discovery.

In a field close to the entrance to the farm, just off The Street, had been dumped the body of a woman. She was wearing a bloodstained nightshirt that featured a picture of a cuddly teddy bear peeping out from under a duvet and saying, "I can see you." The body was bound in another nightshirt covered in love hearts and bearing the words "Give us a kiss at bedtime." It was an ironic and bizarre shroud.

Two pairs of panties and a bra had also been knotted together and used to truss up the body into a foetal position. Another item of clothing worn by the woman was a distinctive pink, grey and white nylon bomber jacket with an elasticated waist and front zip fastener.

Mr Ling had at first thought the bundle was rubbish thrown from a passing car on to the nearby road. But several hours later he made a closer inspection to discover the full horror of its contents. The dead woman had suffered brutal facial and head injuries.

Police immediately cordoned off the spot and made a search of the surrounding area. A fully computerised murder incident room was set up at Maidstone Police Station and detectives began carrying out house-to-house inquiries.

The mystery woman was said by police to be aged about 30 years old, 5ft 2ins tall and weighing about seven stone. Her hair had been

The bloodstained body of a woman was found at Boxley in 1987.

dyed with henna and she had a deformed left foot. Other distinctive marks included some false front teeth and a burn scar inside her right arm.

The discovery stunned many who had lived quietly in the village for years. Just who was the mystery woman? And who should want to murder her?

During the evening massive tailbacks were caused in The Street, a popular rural route between the Medway Towns and Maidstone, as police officers stopped motorists to ask if they had seen anything suspicious.

Two days later an appeal was made on the BBC *Crimewatch* for public help. Later in the same programme Chatham-based WPC Helen Phelps revealed that more than 30 people had rung to help.

One woman had a dramatic message. She whispered, "Listen, quick, I know who killed the woman at Maidstone..." But she hung up before completing the message. The same day detectives revealed they had made a vital breakthrough in their inquiries by identifying her as a 36-

year-old from the Deptford area of south-east London. The woman, who was identified through her fingerprints, was known to police and had served time in prison.

Detectives named her the following day, as divorcee Evelyn Staples, a mother of three who lived at the top of a four-storey block of flats in Pomeroy Road, Deptford.

A post-mortem by Home Office pathologist James Cameron had earlier established the cause of death as strangulation. Kent Police set up an incident room at Greenwich, as well as Maidstone, as inquiries increasingly centred on the London area.

Detectives quickly established that behind the homely sentiments of the motifs on her nightshirts lay the seamier side of Mrs Staples's private life of vice, drugs and crime. Mrs Staples worked the pubs of notorious London vice areas as a prostitute and was frequently away from her Deptford flat for days at a time.

Detective Superintendent David Tully, who led the investigation, said, "She carried all her clothing and underwear around in a couple of bags. She was also mentally retarded and violent. In one incident she smashed a glass in the face of a man in a London pub."

Neighbours of Mrs Staples also spoke of her noisy and disruptive lifestyle. John Dickson, an elderly man who occupied the flat opposite, described her as a 'flaming nuisance'. Stanley Meade, another pensioner who live in the flats, was even less complimentary.

"She used to knock on my door asking for fags, wanting to borrow money. She was a right old cow bag," he said.

Two years later, however, inquiries were being wound down despite the early use of DNA techniques in a bid to catch the murderer.

Detectives had been working on the theory that a client may have attacked her in a haggle over money after sex. Forensic evidence had revealed that intercourse occurred shortly before her death, but inquiries in London had largely been met with a blanket of silence. Mr Tully, who is now retired, said at the time: "She may not have got the money she wanted. It could have turned into a violent confrontation with the man giving her a hiding which went too far."

Detectives believe that Mrs Staples's fatal meeting with her killer occurred on the afternoon before her body was found. She was last seen wandering down New Cross Road in a drunken state and holding up traffic.

But just what was the connection between the sinister, twilight underworld of the capital and a peaceful village like Boxley some 40 miles away? According to detectives, nothing more than the Kent village being a convenient, isolated spot in which to dispose of a murder victim.

Chronology

22 April 1987 — Farm worker Graham Ling finds the dead body of a woman in a field at Street Farm, Boxley.

23 April 1987 — A post-mortem examination by a Home Office pathologist reveals the cause of death to be asphyxiation. Police broadcast an appeal for information on the BBC Television *Crimewatch* programme.

24 April 1987 — Police name the dead woman as 36-year-old mother-of-three Evelyn Staples, from Deptford, south-east London. She has been identified from her fingerprints.

25 April 1987 — A 47-year-old man from Deptford arrested in London in connection with the killing is released by police after being held at Maidstone Police Station for 24 hours.

24 February 1988 — Maidstone coroner Roger Sykes records a verdict of unlawful killing at the resumed inquest. Ten months after her murder police admit they are no closer to finding her killer.

30 March 1989 — Nearly two years after her murder police start winding down their investigation.

Garage Owner's Sinister Case

THE killing of millionaire garage owner and former racing driver Nick Whiting is one of Kent's more sinister unsolved murders. And more than seven years on, officers investigating the murder have not given up hope of a breakthrough in finding the killers.

Mr Whiting's disappearance led to immediate speculation that he had been kidnapped by a gang of car thieves. The former racing driver went missing on the evening of 7 June 1990 — the same night that five high-performance cars were stolen from his showroom in Wrotham Heath.

An intensive countywide search was launched as police admitted they feared for the safety of the 43-year-old father of three. They believed at least two men had broken into the All Car Equipe garage at about 6.30pm and abducted Mr Whiting.

When all the cars were recovered within three days, with no sign of the Ightham businessman, fears grew that he may have been killed. Two of the cars had been abandoned at St Mary's Platt School and the others dumped in different parts of London.

Police said there was no apparent motive for kidnap but admitted, "The longer it goes on, the more we are looking at it as a murder inquiry."

Mr Whiting's younger brother, Andrew, made a public appeal for information and said the family would offer a large reward for help in finding him. He said, "He is so close to his family that if he could have contacted us, he would have done by now."

Detective Superintendent Mick Chalkley confirmed that detectives had probed Mr Whiting's business dealings but ruled out any underworld links.

He said, "We have interviewed thousands of people and no one has said a bad word about him. He was well respected in the car world and known as a man of integrity with a very good reputation."

Mr Whiting made his name as a racing driver at Brands Hatch and cars were said to be his greatest passion. He raced with the *Kent Messenger* team in the 1970s and held many lap records for saloon car racing. He remained a familiar figure at the circuit as a sponsor.

His car sales showroom, All Car Equipe, specialised in high-perform-ance vehicles.

He had sold the business shortly before his death and was planning to redevelop a former garage in West Kingsdown, where his family's roots are. Almost a month after Nick Whiting was reported missing, his family's worst fears were finally confirmed. A badly decomposed and handcuffed body was found on Rainham Marshes, Essex, by conservationists taking samples.

The victim had been badly beaten, stabbed and shot through the head in what was likened to a gangland execution. Dental records confirmed it was the body of Mr Whiting and the search became a full-scale murder inquiry.

His wife said, "I had prepared myself for the worst but I did not realise just how big a shock it would be."

Detectives said they were working on the theory that Mr Whiting was driven to the remote spot in the boot of a car.

Two men from London were charged with the killing, but the case against one was later dropped and magistrates freed the other because of lack of evidence. The police incident room remained open and one year after Mr Whiting disappeared, Mr Chalkley said new leads were still developing.

In 1995 the murder was linked to a squad of highly-trained contract killers hired by underworld bosses. A national Sunday newspaper claimed that a new nationwide police unit was investigating a mercenary hit squad.

Kent Police said they were treating the link with suspicion but would investigate any new evidence. Andrew Whiting also greeted the story with caution and said, "I am still hopeful we will find out one day what really happened to my brother."

Chapter Six

THE PSYCHICS

My World by Yvette Tamara

YVETTE Tamara (her surname is Egyptian for 'Seeing Tomorrow') is a professional psychic consultant living in Kent. She says she has more than 2,500 clients — including businessmen who travel thousands of miles for her advice — and is sought after by television, radio and the press. She appears on TV programmes like *Kilroy* and *The Big Breakfast*, but, however big a name you are, circumstances have a habit of reminding you of your vulnerability, as she explained.

"My daughter, Jenna, was asleep one night. The central heating was on and there was no reason for me to feel cold. Yet, I felt absolutely frozen. I had to get up and fetch a hot water bottle to warm me up.

"As I walked past Jenna's room, I saw she had left her light on. But it had fallen over on to its side. The lampshade was smouldering. It was about to ignite. If I hadn't been awakened, who knows if I'd still have a daughter today?"

Yvette, who suffers from dyslexia and is deaf in one ear, is convinced it was her spirit guide who made her wake up and saved her little girl's life.

"Spirit can give you guidance and say, 'Come on, you've got to get your act together, let's push you in the right direction. But it's not going to happen unless you do something yourself.'"

Yvette, who was born in London but moved to Ashford as a child and now lives in Maidstone, is in touch with two spirits.

"Billy has been with me since I was a child. My childhood wasn't normal. My sister, who was 16 months younger, and I were split up at about the age of eight. Between eight and 13, we didn't have a very secure life. My parents went off and did their own thing. I had different aunts and a very strict upbringing.

"I was married at 17 to a chap who gave me love and affection for the first time. But he wouldn't have anything to do with the psychic side of my life. To him, it was rubbish, so it was suppressed for quite a few years.

"I had two children, Martin and Jenna, but I wanted to get out of the marriage. Billy was lovely. He would reassure me. I was on my own, no husband, two children. Once I was so broke but I found £5 in the road, enough to buy some food, go home and cook dinner."

Yvette began studies in hotel marketing. "I worked all day and all night. Then I blacked out. It was then that I decided to take on clairvoyancy full time.

"Billy is tall, slim. He's a down-to-earth coal miner who, while in this world, enjoyed life to the full. He is — not was — a fun-loving person. He died in a coal mine. He had six children, a wife he couldn't stand. I know that because he's told me. He speaks in a Welsh accent, he's smashing.

"I've also got George who's just come on board because you move up in your spiritual gift. Spirit guides like to work harmoniously with you. If you're prepared to work hard, they will work hard. They're here to do the right thing meaning, if I told a lie, they wouldn't want to work with me.

"George is a professor. He's come along because I've moved up a level. He's well-educated, likes his food, is well-built and comfortable.

"Billy and George travel with me. It's a very intimate relationship. I play a game with them sometimes. When I'm driving down the road, I ask them the colour of the next car that comes round the corner and they give me a colour. It's usually right.

"You have to communicate with spirit guides, talk to them. The strain can be very heavy. They give you information and sometimes it's weak.

You've got to get it stronger. You have to fine-tune everything. The mental work is heavy, the psychic energy you use is a strain. I've got it because I've reached out for it in my life.

"A woman offered me any amount of money to come up with the Lottery numbers. It would make me rich but it's not meant to be. Billy and George help me in the way they wish but not for monetary gain. They like helping me to help other people. If I went off with the Lottery numbers, my gift would be taken."

Psychics can switch off their special powers when they want to, she says.

"You can close down, like a flower. You say to your spirit guides 'I'm closing down, I need some peace.'"

The dead are a key part of any psychic's armoury, but it need not be a morbid subject, she says.

"When I am in contact with those who have passed over, the main concerns are that of telling loved ones that they are fine and very happy where they are."

Yvette explains why there are more female psychics than male: "Women go through lots of different aches and things happen in their lives. There are a few men who are sensitive and a lot who aren't. Women are more sensitive and looking for an answer.

"There are so many entities up there but people just don't tap into them. We've all got a psychic side we can tap into and the energy is out there."

Yvette discovered her gift of clairvoyance at the age of 13 when she unleashed a noisy poltergeist at her parents' pub in Ashford.

"You can have psychic powers when you are 13, 50 or 60. It's a common thing. You can be clairvoyant (seeing), clairaudient (hearing) or clairsensitive (feeling). There are different forms of psychic abilities. We all have them to a certain degree, especially women. It's like having a camera lens. It flashes a picture.

"It can happen at any age. I've been lucky that my gift came as a child. My grandmother was psychic. She lived in Wales and all the neighbours would come to see her. She was a beautiful woman.

"She became very ill. She knew when she went into hospital, she wasn't going to come out and she bought the sexiest nightie. I recently had a reading with my aunt Alice and my gran came through. So she's very much around me.

"My father is psychic but he doesn't like it. It frightens him when the spirits talk to him. He can't handle it and shuts it off. But I've always found it a comfort."

In her late 30s, Yvette is young for a clairvoyant. She studied at the Arthur Findley College, the world-renowned psychic centre in Essex.

Where is the other side?

"If you can give proof of someone who's passed over, it makes people think there is another side. It's a place where we move on. I sometimes think we have to come back. We do our bit in life but, if it's not quite finished, we come back again. The other side is a place of rest. I feel there's life after death."

Yvette sees no conflict between clairvoyance and religious faith. "I believe in God and the Ten Commandments. Anyone who doesn't follow them has a life of hassle. The first spiritualism was Jesus talking to the disciples."

What happens when a psychic passes over?

"I'll make sure everyone has a good time. My life has never been normal. It's been very adventurous but I've enjoyed it. I love what I do. I love getting messages from the other side and if I can give some peace, what could be more rewarding?

"I hope I shall be a spirit guide for someone else. I hope I don't end up on the other side and not be able to help somebody."

To help enlighten people about her psychic world, Yvette has devised a stage show which attracts huge audiences and our reporter went to see a performance at Maidstone's Hazlitt Theatre.

She sits on a stool. No props. The auditorium is packed, mainly with women but a sprinkling of men. She warns her audience that her power is not so strong in a crowd: "It's not as easy as if I had you on a one-to-one basis."

When she invites people on stage, there is some reluctance — some are shy. She tells a brave soul sitting nervously on a stool: "I see your direction changing in July, but, after July, you're going to have a period,

Yvette Tamara says her spirit guides, Billy and George, travel with her.

about August, when something new is going to present itself and you're going to have a choice in your job."

She tells a man in the rear stalls, "The spirit is coming through even stronger and he's saying to me you've really got to cut your losses and move on. You've got to make your mind up very shortly about what you're going to do.

"He's also saying to me you're going to have some trouble with your electrical system, you're going to have someone out to check it. Are you an electrician?" she asks. "No, I'm a multi-purpose man," he replies. Twenty-four hours after the show, the man contacts Yvette, telling her that all his electrics at home had suddenly blown.

Eastenders star Shaun Williamson, who plays Barry Evans, comes on stage as a surprise guest.

"I was about to get married," he recalls. "But Yvette said, 'I don't see that.' She was right. I'm still single. She also saw a new car having a prang. She was right there, too. It cost me £1,400 in repairs."

The show is drawing to a close. Not everything has worked well. The portrait paintings of Nick Ashron, supposed to resemble a deceased relative of someone in the audience, brings no response but several spells of embarrassing silence.

Later someone admits one of the pictures was like a relative who had passed over but was too shy to shout out.

Yvette, still looking fresh after the two-hour show, says, "I'd like to give you one message as you go home tonight. Always think to yourself, 'There's always someone up there keeping an eye on me.'"

The Mia Interview

CLAIRVOYANT Mia lives with her partner Alan, son Shane, daughter Tania, a dog and four cats in an isolated cottage in the village of Bobbing, near the Isle of Sheppey.

Born Marie Dolan, her grandparents called her Mia and she adopted the name when she became a clairvoyant. There was no indication in her pre-teen years of the extraordinary experiences to come, but adulthood brought with it fears that she might be losing her mind before she was able to come to terms with what she calls her 'gift'. Now she is widely respected and consulted and has recently completed a book about her remarkable life. So unusual are her experiences that our interview follows in full:

I understand you had an ordinary childhood and it was some time before you thought you had psychic advantages. Can you tell us how that began?

The first experience I had was at the age of 13 in Minster Abbey, Sheppey. It was a summer evening and next to the abbey used to be a youth disco, held on a Monday night, which we all went to and I remember coming out at about six o'clock, and walking through the abbey grounds to get some fish and chips from the shop at the top of the hill.

I was coming back, munching these chips and I saw a lady in white standing under what I used to call the Wishing Well Gate at the abbey and I thought she must be going to a fancy dress party, but when I was about 25 yards from her, she just vanished. Just in front of my eyes.

I was so shocked. I went back into the disco and said I'd just seen this person vanish and they all said, "Oh yeah, yeah."

What was she dressed in?

All in white. Looking back, I would associate it with a nun. At the time, I thought she was dressed very weirdly and was going somewhere. She seemed to be looking over her shoulder.

She wasn't looking at you?

No, I wasn't there as far as she was concerned. There was no recognition that I was there.

That was the very first thing. A few years went past and then I lived in a flat with my family in a place called Regency Close inside Sheerness Docks. On 21 January, on a Thursday morning, it was a beautiful, sunny day and I came out of the top flat with my elder brother's friend. It was ten o'clock in the morning. I shut the front door behind me and we both heard this scream.

We looked over the stairwell. It was a spiral staircase, the steps were stone and the bannister was wrought-iron work, and we saw this child, this young boy, falling down the stairs. You could hear this awful crunching sound as he banged into the stone steps. We heard him screaming and we were both running down the stairs watching him, holding the rail all the time. As we had just passed the first floor, on the last turn down to the ground floor, he hit the ground floor with a sickening crunch ...and when we were just about five feet away from him, he disappeared.

Up to that point, he was a normal, little boy. Everything was normal, the noise, the sound. But he just disappeared which was absolutely mind-blowing. I was about 15 or 16 years of age and the chap with me saw it all happen, we both saw it.

We both looked out of the door immediately, because your brain won't accept it straight away and we looked up the path...

There was no blood on the floor or anything like that?

No, nothing at all. Outside the flats, as soon as you get out, there is flat grass and a flat path for quite a long distance on both sides; there's nowhere to go, but, even though we had seen this child disappear, we still had to look. It was really odd, especially with someone else there, otherwise you'd think you were losing your mind.

We went to Sheerness Register of Births and Deaths to try to find something out, but we couldn't find anything, so then we went to the Sheerness Library and went through the old papers of the *Times Guardian* and, 50 years to the day, a boy had been killed in Bluetown, falling down the stairs, on 21 January.

At that point, I was very much an atheist. But, I thought to myself, there must be something — it doesn't necessarily mean life or death — it could be a time lapse or whatever.

The funny thing was that when I saw this, I didn't feel frightened — I felt like crying.

Was that because you could almost feel the pain the boy must have suffered?

Mia was suddenly transported from her garden to the scene of a plane crash.

Yes, the emotion of it. Nothing happened for a few years and then, when I was 22, I was married, Mrs Average, in suburbia, with two kids and a semi and I was running my own business.

Where would that be?

In Sheerness. I am very much Island-oriented.

What kind of business was that?

I had my own cleaning company. Anyway, I was 22 and it was an afternoon and the children were obviously very young then. They were watching television in the front room and I'd put their tea on. I did some toast; I think I was doing spaghetti on toast, and I came in the room to check on them and I was miles away, got engrossed in the telly, standing in the middle of the room and a man's voice said to me, "Toast is burning." It was such a shock.

I went into the kitchen and the toast was on fire. I blew it out and I thought it must have been my subconscious ...I must have remembered that I had put the toast on.

I heard the same voice on three or four different occasions. The next time I was going to a friend's house. I had dropped the kids at play school and I knocked on the door — she had a town house in Sheerness — and she said, "Come in, door's open." She was in the back of the house where the kitchen was.

I opened the front door and I was just closing it when the same man's voice said to me, "She's leaving him." Now, I knew it meant her husband and I knew it referred to her, but I thought to myself, goodness me, I'm seriously losing this.

Yes, it must have been very worrying.

So, I didn't say anything to her, but we had been chatting for about an hour and then she said, "We're splitting up."

This voice... I ended up going to the doctor's after about six weeks of it and, at the same time, I was hearing these words: "Wake up." I couldn't move; I had been paralysed and I had a noise, like a thousand untuned radios, in my head. It was so loud it hurt. It was a peculiar sensation and it would last for a few minutes and then it would release me so I could get up.

I remember going to the doctor and saying I can hear this voice and I get these strange noises in my head and I was sent to see a psychiatrist. Obviously, it sounded like schizophrenia; I thought it was schizophrenia.

I was asked all these questions like, "Does it say bad things? Is it demoralising?" I said, "No, it's very factual things." It told me someone was pregnant. When I went to say hello to her and said, "I hear you're pregnant," she said, "I'm not pregnant." But she came back three days later and said, "Guess what, I was pregnant!"

I had no luck there and they said I must be very tired, that perhaps I was stressed out, that it was my subconscious and I was not recognising it.

Then, the final crunch came when I was putting some washing on the line on a Sunday morning. It was about ten o'clock or eleven o'clock and the kids were playing in the garden.

I had been out the night before and I was feeling a bit the worse for wear. I remember thinking I'll stick the dinner on in a minute and I was just putting the washing out, I put my right hand up to put the peg on and my left hand to put the washing on the line and, in this position, suddenly I was gone! The garden was gone and I was standing on the side of a mountain …and this mountain had trees and there was a plane crash.

There were bits of wreckage all over. There were bits hanging off trees, over rocks and not only could I see it — I could turn my head and see it as well; it wasn't just straight down — I could smell it.

I had this acrid taste at the back of my throat and I could hear whirring, clicks and peculiar noises. It lasted about 20 seconds, that's all, and then I was back in the garden with the washing, absolutely terrified. I thought I was going insane, I thought I was losing my mind.

I left everything. I got the kids and went to mum's. I said, "Listen, I've seriously lost it, seriously, seriously lost it." I told her and I was really upset, because I was frightened.

My mum is very practical, lovely, very down-to-earth, and she said, "Look, you've been falling asleep on your feet. You've been out last night, those kids have had you up during the night, you've had a nightmare on your feet, that's all it is. It's nothing to freak out about." She calmed me down and I went off home.

The rest of the day was normal and at five o'clock, at tea time, I was doing some ironing in the lounge and the news came on and there was this plane crash that had happened that morning. And the scene was as I had seen it!

Whereabouts was the plane crash? Was it abroad?

Yes, it was definitely abroad. I think Asia.

Was it the exact scene you had seen?

Exactly the same. It was as if I had been there and come back again, just after it had happened. I hadn't told anyone else that time because I was worried my friends would think I was peculiar. The phone rang and mum said, "Are you watching the telly? I think it's more than falling asleep, don't you?"

I said I didn't know what to do about it. As we were talking, the only things we could think of were places like spiritual churches, but there's nothing in *Yellow Pages*... I remember looking through *Yellow Pages*.

So, we used to go and sit in the back of these spiritual churches and the first impression I had from them was very tacky with housewives with delusions of grandeur and 50 per cent of the people who would give a service, or a demonstration, didn't ring true. I thought I'm not having any of that.

But, at quite a few of them, where I sat, some of the crowd would come to me and say, "Your colours are phenomenal. You're sparkling all over the place, but you're dangerously out of control."

This is the aura, is it, they were talking about?

Yes, the energies coming off me.

I went about five or six times and then, one night, it was announced that a healing would be given at the back of the hall. I was very cynical still and I looked round and saw this lady who was about 50 years of age, but she had something warm and safe about her. Some people just have a presence and I thought, "Well, I don't know, if she can do it, she might be able to take away what I've got."

So, I queued up and took my turn and she put her hands over my head and in 15 minutes she told me everything that had been going on …the chaos, not specifically, but more or less, and she told me how to control it.

So, what do you have to do?

It's all to do with clearing a void in your mind, thinking of nothing and then observing what comes in. You use the same screen as your memory screen. If I asked you what did you do an hour ago, you'd get a picture in your mind. You have to use the same screen, but you don't put anything on it, you leave it blank.

And then, eventually, if you can keep calm, you start picking it from the ether, like radio or television. But, if you have any emotion or reaction in your chest or any feeling, you'll lose it. You are observing what is, not what you might want or might be …nothing must be emotional.

So, I honed this quite well and here I was, 24, with this gift and an attitude, it must be said.

Well, young people have got attitudes, haven't they?

Yes, I was giving these amazing party pieces and people were coming round and saying, "My God, she's fantastic!" I got more and more big-headed and it culminated in this American researcher hearing of me and she asked if I would join a working group, a circle, to see how far my powers could be stretched.

She was very interested in the youth side of it, because it is usually associated with older people. I was very proud of this and very headstrong and I went for a few weeks, but nothing really happened. Then, one night, there was myself, the American writer, a secretary next to her who was taking notes, next to her was someone who was psychic, on my left was a lay person who was interested, on my right was an old lady who was introduced to me as a deep-trance medium, a very frail old lady, and on the other side was a healer.

The writer asked me what was my most scary experience and I started telling her about a haunted house I'd been to. The feelings were very ominous — even though the actual physical activity had not been that much, the feeling was awful. And she said, "Concentrate on it, concentrate on it." And Eric, who is the voice, Eric's my guide, said, "Don't do this, don't do this, stop it." But I remember thinking, "Eric, this is my big moment."

Eric is the guide who told you about the burning toast?

Yes, he tells me when I need advice. Anyway, to cut a long story short, I homed back in on this house and I brought the thing back into the place. The lights all went, there was this black thing going around the edges of the circle the people were sitting in. The lady on my left, who was the lay person, went into convulsions, the lady on my right, who was this little old lady, was in deep trance.

There was this man's voice saying to me, "You know not what you have done." I thought there's no man in here and I looked round to my right and there's the little old lady with a man's face over the top and her jaw had dropped and this voice was coming out.

And I'm thinking, "Eric, Eric, Eric." And he's saying, "Concentrate on the cross." And I said, "What cross? There's no cross."

But, in the middle of the circle, in the air, was a very faint white outline of a cross.

What, not standing up, just floating in the air?

Not moving, just there. So, I start to concentrate and while I concentrated and stopped the emotion, as I had been told, the cross got more and more solid and this blooming black thing went past me and, as it went round, I felt a dreadful, awful feeling. It broke my concentration and, of course, the cross started to dissipate again.

Eric said, "Concentrate, concentrate!" And eventually I managed to get it so that it was solid and, at the moment it was solid, there was, like, a flash and the thing was gone.

The lady who had convulsions was crying, the other lady was a bit shaky, the secretary was scribbling like mad, the American writer was saying, "This is fantastic, this is just what we want, this is fantastic!' She stood up and said, "See you next week." And I said, "I am never doing this again — ever!" I went out and stopped all clairvoyance for eight months.

That night made me believe in God because everything has an opposite. I took comfort from the fact that, if there's black, there's white and I started to look at my life and take the ability seriously and I realised you can't play with it.

So, now I only do it when it's for benefit and not to anybody's detriment. But it was a lesson I had to learn.

Since then, have you had any other experiences where you were perhaps taken to a place and saw an event that was likely to happen and then, subsequently, did?

Not so much taken to a place. The only other one I had like that was when I was giving a chap a reading. He was in his 50s and his wife was pushing to have it done; he didn't believe in it.

I knew he had been in the Army; I knew that before we started, so I expected to see past Army activity. But suddenly I was taken to this place and I was in very dry air and there was a hill and a road going up this hill, a dry, track road.

You could see the side of it and on posts going up the hill were people's heads, white men's heads. There was this jeep, people dead in the jeep and terrible emotion and I couldn't help talking as I was seeing it.

As I came out of it, I could see the man again and he was crying. This actually happened to him — for a couple of years, he was a mercenary in Angola and this was a group of them and this was how he found his comrades. Not even his wife knew that story.

Moving on to the people you see now, I suppose you get a mixture, some who want to find out about their family, some who are not well. Do you get more women than men coming to see you? Are women more receptive or sensitive? Perhaps men throw it off and don't want to get involved?

Seventy per cent are females. But, once a client comes for the first time, most of them come back.

There are a few problems. Firstly, we have the problem of a stigma attached to clairvoyance. It often seems like end-of-the-pier stuff, with women in strange costumes and there is no vetting service. Anybody can advertise as a clairvoyant, so you get a lot of cowboys giving it a bad name.

Secondly, women are more receptive to new ideas. They are more likely to have an open mind. Men are very conditioned to being strong, having to deal with things on their own, anyway. They are not allowed to say that they can't cope with something or need help; women feel easier to do that.

Most of the men who come along are top business people who see me for practical business reasons.

What sort of things have you been able to offer them? Can you give an instance?

They would say, "I've got something coming up," and I would say, "Don't tell me anything; let me do the reading first." And then I'd tell them what situations were coming up. I will describe how they can differentiate between the two choices.

I'll say, "This is what's going to be happening and this is where the money lies, don't be fooled by that one." And they'll phone back and say, "You were right."

I don't say what might be, I tell them what is and what will be — that's the big difference.

Have you ever had to tell bad news to anyone who has come along, or are you not allowed to tell them bad news?

When you say not allowed, there is no magic force that stops you.

You don't want to upset people too much, I suppose?

Coming to me should be pleasurable …it should be enjoyable, spiritually uplifting. I never give death, ever. They always still want me to tell the truth, so if someone's got a bad time coming up — for instance, say someone's going to be unwell, or they are going to have terrible new financial problems, or marriage problems — then I'll say, "Listen, in this month, all hell's going to break loose financially for you and you're going to be in dire straits. But I want you to remember that I knew this was going to start and I will tell you when it's going to finish. And it will be finished by then, because of…"

So, I'm giving bad news, but I'm helping them through that period. Even if they don't believe me at the time, when it happens, and I've said it's going to happen, they can always take comfort from the fact that she knew this.

When you've given somebody advice, is it down to the individual to put it right, or is it fate — it's going to happen, anyway?

It is going to happen. I don't give them advice. At the same time, one of the hardest things for me is if I get a woman who comes along and, say, her husband or lover has walked out on her, and she's absolutely devastated; it's the end of the world. She comes to me to ask, "Will he come back to me? Will we get back together again?"

I have a look and see there's no way this is going to happen. But I also know that, at the end of that year, she'll love someone else. At this point, she can't take that, she can't see it.

So, I say to her, "I can't see it clearly, but in October you'll be wonderfully happy and your love life's perfect."

She'll say, "Are you sure?" and I'll say, "Absolutely sure." So, she'll go away and she'll think he's coming back and then she'll get along with her life. And when she comes again, she'll say, "Guess what, I think you thought it was my husband, but it wasn't."

Clairvoyance is not just the ability to get information; it's the skill of giving it.

You mentioned you have a guide called Eric — has he ever materialised to you? Have you ever seen him?

Yes, the first time was after he had been around for about 18 months talking to me. I was still concerned that I was imagining it and one night, it was about nine o'clock, I was on my own, the kids were asleep. I was in the front room, the telly was off and I was chatting to him and asking him very fundamental questions like, "Why are we here?" and getting brilliant answers.

I said, "Look, I really need you to appear so that I know, once and for all, what you look like and then I can believe it."

He said, "You're not ready for that." I said, "Yes, I am, come on."

It went on for 20 minutes and he kept saying I wasn't ready and I said, "Well, it's just a figment of my imagination."

Then, the next thing, by the doorway, at first there was a small light. The light grew and filled three-quarters of the door and he was suddenly there! I thought, "Oh my God!" My whole stomach turned...

What does he look like?

He is very, very old, a little hair, a proud nose, with wrinkly eyes and face ...very weathered. He wears a brown robe, not particularly clean, with a bit of rope round the middle and he has a stick.

Is he a monk?

No, I asked him. When I meditate, or try to talk to him, he always goes to this place, like in a wood or a forest and there's a clearing. In the clearing, there is an old tree which has fallen over and he's sitting on it and there's a bit of an open fire and he sits in front of this fire. Behind him in the distance, is this peculiar building, a small, perfectly round stone building.

Has he ever told you where he lived?

I think it's Ireland, but it's hundreds of years ago. I don't know anything about it — my history is useless — but I think he may have been an apothecary, a chemist, or something like that. I am not 100 per cent sure.

Does he talk with an accent?

No.

Does he talk in old English?

Sometimes he'll speak in old English. He'll be talking to me when I'm speaking to somebody and he'll say, "Say this and this..." and when it comes out on the tape it sounds old English, but not terribly so.

People say to me, "How come you've got him." I think he's as mystified about how he's got me as I am about him.

An obvious question to ask, I suppose, is what state of existence is he in now? Is he just on a different plane?

A different dimension. Now, I know, rather than believe, that you come back more than once ...you learn so many lessons that you can stay over there, and he's got on to that stage and now he tries to help me.

Does he describe where he is and what sort of environment he lives in? Does he live in a house?

I've talked about this to him. You don't need a house. It's the emotional feeling, the calm, the serenity.

But are there trees and flowers and things like that?

If you want them to be. You can have what you want.

That's extraordinary.

Let me tell you about what I've been doing in the last year. I do a lot of 'ghost-busting' and I deliberately call it ghost-busting to keep it on a lighter level because, obviously, there are lots of worries involved.

Out of a hundred phone calls I get for ghost-busting, only about 15 or 20 have anything to look into. I am called in by major hospitals, I do pubs, homes …a lot of homes are the worst because people don't want anyone else to know about it as it may devalue their property. It worries the neighbours.

I do this with Alan, my partner, and we go all over Kent and about 80 per cent is without publicity, without being paid.

When you say ghost-busting, what do you mean exactly?

Exorcism. I have to go to clear up after a priest has been in and has not been successful. Some priests in different religions are trained in the art of exorcism, but not all of them. So, it's just Eric and I, really, sorting it out. I could not do it without Eric.

I was talking to someone earlier who said there were two kinds of services, if you like: a rescue service and exorcism. He said that exorcism could be used wrongly where you had a confused spirit and that it was only really necessary to give the spirit some guidance.

Yes, exactly, but, saying that, the biggest one I had was at a local psychiatric hospital. I was called in on the night shift because they had had nurses thrown against the wall, levitated, real heavy-duty stuff. One of these nurses was a six-foot fella and he was terrified.

I went in with this very nonchalant air because I had already done quite a few easily in the previous months — and they were rescues, as you said.

We got there about two o'clock in the morning, because the shift started at ten o'clock and we let them get on with what they had to do first. We were walking around this building and there were patients and I was trying not to disturb them, because the last thing they wanted was to know what was going on.

I found this room and I thought it's definitely concentrated here, so I said, "This is where I think I should do it."

Alan stayed with me while the staff went to have a coffee. I opened up and immediately it was terrifying. I stood there shaking violently. My head was full of lots of faces and emotions and noises.

I have to hold it and then Eric comes in and he takes it over. It's almost as though I'm the physical connection.

I said, "Eric, there's no space, it's full up," and he said, "Hold it, hold it, hold it." And I don't even know how it happened, but I held it for about three minutes and then there was the same flashing light, like I said before, and then it was gone.

About two weeks later I got a phone call from one of the nurses and she said there were still a few strange things happening. Could I come back?

I said, "Yes, OK." I went back and opened up in this room again and it was Eric! And he said, "Next time when you do something like this…" and he was shouting at me!

He had brought me back all the way to the hospital and Alan was looking at me and he thought I was doing this exorcism and I was not — I was getting a ticking off from Eric!

I said, "Yes, OK, I understand …we'll talk." What I'd done, you see, was I hadn't been opening up just to talk to Eric. I'd opened up for clients, or for work, and there were lots of things I was doing wrong, through his eyes.

I went back into the rest room and these nurses were waiting and I said, "It's over," and they've never had any more trouble since.

There's been a lot of hype in the newspapers and television and general conversation about the Millennium and how it bodes ill for all sorts of reasons …one or two cult organisations are saying we're all going to get blown up in 1999 and the year 2000 is going to cause so much distress across the world. Do you see anything or have you come across anything in your deliberations which suggests there is a problem ahead?

Not in our vicinity. In the next couple of years, one of the biggest things will be disease in the Third World, new to what we know …different, a new disease.

But I see the year 2000 as a new beginning. I think that the revelations about the future by Nostradamus and others, although I must admit I haven't read a lot about it, are being misunderstood. There is change, but it's different as we know it.

We are not talking about asteroids hitting the Earth, destruction or world wars?

Fifty years ago, if someone said there weren't countries, only Europe, under one umbrella, it wouldn't have seemed feasible, but that's coming to pass — and it's a whole new way of thinking.

Do you think this change will start in the year 2000?

I think it's already started. The year 2000, in the years to come, will be the point when they say it changed.

What about this talk about global climatic change? Is that all part of it?

It comes into it, but it's not going to be as terrible as people think. To me, the biggest thing that's coming in the future is a rebirth, a mass planting of vegetables and trees and a regeneration of the Earth rather than the destroying of the Earth.

That's good. Not many people have said that before. Everybody seems to look at the year 2000 with doom and gloom.

But only because of what's pre-written, instead of looking for themselves.

Well, perhaps they don't know how to?

Everybody has got sixth sense, everybody who walks the Earth.

Centuries ago, do you think we were more acutely aware of it then and we just lost it because of the material world we live in?

Absolutely. It's in all religions or in all histories. They mention the spiritual, or knowing, or the seer, and even in today's society, if you, as a newspaper person, said to your colleague, "I've got a hunch about this story. We're going to go with it." And against all the odds, against all the advice, you pull it off, they will say, "Good hunch, there."

You could have had a sixth sense about it, which is not acceptable. It's exactly the same thing, different terminology.

I suppose one thing you can't do for yourself, or anyone else, is predict the Lottery numbers?

My goodness, I've tried…

Let Your Chil
Back To Nature

by
John Hodgson and Alan Dyer

Illustrations by Sally Reason

The revival of an ancient way to combine stories and fun activities that helps children to become more sensitive to the natural world, and to grow into creative, well-balanced adults.

www.capallbann.co.uk

Let Your Children Go Back To Nature

ISBN 186163 1723

Published by:

Capall Bann Publishing
Auton Farm
Milverton
Somerset
TA4 1NE

This ground-breaking book by two long-experienced educationists challenges the current orthodoxies about the upbringinging of younger children.

It offers both parents and teachers an attractive means to ameliorate the deadening demands of the National Curriculum.

It is crammed with new and stimulating ideas, games and creative activities that have already delighted thousands of children of all abilities.

Alan Dyer is Principal Lecturer in Environmental Education at the Unversity of Plymouth, and founder and coordinator of Education Earthwise, a forum for teachers and environmentalists. His reputation for presenting lively 'magical' workshops on the environment has spread to central Europe, the United States and the Far East as well as throughout Britain. He is also the author of *'Personal, Social and Health Education in School Grounds'*

John Hodgson is a former curator and teacher of the fine and decorative arts, then a full-time Adviser to the National Trust who initiated and organised its educational work over a twenty year period. After retirement he ran educational programmes across southern England, linking landscape and mythology. He is also the author of *'Mabon, The Divine Child and the Sacred Land of Britain'* and *'Living as Ancient Greeks'*.

1

What children have said about the Quests and other adventures:

I really enjoyed it. It was super, exciting and fantastic all put together!

It was the best day I have ever had. I wish we could do everything again.

I learned a lot from what we did. If I get board (sic) I will write a dragon story. I learnt new games that I can play with my friends it was really fun I did tell my mum about it.

What parents and teachers have said:

A tremendous day which all the children enjoyed. Life became mysterious and fun.

The children thoroughly enjoyed the day. It really captured their imagination.

It was a magical day for the boys and girls (and for their headmaster).

What countryside rangers have said:

Some great ideas, good practical hands-on stuff.

Excellent insight! I left feeling full of ideas and can't wait to start.

Very inspiring. It felt great to touch nature.

Chiron

Chiron, the First Teacher

Archaic humans .... still possessed the insight that one had to leave the world, that one could become 'tame' only if before one had been 'wild' .... In order to be able to live within the order, in other words, in order to be consciously tame or domesticated, one had to have lived in the wilderness. One could know what inside meant only if one had once been outside.

HANS PETER DUERR [12]

Chiron was a centaur, half animal, half human: he had a horse's body and human torso, arms and head. The centaurs were wild, like undisciplined children. They represent humanity emerging from the animal state on the way to becoming fully human - just like young children.

Chiron was different: he was wise and gentle and, in the hills and forests of Thessaly, he taught music, astronomy, and the lore of herbs and animals, as well as noble behaviour, so most of the great heroes of Greece went to him to be educated as children. Under the guidance of the god Apollo he taught Hercules, Achilles, Jason, Aeneas, Asclepius and many others. He was particularly suitable as a teacher of the young because his half-animal nature took full advantage of their senses, which develop ahead of the intellect, and their joy in exercising their bodies. Therein lies his wisdom and understanding of the young.

The current educational diktat, seemingly dominated by the demands of the business sector to expand even further our already wealthy economy rather than nurture good and happy citizens, is putting intense pressure on teachers to over-emphasise rote learning and the measurement of basic skills at the expense of time spent on children's physical, cultural, creative and aesthetic development. Of course the mechanical skills are important, but the curriculum does need to be more evenly balanced throughout the school years by those other aspects if our children are to grow up as fully rounded personalities.

There is ample evidence that if the young are deprived of a normal sequence of development, and with no opportunity to learn how to to cope with frustrations, nor to test themselves against physical and emotional challenges in the face of the wider environment, they suffer serious consequences: in recent years we have seen an alarming growth in suicides, violence, escapist drug taking, and other forms of anti-social behaviour among young people as they emerge from malformed childhood years.

The first stage in helping the young to grow up, perhaps the most difficult for parents, is to face the moment when it is time to LET THE CHILDREN GO so that they may have the opportunity to start testing themselves against the world. This should begin, albeit gently at first, in the important middle years of children: on average between about seven and eleven.

It was not so many years ago that most young children were free to play outdoors, to join a gang of friends and climb trees, build dens and create secret hiding places (in the woods if they were lucky country children), and to have exciting imaginative adventures. Today few children have opportunities to go BACK TO NATURE and play in the woods and fields - many spend too much of their time installed in front of television or computer screens, 'safe' from the media-spun threats about prowling child-molesters out there in the world beyond their front doors.

Despite ample evidence to the contrary, there is undoubtedly a perception among some sectors of the public that it is a more dangerous world for children today. Some adults portray the natural world as dirty and full of things that bite, sting or cause dreadful diseases at the slightest contact. Advertising and media campaigns can mislead children into an illusory sterile world where they are actively discouraged from close contact with soil, animals, plants, adults and even each other!

Whatever your perception is, or wherever you live, we offer an alternative approach to what is still a beautiful, exciting and wonder-filled world - just waiting to be explored by eager adventurous young minds. We offer an approach, open to all parents, teachers and leaders, that would seem to be necessary if children are to enjoy normal development like earlier generations of children since prehistory. If we do not do something, we shall see a huge increase in children that are emotionally stunted, physically overweight and under-developed, unable to adjust socially and alienated from the joy and beauty of nature.

Chiron offers one possible solution. We call it DRAGON QUESTING.

All of you with children, take them somehow into the country among green grass and yellow wheat, among trees and by hill and streams, if you wish their highest education, that of the heart and soul, to be completed. Therein shall they find a Secret - a knowledge not to be written, not found in books, a feeling, a sense that fills the heart with an emotion never to be forgotten.

RICHARD JEFFERIES, *19th century nature writer* [21]

If I had influence with the good fairy who is supposed to preside over the christening of all children I should ask that her gift to each child in the world be a sense of wonder so indestructible that it would last throughout life, as an unfailing antidote against the boredom and disenchantments of later years, the sterile pre-occupation with things that are artificial, the alienation from the sources of our strength.

If a child is to keep alive his inborn sense of wonder without any such gifts from the fairies, he needs the companionship of at least one adult who can share it, rediscovering with him the joy, excitement and mystery of the world we live in. Parents often have a sense of inadequacy when confronted on the one hand with the eager, sensitive mind of a child and on the other with a world of complex physical nature, inhabited by a life so various and unfamiliar that it seems hopeless to reduce it to order and knowledge ...

I sincerely believe that for the child, and for the parent seeking to guide him, it is not so important to know as to feel...

RACHEL CARSON, *20th century American ecologist* [5]

Little brother, growing up, becomes aware that life is one ... one vital process with many manifestations, and joyfully he feels his kinship with the earth and its forces. With sudden illumination he knows that he is one with the birds and the ripple of the river ... one with the fledgling and the burrowing mole ... one with the upstanding trees and the quivering

8

dragonfly ... one with rain and mud, starshine and the kiss of the wind ... joyfully, splendidly he longs for harmony with life.

LESLIE PAUL, *founder of the Woodcraft Folk* [30]

Children should live in the world of beauty, games, fairy tales, music, drawing, fantasy, and creativity.

VASILY SUKHOMLINSKY, *Soviet Russian headmaster* [36]

Contents

THE ARGUMENT

The child, archetypal innocent and potential hero; the needs of childhood; the qualities of middle childhood; the senses.

Nature, nurturer and nourisher; restorying the landscape; a mythic history of Britain; Clas   Myrddin; 'The Land Beyond the North Wind; Brutus the Trojan; Brittia, spirit isle of great souls; Island of the Mighty, Arthur's Round Table, the Grail Quest and the Waste Land; Robin Hood and the forest outlaws; the Hollow Hills, the Land of the Ever Young, and other fairy places.

Beauty; 'Once upon a time ....'; nature spirits, fairies and the Otherworld; fairy tale quests; hero and heroine myths; the Hero's quest; the myth of the Golden Age' three cultural resources: ancient Greece, the Celts, the English/Nordic/folktradition.

THE ACTIVITIES

Introduction

The ideas and adventures that you will find in this
book started out as a two-year experiment with
twenty-four Devon schoolchildren, sponsored by the
National Trust. The concept proved so successful that
it has grown over the past twelve years to encompass
many more activities and thousands of children
across southern England.

From the start we were concerned to find ways to
restore to children their traditional relationship with
nature, to help them to empathise with its fauna and
flora, and to become more aware of the landscape and
its forgotten stories.   Particularly, we wanted to
explore the possible range of educational routes into
the environment beyond the traditional ones of
science and geography.   Especially we were keen to
use the arts: we wanted children to sing, dance, act,

paint, write, and tell stories about our beautiful land. We are grateful that both the National Trust and the University of Plymouth provided the time, money and site to enable us to do something about it. We were also fortunate to be joined by an inspired Orpheus in the form of Tim Lacock, talented singer-songwriter, actor and play-wright, by Phillip Hull, a distinguished ethno-musicologist, and by a group of enthusiastic students from The Faculty of Education in Exmouth.

As far as we are concerned it has all been tremendous fun - for us, for our many helpers and, above all, for the children. But enjoyment is all very well, some may argue; what about 'real' education - particularly at a time when the major focus of education policy is on literacy, numeracy, constant testing and hyper-accountability! We have used the methods outlined here with many maintained schools and also with several of the country's leading preparatory schools, invariably of necessity linking them to the National Curriculum requirements. We have poured an immense amount of 'required' information over the children - but strongly reinforced it by direct experience, games and creative activities - as we do with all our programmes. Subsequently many parents and teachers have remarked on how much of the information the children have retained long-term through this method. The children undoubtedly love it, and we have been asked to return again and again - surely the proof of the pudding!

So we offer all readers a rich mixture - an 'Enchanters' Brew' - of ideas and activities with plenty of nourishment for young minds and bodies. Of course we are still trying out new recipes, new ingredients, and we invite you to help us to enrich the mixture further, amplifying this ongoing project.

A word to parents

We hope that you will resonate with the ideas in the first half of this book and try out some of the many activities in the second half as a means to enrich days in nature with your children. And if you are convinced by our arguments but lack the confidence to use them yourself, we hope you will encourage any teachers and/or out-of-school activity organisers you know to try out our approach. We are confident that they - and you - will be impressed by its positive affect on the children.

An explanation for teachers

This book was written primarily for you, following requests from many teachers to make the material available to supplement and enrich all areas of the curriculum. We know that many teaching colleagues share our concern about the narrowing and formalising of the curriculum and that you are making valiant attempts to generate enthusiasm for learning through a range of creative approaches. We also know, from wide and extended personal experiences, that a day of adventuring amid nature such as we offer here can stimulate both the brightest and the most reluctant learners to return to the classroom with renewed energy. All aspects of the national Curriculum, including the literacy and numeracy strategies, can be addressed through our approach.

Some of the advice we offer may seem obvious to you, but remember that we are also addressing parents who do not have your training and experience.

A plea to out-of-school activity leaders and countryside rangers

We have also been pressed to publish this material by many colleagues who work with children as site wardens and youth leaders. Teachers today are under intense pressure to produce

academic excellence and there is a real danger that some of the most important elements in the development of well-balanced individuals are having to be neglected. You have the opportunity to redress the balance and, we promise you, its FUN - for the children *and* for you.

If you are developing similar ideas in your own way and would like to share and discuss your experiences, we would be pleased to hear from you. Please write in the first instance to the address below.

We also periodically run INSET/CPD and other workshops for those interested in our approach. For further information on these please write to:

Alan Dyer
Faculty of Education
University of Plymouth
Exmouth
Devon EX8 2AT

ajdyer@plymouth.ac.uk

Good Dragon Hunting!

Alan Dyer	John Hodgson
Ambrius	*Abaris*

Note: Activities presented in Chapters IV, V and VI that are suitable for families or very small groups are preceded with **F**. Those that seem to work best for groups of ten or more are marked **G**. Most are suitable for both types of group. These are marked **F/G**.

Dragon Quest

Despite the fact that most of us now live in towns, we must never forget that we humans are still part of Nature as much as the trees and birds are, and we cannot escape our connection to the dynamics of the living and the non-living world wherever we live. We are allowing ourselves, and our children, to become increasingly separated from our earthly roots, and forgetting our symbiotic relationship with the earth and its systems.

Dragon Quest aims to help pre-adolescent children realise that they belong to nature and need to keep in intimate physical, emotional and psychological touch with it throughout life for their own delight, spiritual enrichment - and survival. And the method? To take them on romantic adventures in the woods to meet some of its mythical inhabitants, especially DRAGONS!

There are five powerful dragons waiting for us out there in the woods and hills:

The Dragon of the East, which guards the beauty of the world;

The Dragon of the South, which guards the fecundity of nature;

The Dragon of the West, which guards the treasures of the earth;

The Dragon of the North, which represents the wild forces of the elements; and

The Dragon Within, which we all have to learn to control.

But what do the dragons really represent, and why do gods and heroes always *kill* the dragon? First, it needs to be understood that the gods of Olympus and Asgard are not just discarded nature gods as some have thought: they are also *human-* nature daemons that still live *inside* all of us.

And the dragon/serpent? What does he represent?

Dragons and serpents traditionally represented the elemental powers of nature and therefore, in ancient times, they were seen as fierce protectors of the land, so they often became symbols of sovereignty such as the Dragon Emperors of ancient China, Cecrops, the first king of Athens, and the Pendragons, the early rulers of Celtic Britain. As the established king was only allowed to rule during his prime, by the archaic law of 'The King of the Wood' (cf. Sir James Frazer's *The Golden Bough*'), the young hero and future king had the task of overcoming him: the old king in decline must be replaced by the young 'prince' to ensure the continues fertility of the land. The hero slaying the dragon was a symbol of this.

Since the dawn of consciousness people have attempted to understand the mysteries of life by devising myths and fairy-tales about dragons and giants, that justify their feelings of awe, terror, wonder and delight in the face of natural phenomena. Most of these stories emerged from tribal societies very different from ours today, though the stories are still valued by many parents and teachers as part of our cultural heritage which we pass on to our children, though their significance is often not fully appreciated. Once we really study them we discover that they often contain profound truths about human existence, and they can still speak to us at a very deep level of consciousness.

Myths and fairy-tales help children, who are still at a pre-conscious stage of development, to adjust themselves to the world. They are also immensely satisfying. Every child is born into nature and remains part of it until detachment begins with the arrival of adolescence. The dragons are still powerful symbols, attractive to young children, which can help them come to terms with the choices and dilemmas on their journey to adulthood.

We adults need them too:

Modern man has freed himself from 'superstition' (or so he believes), but in the process he has lost his spiritual values to a positive and dangerous degree. His moral and spiritual tradition has disintegrated, and he is now paying the price for this break - in worldwide disorientation.

Anthropologists have often discussed what happens to a primitive society when its spiritual values are exposed to the impact of modern civilisation. Its people lose the meaning of their lives, their social organisation disintegrates, and they themselves morally decay. We are now in the same condition.

C G Jung [22]

Traditional people - and young children - are not separate from the rest of creation; and in their thinking they animate the whole of nature with spiritual life: every tree and stone has, they believe, a personality with which it is possible to comunicate (just as young children converse with their teddies), and there are spirits everywhere - fairies, dragons, giants, and so on.

But why do we still have to *kill* the dragon? There came a point in our ancestral development, just as puberty comes to every child, when we began to see ourselves, for the first time as individuals *separate* from each other and from the rest of nature, and that is the point when we 'kill' the old nature spirits in our minds, and become 'rational' beings. So the adult world demands that the dragon *has* to die so that we can 'fit in' with whatever are the current dominant mores of society. But, we beg you, help the child to *tame* his dragons rather than kill them. Let them live, for the young child *needs* his dragons, and elves and tree-spirits, if he is to enjoy a full, creative life into maturity. Dragon Quest helps them to live in the child's mind, waiting to be conquered not killed.

They should also be allowed to live in children's minds as fierce protectors of the environment who will ensure that we suffer if we harm nature and destroy trees, plants and wildlife.

So who is right? Our earlier ancestors and and children, both in intimate contact with nature, within themselves and without, or 'rational' adults who have long lost touch with the whispering woods, the singing streams? We know where we stand.

Enchanter

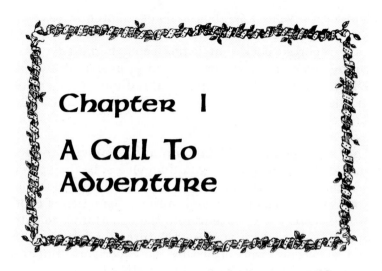

Chapter 1
A Call To Adventure

The time of trial has come: all who feel brave enough to take up the Quest have assembled, and the Enchanters prepare them for the ordeal with campfire tales of the great deeds of past heroes and heroines.

Then they take them deep into the forest and teach them the wisdom of the woods, the secrets of the furred and feathered brethren, the art of self-control, and how to build a woodland shelter, how to communicate with the animals, how to keep warm and well fed, and to develop many other skills, before they face the final challenge: the Quest to find and face the dreaded Dragon and rescue the Lost One.

* * *

For several years now thousands of children across southern England have undergone this experience, and many of them have reported back that it has been the best day in their young lives. They return for more, over and over again. Why? What are the magical ingredients that evoke this reaction? How is it organised? What is the inspiration behind it?

This handbook aims to explain, and to provide the tools to enable other, prospective, guardian elders, be they parents or teachers - or 'Enchanters' as we prefer to call them, for our aim is to re-enchant our land in the imagination of children - to give more young Adventurers the opportunity to enter the magical and perilous worlds of Nature, Landscape and Myth, and to become transformed by the experience. But first we must consider the background to childhood:

* * *

The child: archetypal innocent and potential hero

It is the Child that sees the primordial Secret in Nature and it is the child in ourselves that we return to. The child within us is simple and daring enough to live the Secret.

CHUANG TZU

The study of the child in nature, culture and society reveals that there is a special period, the little understood, prepubertal, halcyon, middle-age of childhood, approximately from five or six to eleven or twelve - between the strivings of animal infancy and the storms of adolescence - when the natural world is experienced in some highly evocative way, producing in the child a sense of some profound continuity with natural processes and presenting overt evidence of a biological basis of intuition.

EDITH COBB [7]

26

In archaic Greece, as in most traditional societies, it was the custom to subject young boys to a period of training, testing and questing in the wilderness. There are indications that this started when they were about nine, though Achilles began at six. The boys were taken from their mother's protective care to spend their time exploring and getting to know the countryside, its flora and fauna, playing hunting games, taking part in races and other sports, and fighting mock battles, with the training culminating in a challenging adventure. In Minoan Crete this process lasted two months, probably finishing at Midsummer. The process then continued with more civilised activities right up to eighteen.

Selected Greek girls of the same age were transformed into *arktoi* - 'She-bears', and they followed Artemis, goddess and 'Lady of the Wild Things', into the wild woods and hills for a similar form of initiation.

This experience usually took place in forest surroundings where the children could learn to master their fears, develop new skills, and discover self-reliance. They faced a series of hazards and strange encounters prepared by their elders who would act as guides, guardians and challengers.

Throughout the ages in all traditional societies the latter would sit them round a fire at twilight and recount the myths, legends and wonder-tales of the tribe: stories in which a hero or a heroine enters a Dark Forest and overcomes fearsome foes - wily dragons, threatening ogres, malevolent witches, or evil knights. In the stories they learnt that the forest is a place of challenge, discovery, transformation and shelter, which provides the brave and virtuous with unexpected help, often in the form of magical animals who reward kindness with rescue from dangers.

This story-telling was an essential preliminary, offering warnings and helpful advice to the apprehensive novices about to embark on their first great adventure in life.

* * *

Children today have few opportunities to adventure in the wild: the playgrounds which may be some children's only experience of the 'outdoors' can be sterile and vegetation-free - no place for nests, dens, tree houses or tunnels. If 'wildwood' is nearby, it is often carefully protected as a nature reserve, in private hands with no access or in some other way off limits to adventurous children.

With a few notable exceptions round the country most children on educational visits to the countryside today make contact with nature only as detached observers, often insulated from the elements by kagouls, jeans and wellies, and armed with clipboards and questionnaires, so they have no opportunity to become physically and emotionally integrated with it. This is unfortunate for, while many children worry about the destruction that people are inflicting on the environment and wildlife, they, like the perpetrators, have been deprived of intimate contact with nature and at best only understand its processes in theory.

Yet when children, both boys and girls, from about six or seven to twelve or thirteen, whether from inner city or suburbia, from privileged or deprived backgrounds, are taken on a Dragon Quest or other wildwood adventure, they quickly forget their modern cultural conditioning and return to the primordial state of their distant ancestors: the thin veneer of civilisation falls away, and they exult in a new sense of freedom and wonder in the face of the beauty and mystery of the natural world. And, given the opportunity, they return again and again: the spirit of the Forest has entered their souls and imagination. It has become precious to them and they yearn to be at one with it. Ultimately at least some may be permanently changed by the experience.

Don't think this is a difficult or potentially disruptive situation for the parent or teacher - in our long experience, adults invariably have at least as much fun and as many moving experiences as the children! Perhaps for many adults it fulfils something missed from their own childhood ....

The needs of childhood

Dragon Quest and other wildwood adventures outlined here aim to bring young children into direct, intimate contact with nature, refining their perceptions, especially through the senses. In this situation they can experience moments of wonder and awe, beauty, joy and freedom found in no other environment and, hopefully, hold on to their essential sense of oneness with all creation.

For millennia these activities have engaged children because they answer specific needs at this stage in their development. Unfortunately most children today are being deprived of them. No matter how the centuries turn and the cultural paradigms shift, the older generation will always despair at the antics and mores of the young; but we seem to be facing a very new challenge in the 21st century. Our modern urbanised, work-pressured, pseudo-sophisticated and neurotic age unwittingly encourages some young people to embrace self-destructive behaviour which may well resonate throughout their lives.

Unfortunately we ourselves face something of a dilemma here: the traditional purpose of the initatory experience on which we base the Adventures was precisely to provide a rite of passage *out* of childhood into well balanced maturity - ultimately to 'kill' the wild child within us. In most myths the

Hero 'dies' young, i.e. through initiation he passes out of the adventures of youth to become a mature and rational adult. This *rite de passage* needs to be restored, but too often two other important things could be killed at the same time - *imagination* and *creativity*. We believe that Dragon Quest avoids this danger.

Edith Cobb studied the biographies of 300 historically outstanding creative individuals, and the overwhelming majority revealed that the most formative period in their lives was from about the age of six to twelve [7]. You don't have to look far to observe how many creative people never shed their immaturity. Do we really want to destroy potential high creativity just to recruit everyone into staid 'adult' society? Furthermore, as the Bible warns us, we stand to lose out on entry to the Kingdom of Heaven unless we keep the Child alive within us; so our intent is to preserve the *childlike* in people (as opposed to the *childish* and destructive). Our adventures use the initiatory idea first, to give children an intimate and joyful experience of nature and to help them to appreciate their place in relation to the natural world; second, to challenge them within their limits as young children so they can begin to realise their potential in practical situations and as part of a cooperative team; and, third, to give them lots of fun.

The qualities of middle childhood

We are each of us an amalgam of animal body and animating spirit. Maturation is a process of development from the un-self-aware animal-like nature of the three-year-old, via middle childhood when we are slowly learning to distinguish between the worlds of imagination and reality, to adolescence and beyond when most of us have become confined by 'shades of the prison-house'. The natural world is the appropriate environment for that delightful period between the ages of about 6 and 12 when our pure animal nature is giving way to a collective tribal stage. Most healthy children start to revel in a sense of *physical freedom* and delight when offered opportunities to roll in the grass, to climb trees, to race the wind and bask in the sun, to dance ecstatically in pouring rain and to get thoroughly messy.

Children are highly energetic in short bursts, but they are also more sensitive than most adults. In the first place children, born romantics all, spend much of their time in the world of the *imagination*, and living out their day-dreams. Myths and fairy tales, accumulations of centuries of folk-dreams and of deep psychological import, offer far richer food for the imagination - and the intellect - than most children can create on their own. It is perhaps not surprising that our wildwood adventures have proved to be particularly attractive to many of the most able children, who tend to be more responsive to imaginative stimulae as well as often being more adventurous and less inhibited than the average child. Unfortunately there is a long-held misbegotten idea that bright children should only have their rational intellect developed, not their other faculties.

There is no better setting in which to develop imagination and creativity than the world of nature. Nature has the capacity to give us so many *aesthetic experiences* : not only the obvious beauties of sunset, of autumn colours, or a stand of tall trees, but also the exquisite smaller beauties:

> *...the stirs*
> *Of a swan's neck unseen among the rushes:*
> *A linnet starting all about the bushes:*
> *A butterfly, with golden wings broad parted,*
> *Nestling a rose, convuls'd as though it smarted*
> *With over pleasure - many, many more,*
> *Might I indulge at large in all my store*
> *Of luxuries ....*
>
> JOHN KEATS: *Sleep and Poetry*

In our adventures we always endeavour by specific activities to enrich children's experiences of Beauty. As the English naturalist, Richard Jefferies once said, 'The hours when we are absorbed by beauty are the only hours when we really live. These are the only hours that absorb the soul and fill it with beauty. This is real life, and all else is illusion, or mere endurance'.

The nearest young children can get to a true sense of *the spiritual dimension* of life is in the natural world where they are faced with the wonders and mysteries of creation. It is especially during childhood that most people, if they are lucky, enjoy those brief visionary moments of heightened awareness of total oneness with all creation. These are impossible to engineer but they can sometimes occur in Greenwood Vigils (see page 179).

The senses

Children of the age-group we are concerned with experience the world much more through the senses than through the intellect so let us devote a little space to them. They are much more alert in childhood than in later years. Consider seven of them - not all of them the ones you might expect:

At a conscious level *touch* is the most important to children: as the art historians Bernard Berenson[1] and Kenneth Clark[6] have both asserted, the young child's guarantee of reality is neither sight, nor sound, nor smell, but touch. Wordsworth said much the same in his introduction to the ode *'Intimations of Immortality'*:

> *I was often unable to think of external things as having external existence, and I communed with all that I saw as something not apart from, but inherent in, my own immaterial nature. Many times while going to school have I grasped at a wall or tree to recall myself from this abyss of idealism to reality.*

Some readers may recall a special 'touch' on the way to school - the railings that you ran your hand along as you passed, the hedge that was soft and woolly, or the spongy dampness of a moss patch on the churchyard wall.

Touch is the essential means by which we grow into the material world. To the distress of museum curators children want to touch everything *because of all the senses they learn most easily through touch*. Touch therefore plays a major role in all our adventure programmes: children are encouraged to explore the textures of bark and leaf, rock and mud, fur and feather, and as the whole skin surface is a sense organ, we encourage them to use as much of their bare body-surface as they individually desire - face, arms, legs and torso - and how they enjoy the sensuous thrill of it! If you can get them into sand or long grass, wearing the minimum of clothing, just watch them crawling, rolling, and squirming in it in sheer delight. Notice too their enthusiasm for body-contact games like British Bulldog, alas now forbidden in many schools.

In an unfortunate, and we believe sadly mistaken, desire to protect children's physical integrity some paranoid guardians of 'political correctness' have made many adults terrified of touching children. This is a tragic mistake: children *need* to be hugged, they need to rough-and-tumble with trusted adults who, unlike other children, know their own strength and when to stop before there are tears: like puppies and kittens children relate to the world most happily through touch.

Of course one must always be sensitive to the fact that there may be the odd sad child who, for one reason or another, is shy of any physical contact with adults. If this attitude is encountered it must always be respected, though we have found that such children do not seem to attend Dragon Quest type activities.

For the most part children use the senses unconsciously. For example the *kinaesthetic faculty* - experience of space through movement - is working all the time entirely unconsciously, yet it is highly important to the development of the growing child. In moving silently through undergrowth on uneven ground or in climbing a tree this sense is being exercised very hard. Devising activities which focus on and develop this sense is very important. As with touch it can be further trained by occasionally blindfolding a child for an exercise.

Sensory deprivation, especially blindfold games, are particularly useful in helping children to become more conscious of the sense of *sight* too. A wide range of observation games are employed in the adventures under the romantic pretence that they provide training for hunting and stalking.

The sensitivity of *hearing* is being atrophied in many young people by the high decibel level of modern living. Somehow we must ensure that children can also be allowed to enjoy the many sweet small sounds that the natural world offers. Again sensory deprivation can be valuable here: by temporarily muffling their ears it may be possible to make some of them aware of the loss they will sustain by bombarding their eardrums with over-loud noise.

Most adults neglect the sense of *smell* until they pass a rose or a sewer, yet we are surrounded by a rich bouquet of scents all the time and barely notice them. It may be significant that sometimes adults can encounter a particular smell that immediately evokes a recollection of a certain place or time, invariably from these most significant years of childhood. Psychologists tell us that smell is one of the most powerful triggers of memory. Few places provide more delightful scents than the countryside, and by sense-training games that focus on some of the most pleasurable in an adventure, our hidden store of memory-triggers can be enriched for ever.

The sixth sense is of course *instinct*. This is important as a means of self-preservation, and we encourage children to talk about it and exercise it.

Finally we aim to develop that sense, rarely recognised as such: *feeling*:

....we must constantly remember that it should not be the education of the intellect but the education of feeling should receive the place of honour in schools ....
RABINDRANTH TAGORE: *Siksa*

At this stage in their development children are naturally animistic - they assume that even inanimate objects have feelings.

Children are often reluctant to admit this to adults who, they discover, think differently. However it is vitally important to cultivate this faculty. The child's readiness to empathise with other things is much used in the adventures, not only because it is natural to children, but it provides opportunities to help them to appreciate the needs of other creatures. Apart from encouraging them to freely express their feelings in an non-critical atmosphere, they are often given exercises in 'shape-shifting' into other creatures by observing, then role-playing them.

All these senses were highly developed in tribal societies, and the middle-age children we are concerned with here do retain vestiges of them. But, in our advanced civilisation, what is the point of bothering to cultivate them? And why should we seek to exploit this transitory tribal phase in human development by giving the child opportunities to revert, albeit briefly, to the character of a wild hunter-gatherer in the forest?

First, children have to live through the tribal stage in one way or another. If it is stifled the child can become emotionally frustrated and behavioural problems are likely to occur during adolescence or later.

Second, it provides direct experience of nature at its most basic - rare today, particularly for children at the age when they are potentially most ready for it. This can lead to a richer appreciation of nature, its beauty, it's wonders - and its perils - than is normally available to the modern child. This, in turn, is likely to lead to a deep appreciation and concern for the natural environment at a time when it is under great threat.

A belief in the therapeutic value of nature is not new. It was an integral part of the education of the young in ancient Greece, in the Forest Schools of India, and even in the 20th century youth movements. However with dragon Quest we have re-introduced an element largely ignored by our more recent predecessors and neglected since the Renaissance: the re-creation of myth and fairy tale through role-play, in suitably primitive costume, amid nature*. Psychotherapists have relatively recently come to realise the profound importance of these ancient stories to children, and now, in Dragon Quest, children can exorcise the monsters in the Dark Forest of their individual psyches through imaginative adventures in a real forest as the 'Tribe' lives out a hero-quest under the guidance of wise and protective 'Enchanters'.

We also aim to sensitise children to the *landscape* and its features. Children mostly don't notice landscape - it doesn't

---

* Our only modern predecessors (and inspirers) have been the delightful pastoral romances of Sannazaro, Ariosto, Tasso, Sidney, Spenser and others, and especially, the court and civic masques of the late 16th and early 17th centuries, which often took place in park and woodland settings.

move, it's just a background to more interesting things close at hand. Children love stories, yet they are rarely told that every landscape is rich in stories - of dragons, giants, fairies and their enchanted realms, and of the heroes and heroines of romance. The adventures outlined here attempt to 're-story' the landscape in the ancient tradition, and bring it alive in the child's imagination.

They also provide lots of fun, self-discoveries, creative opportunities and spell-binding experiences.

Chapter II
Nature And The Land

More things are learnt in the woods than from books: trees and rocks will teach you things not to be heard elsewhere.

ST. BERNARD OF CLAIRVEAUX

Nature, nurturer and nourisher

Our lives today are very different from those of peoples of the Dawn. Why, then, do we think education in the woods is so important? Surely it is irrelevant at the beginning of the 21st century?

Firstly, people are still strangely attracted to Nature, none more so than during childhood, when we feel drawn in body and spirit towards the sun and the stars, the sky and the wind, and towards fields, trees and plants. Nature calls to us, offering a joyous sense of freedom and space. Close contact with Nature is refreshing and vitalizing; it develops sensitivity and awareness of the beautiful. It can promote spiritual awakening and realisation of the kinship of all life. Vinoba Bhave, the great modern sage of India and friend of Ghandi, once said:

....the more closely we can live in harmony with Nature, the greater our welfare and happiness will be; the more we are cut off from Nature, the less contented we shall be. ...Human lives are like trees, which cannot live if they are cut off from the soil which nourishes them.

VINOBA BHAVE [2]

D H Lawrence took this further, using similar imagery:

We must get back into relation, vivid and nourishing relation to the cosmos and the universe.

He urged that this should be through daily ritual and reawakening, celebrating the dawn and noon and sunset, the kindling of fire and the pouring of water; celebrating the moon in her phases, the morning and evening star, and the turning of the seasons, marking them with procession and dance.

To these rituals we must return: or we must evolve them to our needs. For the truth is, we are perishing for lack of fulfilment of our greater needs, we are cut off from the great source of our inward nourishment and renewal, sources which flow eternally in the universe. Vitally, the human race is dying like a great uprooted tree, with its roots in the air. We must plant ourselves again in the universe.

D H LAWRENCE [25]

One of the ways we can reconnect ourselves is by restoring an old relationship with our own land. We feel close to friends if we know their story. The same applies to landscape.

Re-storying the landscape

Once upon a time - in the childhood of the world, and of every man and woman - the land was full of an ineffable magic: every hill and stream, every rock and tree, was mysterious and wonderful, if often threatening. And by the ancient rules of magic the only way each perilous Thing could be mastered was by naming it, and knowing its story. And thus it could become safe, and ultimately accepted as a necessary and valued part of the human environment.

We not only observe this process in the development of every young child, but we can discover the traces of society's childhood in the remnants of story that linger still in the landscape. In every corner of the world, in every traditional culture, places and natural objects have been given a name, a personality, and a story.

In names and traditional tales gods, giants and heroes, fairies and dragons still inhabit the British landscape: Baldersby, Sarn Elen, the Devil's Punch-bowl, the Giant's Causeway, Arthur's Seat, Pixies' Pool, Drakelow, and so on. A few of the tales are still familiar - Jack the Giant-killer at St Michael's Mount, the child Merlin Ambrosius at Dinas Emrys, the Lambton Worm at Penshaw Hill, and so on - but most have been forgotten by a society which sees the countryside only as a place for a picnic.

These days most of us are blind to the landscape - in the words of the 17th century divine, Thomas Traherne, 'The World is a Mirror of Infinit Beauty yet no Man sees it' (*Meditation 131*).

It is sad that children, who enter this world marvelling at its strangeness and beauty, quickly learn from their parents to become *blasé* about the world around them: their sense of wonder atrophies and, while they still mostly love animals, and trees and flowers, they fail to notice the wider landscape, possibly, because it is just there and doesn't 'do' anything. That infant awe and delight in the face of creation needs to be revived, and that is what we are about here.

We must not forget, however, that it is mostly during childhood that some individuals recover, if only for fleeting moments of glorious revelation, the realisation that they are *one* with all Creation, perhaps sharing the feelings of the Irish writer and visionary, AE George Russell: 'I longed to throw my arms about the hills, to meet with kisses the lips of the seraph wind.', or those of Thomas Traherne, recollecting his childhood vision of the world:

> *All appeared New, and Strange at first, inexpressibly*
> *rare, and Delightfull, and Beautifull .... All Things*
> *were Spotles and Pure and Glorious: yea, and infinitly*
> *mine, and Joyfull and Precious .... I was entertained*
> *like an Angel with the Works of GOD in their Splendor*
> *and Glory; I saw all the Peace of Eden, Heaven and*
> *Earth did sing my Creators Praises, and could not*
> *make more melody to Adam, than to me. All Time was*
> *Eternity, and a Perpetual Sabbath. Is it not Strange,*
> *that an Infant should be Heir to the World, and see*
> *those Mysteries which the Books of the Learned never*
> *unfold?*
>
> THOMAS TRAHERNE: *Meditation 302* [37]

If we are to become fully sensitive to the world about us - and that is the way to enjoy it most - we must not only be aware of its physical qualities, but also its 'story', both historic and mythic. In Dragon Quest and we mostly make use of the

British mythic story and it may be worth rehearsing some episodes in outline here:

A mythic history of Britain

All things Begin and End in Albions Ancient Druid Rocky Shore.

WILLIAM BLAKE

The English are notoriously ignorant of their cultural heritage, and few are even aware of Britain's ancient reputation, across Europe and beyond, as one of the most sacred places in the western world. Once it was known as the home of gods and wizards, a place of marvels and mystical power. Even the Tibetans have a story about its ancient spiritual sanctity. Perhaps our history has been too rich. To appreciate the depth of mythic history we have to dig through layer upon layer of cultural immigrations - Greek and Roman, Celtic, Teutonic and Nordic in the past, and many new influences today.

Clas Myrddin

According to legend, the first name of Britain, before it was inhabited, was 'Clas Myrddin'.This has often been misinterpreted as 'Merlin's Enclosure'. However it is more likely that the name given to the mysterious island seen dimly across the Channel meant something like 'the sea-girt enclosure'. In the Celtic mind islands were always associated with the Otherworld - and the British Isles more than any other - and Britain and Ireland were soon to gather many magical legends round them. According to the Welsh Triads the next name of Britain was Ynys Veli which has also probably been misinterpreted as 'Honey Isle'. It is more likely to mean 'Isle of Bel' - Bel/Belenos was the local sun god and healer, cognate with Apollo.

'The Land Beyond the North Wind'

Many ancient Greeks identified this island (or its Otherworld
reflection) with a place they called Hyperborea - The Land
Beyond the North Wind. They said it was the birthplace of
Apollo's mother, the gentle Titaness, Leto. It is likely that the
god himself originally came from here too, for classical
scholars say that he was a late-comer to Greece, coming down
from the north. Sophocles called the land Phoebus' ancient
garden - 'Phoebus' (= 'pure', 'radiant') was a title of Apollo.

Even the alternative story that he was born on the island of
Delos says that as soon as he was presented to his father Zeus

on Olympus, he begged for a swan-chariot and immediately flew off in it, along the Milky Way, to Hyperborea where he spent a whole year with the rejoicing people. He was said to return for some months every year.

The many Greek descriptions of the island make it a delightful paradise: a temperate climate, fertile land, rich in every crop, with a city dedicated to Apollo, a magnificent sacred precinct, and a famous circular temple built 'in the pattern of the heavens' - this was probably Stonehenge. Most of the natives lived in the woods and groves, and praised Apollo continuously in song and dance.

> *The Muse never leaves that land*
> *For this is their life:*
> *Everywhere the girls are dancing,*
> *And the sound of the harp is loud,*
> *And the noise of flutes.*
> *They feast and are glad,*
> *They bind their hair with bay-leaves of gold,*
> *Neither sickness nor cursed old age*
> *Touches their holy bodies:*
> *Without toil, without war*
> *They dwell, and do not trouble*
> *The stern scales of Fate.*

PINDAR: *Pythian* X [31]

Like the people of the world's Golden Age the inhabitants were reputed to have characteristics which we could do well to encourage the children to emulate. They included:

Alert senses, sensitivity to all around them.
Grace and Beauty, perfection of movement and action.
Instinctive perception and knowledge.
Conscious unity with nature and the tribe.

The description of the climate accords with that of Stonehenge III (c.1500 BC), a period of peace and prosperity. The henge was certainly linked to sun-worship - among Apollo's many attributes was that of sun god - and objects of probable Greek origin have been recovered from the area.

Brutus the Trojan

By the 6th century BC this island was called Albion. There is a story going back to at least the 7th century AD that it was inhabited solely by giants until Brutus, great-grandson of Aeneas the Trojan (i.e. in about the 11th century BC), arrived with some comrades at Totnes, defeated the chief of the giants, Gog Magog and the other giants, and gave his own name to it. The stone on which he is said to have taken his first step can still be seen in Totnes Fore Street, but modern historians dismiss the story as romantic nonsense. However it seems strange that we claimed our descent from those who were defeated at Troy, rather than from the victors. France too claims to have been founded by Francus, descendant of King Priam of Troy, just as Italy claims Aeneas himself as its founder.

Brittia, spirit isle of great souls

Merlin, originally either a prehistoric god or a druid priest, was probably the presiding genius of Britain's forest groves long before the Celts arrived to embrace the native druidism. That the druids were here before the Celts is suggested by the fact that the high college of druidism was here in Britain, while the Celts themselves had spread outwards from central Europe. The Celts of Gaul looked with awe towards 'Brittia', and employed boatmen to carry the souls of the dead across the channel to this magical isle where they were greeted by a disembodied voice welcoming each ghostly arrival by name and rank.

46

Island of the Mighty: Arthur's Round Table, the Grail Quest and the Waste Land

Stories of Britain's great hero-king, Arthur, spread throughout western Europe in the Middle Ages. Arthur, too, may have been a prehistoric sun-god but it is the exploits of the Round Table that still grip the imagination. Arthur and other Round Table heroes appear in the Mabinogion, in the Triads, and other ancient books of Wales, wonderful sources of stories for our purpose, especially the search for the Divine Child hero/god Mabon, and the quest for the Thirteen Treasures of Britain. The Holy Grail, another stimulus to questing, may have originated in the Celtic cauldron of re-birth, but stories of the Grail Quest first appeared in Little Britain - Brittany (Chretien de Troyes: 'Perceval' 1180), though Chretien claimed that the story was not original. Then, over the next fifty years there was a veritable explosion in Grail Quest books across western Europe, including Wolfram's great 'Parzival' and the Celtic 'Peredur' (also in the Mabinogion) which we use frequently in our adventures.

The concept of Great Britain as the Waste Land which had to be restored to fertility first appeared in ancient Celtic stories and was adopted by the Grail authors. It has obvious relevance today, and we often employ it.

Robin Hood and the forest outlaws

There is little evidence of an historical Robin but he may be a form of the forest elf Robin Goodfellow, and Robin's green costume and hood also suggest fairy origins. Certainly communion with all such beings was outlawed by the Church in the Middle Ages. Robin can also be equated with the Green Man, ancient spirit of the forest throughout Europe, whose foliate face can be found lurking among the corbels of many British church roofs. Today the Green Man has returned to the imagination of many who are concerned about the

protection of nature. He is the Guardian at the Gate of the 'Wood Beyond the World'.

The Hollow Hills, the Land of the Ever Young, and other fairy places

The landscape of the British Isles is exceptionally rich in tales of fairies, giants and dragons: the barrier between worlds has always been thinner here than almost anywhere else in the world.

Every nation has its own mythic history which can be transformed into Dragon Quest adventures. The nations of Europe share many of the same cultural influences with Britain, thanks to successive invasions and the exchange of cultured tourists, and our ideas here can readily be transferred to other parts of the continent with very little alteration. Running workshops farther afield has provided opportunities to share our ideas with colleagues in more distant parts of the world and they assure us that they would find the concept easily applicable to their own cultures.

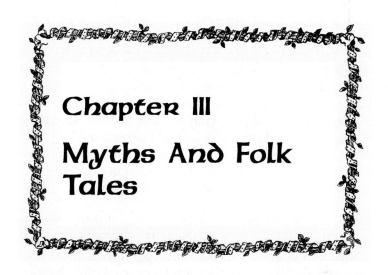

Chapter III

Myths And Folk Tales

The primitive mentality does not invent myths, it experiences them. Myths are original revelations of the pre-conscious psyche...

C G JUNG [23]

Myth is the foundation of life; it is the timeless pattern, the religious formula to which life shapes itself, inasmuch as its characteristics are reproductions of the unconscious.

THOMAS MANN:
Joseph and his Brethren

What are myths and fairy tales? Who are the 'gods'? And what is their value to us, and particularly to children? There have been many theories about myths - people have speculated about them since at least the time of the ancient Greeks; and scholars are still arguing about them. Whatever they are, a growing number of people today are beginning to appreciate the vital importance of myth not only to the health of traditional societies, but to our own too: myths present the eternal underlying patterns of life in story form. If we wish to understand ourselves and the way we behave, if we wish to look for solutions to our problems, we could do well to familiarise ourselves with the great classical myths, and the gods, who all represent aspects of ourselves; and to analyse their meaning. *History* is only about the dead; *myth* is ever-living, past, present, future.

Mythology is enormously attractive to children because it avoids the abstract: it is all about People Doing Things; and children can appreciate, and talk about, things like Goodness, Truth and Beauty when they are translated into stories about people who are involved in magical adventures.

In our adventures we always ally the children to positive archetypes. When they seek mythological characters with which to identify themselves, it is far better that they should be the traditional questing heroes and heroines, images of the journeying soul, than the short-lived fantasies created as money-spinners by Hollywood, and that they enrol themselves on the side of Sweetness and Light against the growing army of Barbarians and Philistines. All our activities aim towards healing and wholeness through experiences of Beauty, for as a wise man once said, 'it is by Beauty alone that the mind is refined and the soul grows'.

Beauty

Why are all the gods and heroines in these stories beautiful, all the heroes noble and handsome? It is because they are aspects of the soul on its journey through our life.

In recent years there has been a resurgence of interest in the soul as an integral part of human being. Myth and folk tale, which are timeless, and experience of otherworlds, which is universal (though not shared by all), can be said to be adventures of the soul. At certain times of heightened sensitivity in our lives, especially in childhood, we can descend into the unconscious and directly experience the life of the soul. Myths and folk tales can help us find our way in this hidden world.

The soul is incorruptible, pure, innocent and beautiful, and it grows in Beauty but, deprived of experiences of Beauty, it becomes starved and shrivelled. Myths and folk-tales, like the natural world, are rich in beauty, and essential food for the growing child.

Dragon Quest adventures are based on selected myths appropriate to children in their middle years. At least some of these marvellous stories, especially those about adventures of a hero or heroine, were devised specifically to prepare children for their rite of passage into adulthood, and these are the ones we use with just the right age-group.

Most of our adventures are based on one of two major mythic themes, each appropriate to a particular age-group: the 'fairy-world' for children aged six to nine, and hero-myths (including the disguised initiation tales about girls such as Briar Rose, Beauty and the Beast, and Vasilisa the Beautiful) for eight to twelve-year-olds.

Once upon a time ....

The re-creation of tribal myths through story-telling, drama and ceremony was of vital importance to our ancestors: they gave meaning to their lives and they ensured the continuity of the gods. Creation myths and the adventures of gods and heroes take place outside time, in eternity. 'Once upon a time', like the aboriginal Dreamtime, is time-less: it is not just in the past but also in the present and in the future - and it is re-created every time the story is re-told or re-enacted.

It may be outside time, but there are certain times when it is easier to enter the Magic: at midday and midnight, at dawn and dusk, or on May Day and Hallowe'en; and it always has a locality, an enchanted Place, and to enter there we have to cross the Edge, beyond civilisation.

Strictly speaking then, the correct time and place for story-telling is at twilight and round an open fire. As the gloaming settles outside the huddled circle of listeners, everyone feels safe in the company of others, and all are at their most vulnerable and open to the magic that the story-teller weaves into the tales.

Nevertheless when the enchantment has broken at the end of the session, there are children who will ask 'Did it really happen?' or 'Is it true?', and the answers must be 'No, it didn't really happen' and 'Yes, it really is true', for most myths and fairy tales contain profound and universal truths about human life and its meaning which can be absorbed unconsciously during childhood. Because the child before puberty is living in a largely mythic world - the same world inhabited by the gods and heroes - it is important that the stories should never be explained rationally. Once you do that you destroy the value of the story to the child; it loses all its magical power and therapeutic value.

Nature Spirits, Fairies and the Otherworld

Come away, O human child!
To the waters and the wild
With a faery, hand in hand,
For the world's more fully of weeping than you can
understand.

W B YEATS; *The Stolen Child*

In every culture in the world people have believed in the existence of some form of spirit world and creatures somewhat similar to the European fairy. The British Isles has for millennia had an international reputation as the place with close contacts with the spirit world: we have more ghosts and fairies to the square mile than anywhere else in the West.

For all that, there have been endless reports of the retreat of the fairies from our islands. At the onset of the Iron Age in prehistory, the invading Milesians came to Ireland and banished the beautiful and magical people of the goddess Dana (the Tuatha De Danann) who had arrived via northern Britain, and drove them below ground where they still enjoy a paradisal life as the fairy Sidhe within the Hollow Hills; and from Chaucer onwards there have been reports of the departure of the fairies - yet there are many gifted and sensitive people who claim to have encountered them even today. How can we *rationally* account for this?

The story of the banishment of the Tuatha de Danann may well provide the answer: Underworld might be a more appropriate term that Otherworld. Traditional people, many children and sensitives can still get in touch with the Unconscious, our personal underworld, an ability which most of us have lost, except in sleep. The belief that fairies and other denizens of the spirit world are only discernible below the levels of consc- iousness, explains why only certain people can see them, though it doesn't explain whether they are 'real' or not.

At present, however, the disbelievers appear to have won over most children: the majority of the middle-age children that we are concerned with now claim to be as sceptical about fairies as most adults - at least in front of their peers: fairies just aren't 'cool'. Nevertheless we have found that there is no shortage of children keen to attend Dragon Quest programmes about elves and fairies - as long as they know they are with other like-minded children, and we have found that provided one avoids the word 'fairy' and speaks instead of elves and dragons, even the 'coolest' children are prepared to drop their sceptical front. Incidentally, the word 'fairy' was not generally used until the 13th century and they only started growing wings in the early 17th century. Before that 'elf' was the normal term.

The idea that this is a magical world where strange and frightening and beautiful things can happen - just as in myths and fairy tales - is very important to the child's developing understanding of existence. It can keep alive a sense of awe at the wonder of Creation and it can continue to feed the creative imagination into adulthood - as long as we foster it in children. And the classical concept that every place, every tree, every flower has a guardian spirit that looks rather like a human being can help young children empathise with and respect other forms of life.

As far as our programmes our concerned, we aim our 'fairy' activities at six- to nine-year-olds. Unlike the Adventures for the older children, which are often based on specific myths, the 'fairy' programmes are only occasionally linked to an identifiable story. We do tell them folk-tales - lots of them, and they love them - but the activities are centred on helping the children to enjoy the beauty and wonders of the natural world. Of course we do subject them to lots of elvish 'glamour' or 'grammarye' (ancient words for fairy enchantment) in a Wood of Wonders, and they are likely to meet witches and wizards (none too frightening) who end up helping the children, and, perhaps, a (pantomime) dragon for them to chase. We see no advantage in making the experience in any way fear-inducing - we want even the most timid to come again.

We have found few fairy-tales that can be used specifically to focus children's attention on the natural world, but they are of the greatest importance to the child's development, and most take place in woods and wild places. See the bibliography for sources of suitable stories. Apart from the classical tales of Pan and the nymphs, we would especially commend the wonderful stories that originate in eastern and central Europe, especially those from Russia, Poland, Hungary, the Czech Republic, Slovakia and Bohemia. It may be that these seem so very rich - and beautiful - because they are still alive to a peasant community that continues to tell them to their children - and to pass them on to professional writers.

Fairy tale quests

In Dragon Quests we centre many of our programmes on the perilous journey of a hero or heroine in search of 'fortune'. As with myths there are plenty of examples in fairy stories of this Quest pattern but, of course, the majority of these tales seem to be about other things. J C Cooper, in her highly illuminating study of the subject, offers a broader perspective:

The most constantly recurring themes are those dealing with the descent of the soul into the world, its experience in life, initiation and the quest for unity and the trials and tribulations that beset its journey through the world. Possibly the best-known and most frequent of motifs is that of Paradise Lost and Regained, of which the story of Cinderella is the classic example, though the theme runs through most fairy tales in the form of initial misfortune leading eventually to a happy ending.

J C COOPER [8]

She goes on to list and explain some of the most common features in these tales, found in every culture across the world:

> The breaking of a taboo, e.g. entering a forbidden room;
> helpful or grateful animals;
> the loathsome suitor, transformed into a prince or princess; metamorphosis into a bird, often a swan.

Fairy stories of the Quest type often involve three brothers, each in turn setting out on a quest, and it is always the younger brother, the 'fool', who achieves the princess and the kingdom. What are such stories trying to tell us? The innocent responds to life spontaneously, allowing his intuition to guide him, while his older, unsuccessful brothers are restricted by their determination to rely on reason alone: they cannot adapt, whereas the 'dummling' is open to learn from experience.

Furthermore the innocent, unlike his brothers, welcomes the advice and aid of animal-helpers. These represent his own instincts in reacting to situations, whereas his brothers ignore theirs.

We believe that there are valuable lessons to be learnt here, and our adventures we are always encouraging the children to become aware of and remain open to their natural instincts and intuition.

Hero and heroine myths

The stories of the great heroes of ancient Greece - Hercules and the Apples of the Hesperides, Jason and the Golden Fleece, Perseus and Medusa, Theseus and the Minotaur - are among the most popular of all myths, especially among young boys. They are all hero quests and, while the children are not conscious of the fact, they all represent rites of initiation for boys as they approach puberty. This may explain their attraction to the age-group, albeit at an un-conscious level.

For clues to the initiation of girls we mostly turn to folk-tales - Cinderella, Briar Rose, Beauty and many more. Folk-tales are mainly for the chimney-corner, and in most cultures female initiation was concerned with sexual and domestic matters. The splendid exception, from our point of view, is centred on the Greek goddess, Artemis, who took young girls into the wildest places for activities similar to those of the boys. This is one of several reasons why we make much use of the classical stories.

The word 'initiation' worries some people, yet initiation is part of everyday life, taking many forms: most of us undergo initiations frequently in our lives, whether it is in changing schools, starting a new job, getting married or merely learning to use a computer.

The most important initiation in all tribal societies has always been the rite of passage from childhood to adulthood. Some traditional societies believed that the child does not have a soul until the initiatory experience, after which the individual can take a full part in the spiritual life of the community. So the Hero Quest is a rehearsal of the journey of the new-born soul in its search for the treasure of spiritual enlightenment.

In tribal societies initiation invariably took place at some time before the onset of puberty, from seven or eight to twelve plus, and it could last from two months to nine years - Arcadian youths could stay as 'wolves' in the wilderness for nine years, until they were eighteen - this is prossibly the origin of 'were-wolves'. It took various forms, from terrifying ordeals involving physical mutilation to relatively benign formalities - though still with an element of fear, or at least trepidation, involved. It always included story-telling, drama and mimetic role-play, and dancing.

Dragon Quest makes no grand claim to provide such a significant revelatory experience but it uses the traditional pattern, not only to provide a day of high enjoyment, but hopefully also to raise the awareness of the children towards the natural world and their place in it. When successful such an adventure has the potential of making children also aware that they are at the start of a lifelong journey of fulfilment which, for some, will turn into a spiritual quest for the Heavenly Paradise.

The Hero's quest

Right across the world in every culture the hero-quest follows much the same pattern: it must be ingrained in human genes. Because we have long lived in a patriarchal society we know far more about male initiation than female, no doubt because the latter was always shrouded in secrecy. Those forms we do know are usually about the story of a youth and his development from innocent childhood to 'King'. As we have already made clear, it is not about a real person but about the journey of the human soul.

Ruminating over the structure of traditional initiations, and the part that gods play in them we have become convinced of the importance of the Divine Child archetype, especially in Indo-European cultures. Specialists in myth and psychology have long recognised and discussed this figure. Psychologists take the view that he represents 'the Child Within' us all (i.e. he is a part of our personality) and that too many adults believe that he must be suppressed or discarded if we are to mature. Mythographers, on the other hand, see the Divine Child as an important external god-form who reappears at significant times throughout history.

> *The mythological idea of the child is emphatically not a copy of the empirical child, but a symbol clearly recognised as such; it is a wonder- child, a divine child, begotten, born, and brought up in quite extraordinary circumstances, and not - this is the point - a human child.*
>
> C G Jung [23]

We take the view that the Divine Child is both transcendent and immanent, and that he can not only inspire the young to grow, adventure and be creative, but is also an ideal we need to keep in touch with *throughout* life if we are to remain young at heart and retain our ideals and creativity. The

Young Hero

archetype can be especially inspiring at the creation point of any new projects. Nearly all of the greatest creators in history maintained that contact and there is plenty of evidence that the Child must have remained alive in them throughout their lives.

The initiation of the hero follows seven stages:

1. Separation from the mother
The young child sees Mother as protector, and as the first stage in the making of the 'hero' the Mother has to LET THE CHILD GO before he can be persuaded (or compelled) to take his first independent steps into the world. In all the traditional stories the child hero is a lone traveller, learning to stand on his or her own two feet.

2. The Call to Adventure
The Quest starts with an invitation to adventure outside society - 'at the Margin'. Sometimes, according to the old stories, it is refused, but then something or someone forces the issue: the young Jason's uncle sends him to recover the Golden Fleece, Perseus is challenged to behead Medusa, the wicked step-sisters send Vasilisa out into the forest to call on the witch Baba Yaga. Our adventures sound so attractive to most children that there is little difficulty in encouraging those first steps which are intended to lead the child to 'die' to the old life, then to be 'reborn' in the new.

3. Entering the Margin: the Forest of Challenges
In the old tales the hero or heroine most frequently entered such a forest but sometimes it was the underworld, or the belly of a serpent or whale, or a perilous sea journey. All of these represent attempts to reach the Earthly Paradise and it's treasures. At the entrance there may be a challenging guardian, clashing rocks, a perilously narrow bridge, or a labyrinth to negotiate.

Traditionally this period at the Margin provided the time and place for teaching the novices how to become independent, standing on their own feet, and surviving in the forest - building huts, practising archery, learning to appreciate and communicate with the natural world, and taking part in more or less serious war-games or ritual contests - all, as it happens, highly attractive activities to the age-group, girls as well as boys, even to the present day.

During the sojourn in the forest they were also taught the myths, songs and dances of the tribe as well as secret sacred knowledge, probably - for we don't really know - about the cycle of nature: birth, life, death and rebirth. We do know that it was usually presented in the form of a dramatic re-creation.

4. Shape-shifting or Metamorphosis
Often the hero or heroine is taught 'shape shifting' through a series of exercises which, through observation and meditation, enable him to transform himself imaginatively into an animal form, and to make dream journeys to other places.

5. The Great Quest
The experience frequently includes a journey in search of a priceless sacred treasure such as the Water of Life, the Holy Grail, the Cauldron of Rebirth, the Golden Fleece, or the Apples of the Hesperides. Often the hero/heroine sets out on the journey without knowing either the destination or the object of the quest.

6. Overcoming the Powers of Darkness and Chaos
On the journey the hero/heroine is faced with a series of ordeals which might include temptations or, almost certainly, the overcoming of a dragon or an ogre, a giant, evil knights, or other hazards such as having to 'cross a bridge no wider than the edge of a sword'.

Unexpected helpers may be encountered but they also act as challengers so that the quester is encouraged to find solutions for himself. Sometimes these helpers take the form of a Wise Old Man, or magical talking animals. In the stories the successful Hero or Heroine is invariably courteous and helpful, and the kindness is returned multifold. As we have already explained above the animals represent the individuals own instincts.

7. Rebirth and inheriting the Kingdom

At the end of all the ordeals the quester emerges to the life of a mature, spiritualised 'King' or 'Queen' to live 'happily ever after'. In the process of initiation the children of the tribe would experience this sequence through story, ritual drama and role-play. Sometimes they would *be* the youthful Hero or Heroine themselves. In other traditions they would become 'companions' who helped or rescued the Divine Child-Hero. Examples are the company of seven who rescue Mabon, Robin Hood's 'Merry Men', Arthur's Round Table, Roland and his peers, and the Little Bears of Artemis. In our Quests we tend

to use the 'companions' form, though we also frequently appoint older children to play the main roles.

The myth of the Golden Age

Often linked with the quest of the hero is the concept of the Golden Age, ruled by Kronos (Saturn). Indo-European cultures have shared a belief that the world has been in a state of long decline since a glorious Edenic dawn. This decline proceeds from a paradisal Golden Age when the gods walked on earth, through Silver and Bronze Ages to the present Iron Age, a time of wars, depravity and suffering, possibly ending in a great destruction (which, some say, we are currently living through). Then the cycle will eventually move on to a new Age of Gold.

Kronos was banished by his son Zeus to an Otherworld kingdom where he still enjoys the Golden Age conditions of abundance, peace and harmony. This land has long been identified as the British Otherworld.

The Irish poet and mystic George Russell (AE) was among many who have insisted that the Golden Age is here, all around us, could we but see it:

> So did I feel one warm summer day lying idly on the hillside, not then thinking of anything but the sunlight, and how sweet it was to drowse there, when, suddenly, I felt a fiery heart throb, and knew it was personal and intimate, and started with every sense dilated and intent, and turned inwards, and heard first a music as of bells going away, away into that wondrous underland whither, as legend relates, the Danann gods withdrew; and then the heart of the hills was opened to me, and I knew there was no hill for those who were there, and they were unconscious of

*the ponderous mountain piled above the palaces of
light, and the winds were sparkling and diamond
clear, yet full of colour as an opal, as they glittered
through the valley, and I knew the Golden Age was all
about me, and it was we who had been blind to it but
that it had never passed away from the world.*

George Russell (AE) [34]

The ancient legend tells us that the king of a new Age of Gold
will eventually appear to all in the form a Divine Child Hero
of peerless purity and innocence who first has to be sought
and found by human seekers, like Culhwch and his band, who
have only to quest then, perhaps like Parzifal, to ask the right
question. Virgil said the new ruler will be Apollo, whom the
Vikings call Balder, and the Celts Mac Og or Mabon; then

*.... the Sequence of the Ages starts afresh. Justice, the
Virgin, comes back to dwell with us, and the Golden
Age is restored. The Firstborn of the New Age is
already on his way from high heaven down to earth.*

*With him the Iron Race shall end and Golden Man
inherit all the world. Smile on the Baby's birth,
immaculate Lucina; your own Apollo is enthroned at
last.*

VIRGIL: *Fourth Eclogue* [41]

As this seems to be an archetypal theme deep in the psyche of
all the European races, and therefore unconsciously
recognisable to the children, the pattern is a good one to be
drawn on in adventures, perhaps in the form of a rehearsal
for the search for Mabon, who can unlock wonders and glories.

Three cultural resources

Thanks to a series of cultural invasions over the past three
millennia - which continue to this day - Britain shares with

Europe an exceptionally richly endowed in mythical resources, especially classical, Celtic,and the English/ Nordic/folk tradition of elves and fairies. We concentrate on these rather than the equally attractive myths of other cultures because they have now become deeply ingrained in European consciousness. There is no reason, however, why one shouldn't apply the basic Dragon Quest principles outlined here to any other culture in the world.

Ancient Greece

Classical myth is of primary importance because it has influenced European culture and civilisation for over two thousand years, and it continues to do so, perhaps more than any other with the possible exception of the Bible. This is one of the reasons why we make it the principal source for our activities.

There are several other reasons too: Greek mythology provides an exceptionally rich collection of stories, many of them related to the natural world; they are infused with a magical beauty yet have great clarity: the gods and goddesses have well defined characters - very different from the ever-shifting magical nature of the Celtic deities. Even today they are still very much alive as archetypes in our psychology and they continue to influence our behaviour: if we are to understand people's actions we have only to familiarise ourselves with these gods and their stories. Finally, the British Isles have associations with ancient Greece which go far back into prehistory, and there is evidence for this remarkable relationship in Greek literature and (less certainly) in British archaeology.

For our adventures we draw on a few stories that can most easily be translated to a woodland setting, and we encourage the children to dress as Greek gods, heroes and nymphs.

Costumes

In appearance most goddesses wore the long chiton (except Artemis the huntress and her young followers, who wore a short one); the gods were invariably depicted naked except for a chlamys (a cloak). Greeks of the Homeric period wore a sort of kilt, while later Greek youths, like the gods, were mostly naked or at most wore only a hymation (a sort of toga) or a cloak. We are not suggesting that you should expect today's boys to copy this too literally! Costumes that children wear in our programmes can be seen in some of the accompanying photographs.

The Celts

The Celtic stories used in our adventures are taken from the Mabinogion, the principal collection of Celtic myth in Britain, from the Arthurian corpus, and from the Irish sagas. They are full of magic and wonders. There is an enormous quantity of material here but Celtic myths and gods are much less clearly delineated than the Greek and they have fewer obvious links with specific aspects of the natural world: they are as changeable and insubstantial as the mists that often enshroud the Celtic lands. To further complicate matters the Celtic tribes were noted for their quarrelsomeness; as a result of this each tribe had their own name for each of the gods. The Romans tried to overcome this by identifying each Celtic god with a classical deity. Thus the god of the woods (Roman: Silvanus), was called Nodens in Gloucestershire, Cunomaglus in Wiltshire, Cocidius round Hadrian's Wall, Callirius in Essex and, possibly, Cernunnos in Dorset - depicted as the Cerne Giant.

Again we help the children to dress appropriately. Unfortunately there are also few descriptions of the appearance of the Celtic gods, though the stories do frequently give a detailed description of their ornaments. We know the people wore short colourful tunics with plenty of barbaric decoration and jewellery, bare legs (except the Gauls, who wore trousers), a tartan cloak, and blue tattoos of woad all over - the Romans reported that the British Celts went into battle naked and they looked terrifying.

The English/Nordic/folk tradition

> *Widespread they stand, the Northland's dusky forests,*
> *Ancient, mysterious, brooding savage dreams;*
> *Within them dwells the the forest's mighty God,*
> *And wood-sprites in the gloom weave magic secrets.*
> JAN SIBELIUS : *Tapiola*

While the general principles underlying Dragon Quest are equally applicable in the northern world - they certainly had more than enough dragons and giants to battle with! - their stories tend to be very violent and blood-stained, and they make few references to nature except as an hostile force. However, apart from the Norwegians and Icelanders, the northern folk who came to Britain were mostly Danes and Saxons who lived at the edge of the seemingly endless Teutoburg forest which then spread across modern Germany and Poland, and from which Arminius ('Herman the German') and his wild guerillas were able to pounce on and destroy a whole Roman army.

The remains of that great forest have however also given us the wonderful magic-filled folk and fairy-tales of Scandinavia, old Germany, Bohemia, Hungary, and other central European peoples, and their characters are readily adaptable to woodland adventures.

As far as costume is concerned, the appearance of the early Teutons was somewhat similar to the Celts, though less colourful and without the tatoos and tartans.

72

Of course we have our native fairy tale characters, nearly all associated with the woods, mostly originating in the Middle Ages (e.g. Robin Hood) or the Elizabethan period (Queen Mab, Puck and the little Shakespearean sprites). These too are ideal for Dragon Quest adventures.

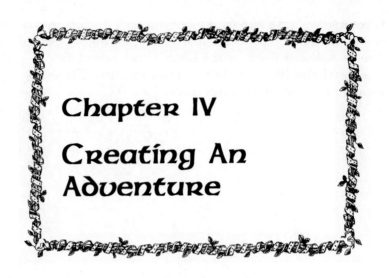

Chapter IV

Creating An Adventure

*The mythical Kouretes (who protected Zeus as a child)
still show traces of their function as masters of
initiation: they bring up boys in the bush, teaching
them the archaic techniques of hunting and gathering
wild fruits, of dancing and music.*

MIRCEA ELIADE [14]

For various practical reasons, the majority of the
adventures we offer here have been designed to fill one
or two days, though children invariably beg for more.
However it is better to stop before they have become
sated.

Whenever we do advertise proper camping, we are invariably overwhelmed with applications.

The day programme is usually divided into two parts - an introductory training session ('tuning-up' for the main activity) followed by the Adventure itself ('tuning-in'). Of course this is not an immutable rule: with the younger children there is rarely any obvious division.

When we do divide the day, the training session often takes up *at least* half the total time available, and it consists of games, stories, and opportunities to try out unfamiliar activities and learn new skills. The Adventure may be very brief if time is limited - perhaps just a game based on the theme for the day. Alternatively it may be an extended focus of all the earlier training and include some of the ideas given in this chapter.

We invite you to draw on this collection of activities, all of which have been tried and tested, and pluck out whatever seems appropriate to the Adventure you are planning. But first we must start by ...

PART I: PREPARING THE GROUND

Creating your own Special Place

We think it is really important that you should find some way of identifying any place you choose to play in as 'special', so you need to provide it with a magical threshold - a way of 'entering' what then becomes a mythical 'enchanted' landscape. If you regularly use one place for your activities (a nearby wood or your school grounds) then create some form of portal or a maze or a dancing place as somewhere to begin your quest. If it is a temporary site, then a simple gateway of bent branches and some colourful ribbons can be quickly erected.

Beating the bounds

It was the custom in some parishes, before many people could read or write, to continue an ancient Roman custom and take young boys round the boundary during Rogation Week for a ritual 'beating' at certain sites round the edge of the parish. This beating was never more than rough fun with volunteers and the victims were usually rewarded with a shilling for their pains.

Most children enjoy a 'Dragon Quest' version of this as we go round identifying the bounds of our activity area in a wood: at each easily identifiable landmark during the perambulation two adults take young volunteers by their wrists and ankles and 'throw' them high in the air (without letting them go) three times before letting them down again gently. There are always far more demands from both girls and boys to be subjected to this 'ordeal' than most of the available throwers can cope with. Needless to say the 'privilege' of participation in this ritual is its own reward. (NB Be very conscious of the safety aspect of this part of the activity, and if you are at all unsure about the capability of the adults to do this, then we suggest you do other activities at each site).

Entering the Mythic Landscape

We often use these activities to take us into our magical world and leave the troubles and concerns of the 'real' world behind. This is particularly valuable if the site you are using is close to modern buildings, roads or on the edge between developed and natural areas.

To start and end most programmes the children enjoy performing the ancient 'Geranos' dance. After Theseus slew the Minotaur over three thousand years ago, he invented the Geranos - the 'Crane Dance'. Originally this 'high-stepping' (i.e. stamping) dance followed the pattern of the Cretan or Trojan maze. We have simplified it to resemble a traditional folk dance that may well have once descended from the Geranos. Now the dancers, boys and girls alternating and hand in hand, start in a circle. The leader breaks the circle by only holding the hand of the child on his/her right. The leader then leads the line in an inward spiral to the left ('sunwise') and towards the centre to the beat of a drum or tambourine. The line follows the leader at a walking pace, stamping the ground with knees raised high. At the centre the leader and neighbour, without breaking from the line, form an arch with their hands then they start anti-clockwise with their hands joined over the children's heads, to spiral outwards to reform the circle.

The inward, sunwise spiral represents the path of the sun and moon; the outward spiral represents the way of the stars. Both at the start and at the end everyone stands still because, until Pythagoras revealed the truth, the early Greeks believed

that the Earth stood still. The result surprises the children: they started facing inwards and end facing outwards! This a truly magical, cosmic dance, and the children love it, often begging for a repeat.

Part II: THE TRAINING OF HEROES

Note: Activities suitable for families or very small groups are preceded with **F**. *Those for groups of ten or more are marked* **G**. *Many are suitable for both types of group.*

This is the Training or 'Tuning-up' section of any programme. Select ideas from here that seem appropriate to the later adventure.

The training is usually in 'game'-form, and you can draw on the ideas below and on the games in Chapters V and VI. As an invaluable supplementary resource for nature games we would particularly commend '*Sharing Nature with Children 1 and 2*' by Joseph Cornell [9]. We draw on Joseph's books extensively in training sessions as well as '*Earthworks*' by Steve Van Matre.

F/G The silent trail: the woods are full of wildlife which you can meet, especially if you are alone and moving silently, early in the morning or in the evenings. Unless you can persuade children to be very quiet for an extended period (as in Green Vigil - see below), they are unlikely to enjoy such an experience. As a first stage in training, show them how to walk silently. We frequently do this over quite a short distance (c.100 metres) on first entering the wood.

First we show them how the woodland tribes of north America walk in the woods - in single file behind the leader, with bare feet or in thin-soled moccasins pointing straight forward in order to cover the maximum distance with every step; the ball or side of the foot is placed down first to feel the ground for any stick that might snap, then the heel. They should also attempt to step in the footprints of the hunter in front so that they leave the minimum evidence of their passing. At the same time they need to keep their eyes skinned on all sides and above their heads - you could also encourage them to train themselves in peripheral vision - 'seeing out of the side of your eyes' - which we all have and seldom use to full potential. Use you hands to 'weave an (imaginary) veil of silence' over them so that no-one talks, and challenge them to follow you in single file so silently that you are not sure whether you are being followed. Warn them that you may suddenly freeze. Keep your own eyes open all about you and if you notice anything of interest during the walk stop and point it out silently to your immediate follower. Don't forget to congratulate them when they finish and lift the veil that held their talking.

F/G The Whispering Wood, sometimes called the Green Vigil

Children rarely have the opportunity to be completely on their own these days, yet solitude is the breeding ground of imagination. Most of the best writers and poets faced often long periods of solitude during childhood, and they were forced to fill the void with their imaginings.

Many people, including adults, are nervous at the thought of being alone in the wild, yet Britain's woods are among the safest and friendliest places anywhere.

Naturally with other people's young children one must not really leave them alone in the woods, but we do try to give them the feel of it to help them to empathise with nature.

Find a place in a wood away from traffic noise. Invite the children to cup a hand to their ear and ask them if they can hear the wood whispering. Encourage them to be very still and listen carefully and explain that there are the most wonderful sounds and songs in the wildwood if only we can take the time to listen. Unfortunately a group of excited children inevitably frighten the birds and animals away as soon as they arrive - particularly if they are all dressed in bright clothes.

Now if they could only merge into the background, for even a few minutes, they would be rewarded. The idea is to find somewhere to sit comfortably alone within a restricted area, maybe snuggled into the base of a tree or beside a leafy bush. We have collected enough green and brown material from remnant shops to make a set of simple woodland tabards (see Chapter V for details) which the children can wear throughout the day. But many enjoy burying themselves in leaf litter, propping a few dead branches up and hiding behind them or simply covering themselves with leaves - an effective camouflage. It also helps them to be still.

Once silence has fallen, the resident wildlife will begin to emerge again - we have had children report seeing deer, foxes, woodmice, squirrels and many birds.

The children should know that they will be expected to stay there for c. 15 minutes, until they hear the signal to return.

Many children have told us that this was the best activity in the day. Others fear they will be bored, and we give them a clipboard, paper and pencil to draw what they see. A few young or insecure children are too nervous to be out of sight of an adult, and we permit them to stay in view or to sit beside an adult.

Alternatively give everyone a plain postcard and a pencil, then explain that when they are all settled and everyone is quiet they will be able to hear the voice of the Wildwood. They should then try to record the sounds they hear in any way they wish on the card - simply letting the sounds come into their ears and flow out through their hands onto the card. It is a good idea to show them an example. Give them five minutes to find a site and get themselves settled in, then give a bird call (see Chapter VI) which is the signal for quiet and stillness,

We encourage all the adults taking part to join in - they find it as rewarding as the children - try it yourself if you haven't done it before. With younger children at least one of us remains standing and observing, but we don't move about as it will only disturb the wildlife. There can be a magical atmosphere with 30+ people looking like elves in a glade all tuned into the natural sounds. Try it!

When they return encourage them to share their results with each other.

F/G Stalking
Children particularly enjoy stalking but are not very good at it unless they are trained.

Here are a few basic principles (though it will be difficult for impatient young children to adhere to them!):
(a)   If you are stalking an animal approach downwind - most animals have a better sense of smell than of sight.
(b)   Wear clothes that blend in with nature - this is why we provide green tabards - and camouflage your face (see below).
(c)   Move very slowly and smoothly, and be ready to freeze for a prolonged period.

(d)   Learn to walk silently, looking where you are stepping, and placing the ball of the foot down before the heel, 'feeling' the ground as you go. Good balance is important.

(e)   Practice crawling flat, bottom down and using one leg at your side to push you along.

(f)   When peering round a tree avoid showing your head at the expected height - keep low.

(g)   All traditional hunters learn to study, then copy, the natural movement of the animals they are hunting, e.g. 'grazing' towards a herd of deer, gradually moving closer.

Try these games:

F/G The Watchers in the Wood: two players stand back-to-back in the middle of a reasonably dense wood while the rest go out of sight. The latter are challenged to see how close they can creep up to the Watchers before they are named. Once spotted and identified they must go back and start again.

G Forest Shadows - a silent moving exercise: give the children time to disguise themselves in any way they wish, then send them with an adult to spread out along a woodland boundary some distance away to await a signal from you. After they have gone, send out any spare helpers to stand still, silently watching, between you and the children. These are 'The Watchers'. Emphasise that this is not a race; it is a challenge. At your signal the children have to move 'like shadows' to reach you without being spotted by the Watchers. At the end of the exercise the latter should report critically on what they have observed.

F/G Camouflage and Disguise

Stalking becomes more exciting if the children can dress for the part. Forewarn them so that they can if possible wear suitable clothing - dull green, fawn or brown colours, nothing bright. Some may have army-style camouflage clothes. We invite other children to wear our green tabards (see Chapter V for details). We also offer them the opportunity to have face-paints on face and arms (or alternatively, mud), and in the summer they can add some foliage, though this, like the face-paints, calls for adult supervision: all they need is one or two small sprigs of leaves, just enough to break up the shape of their face. We do not want the children tearing at trees. Garden netting over the head can provide a useful foundation for the foliage.

F/G Naming creation

Many adults are likely to feel very insecure when it comes to naming trees, flowers, birds and so on. Don't worry about this. Country people didn't know the naturalist's names for these things either; instead they invented their own, often delightful names: 'Angel's Pincushion', ' Bachelor's Buttons', 'Betty-go-to-bed-at-noon', 'Bread and Marmalade', 'Chopped Eggs', 'Huggy-me-close', 'Humpy-scrumples', 'Mother Shimble's Snick-needles', 'Pop-guns', 'Witches' Thimbles', and many more. Make sure that you have a few good examples and set the children the task of naming particular plants and animals. A researcher recently collected over 400 different regional names for the woodlouse so it shouldn't be too difficult! This is a good activity for the school grounds, or somewhere the children will visit regularly.

F/G Traditional children's country activities

Few children these days have enjoyed the pleasure of making a daisy chain, of putting a buttercup under a friend's chin to find out if they like butter, of discovering the time by blowing on the seeding dandelion head, of making a necklace out of seeds, little people out of acorns, or little grass dolls with long stems of well-soaked dry grass. Try it.

F/G Dowsing

Dowsing is easy! Just about everyone can master it with a little patience and practice. Without going into scientific arguments of how or why it works, maybe you can accept for the moment that it does work! There are many explanations - usually relating to the subtle flow of energy around particular places, rock formations, minerals or features such as underground water. Once you have decided what you are seeking (e.g. water), all of your senses are reacting to those particular energy changes and amplifying them by subtle unconscious reflex actions in your wrist muscles. Many people ascribe the response to 'Earth Energy' and in the absence of any other 'scientific' explanation, this fits nicely with our themes in this book!

A famous dowser in Devon was recently employed by an oil company to dowse for oil in China. They did not fly him out to China, but provided him with maps of the likely areas. He dowsed the maps, indicated the suitable sites for drilling and had an amazing success rate.

Outline the above in your own words and demonstrate to the children. Provide each child with two dowsing rods - wire coat hangers cut and bent into a right angle, about 10cm by 30cm. Hold the rods loosely in each hand so that the long ends are horizontal and can swing freely. The rods should be level, pointing away from you, then walk slowly forwards. When you cross a point of energy or an underground water source the rods will swing together and cross (or they may swing outwards). Take the children to a field that you have checked beforehand to be sure that they will find something. Space the children out in a straight line at one end of the field and all walk forward together. When someone's rods cross they should stop and stand still. When everyone has stopped they have indicated the course of an underground stream. Each time we have done this it has produced a remarkably accurate map of the course of a stream or drain. Once we came upon an electric cattle fence and it was an amazing site to see a group of people holding their rods near the wire and all of them swinging in time to the pulses of electricity through the wire!

Another way is to make a pendulum from a crystal, a stone or a piece of metal and a piece of thin thread. Hold it over the palm of your other hand and ask the pendulum to work for you. Ask it to swing in response to a simple question to which the answer is Yes ... e.g. 'I am wearing green trousers', or 'My name is Sam'. Hold very still and note which direction it swings. Now ask a question to which the answer is No and again note the direction of the swing. You can now ask questions like 'Is there water here?', 'Should I turn right at this path junction?' and note the response. We often use this to find things that are lost or to discover the site of sacred places and important happenings. Try it - it really does work!

F/G The Hero at Arthur's Gate

When those who hoped to become knights arrived at King Arthur's court at Caerleon, the Porter at the Gate would only grant them admission if they were of royal blood or they could demonstrate that they had a talent to offer the king. Before qualifying to take part in the Great Adventure each child should demonstrate some sort of talent at a level that the Enchanter acting as Porter judges commensurate with the individual's ability.

F/G The heroes and the giant Ysbaddaden

The first time that seven of King Arthur's heroes visited Ysbaddaden's castle to ask for the hand of his daughter for one of them, he flung a poisoned spear at them. One caught it and threw it back, hitting the giant in the knee. He threw his spear at them again on their second visit, and again it was caught and returned, hitting him in the chest. On the third visit the same happened and Ysbaddaden was hit in the eye. At this he reluctantly agreed to the marriage - as long as the heroes accomplished 39 impossible tasks, including finding Mabon (see The Great Adventure) and taking the shears from between Torch Trwyth's ears (see Fun Games). Needless to say, they succeeded.

A catching and throwing skill: first create a giant out of logs. Use acorns, fir-cones, etc. as missiles. The Enchanter, on behalf of the giant, throws the missiles at a child who has to catch it and throw it to hit the giant.

Part III: THE GREAT ADVENTURE

Something hidden. Go and find it. Go and look behind
the Ranges -
Something lost behind the Ranges. Lost and waiting
for you.
Go!

RUDYARD KIPLING: *The Explorer*

Go forth to seek: the quarry never found
Is still a fever to the questing hound.
The skyline is a promise - not a bound.

Therefore go forth, companions: when you find
No highway more, no track, all being blind,
The way to go shall glimmer in your mind.
Adventure on, for from the littlest clue
Has come whatever worth man ever knew;
The next to lighten all men may be you.

JOHN MASEFIELD

Who hath smelt wood-smoke at twilight? Who hath
heard the birch-log burning?
Who is quick to read the noises of the night?
Let him follow with the others, for the Young Men's
feet are turning
To the camps of proved desire and known delight!

RUDYARD KIPLING:
The Feet of the Young Men

The Enchanter has returned, cloaked and hooded, and
carrying his long stave-wand. This time he has come straight
from Mount Badon where King Arthur is preparing for his
great battle with the Saxon horde. Years ago Merlin had taken
the great Sword of Light, Excalibur, into his keeping and
hidden it in a time-warp against the needs of just such a day -
and he hid it in this very wood! Now he has sent the

The Great Adventure

The Great Adventure

The Great Adventure

Enchanter to recover it, and he needs a group of Adventurers to help him break the protective spell. First they have to prove their worth in a series of tests, then they must seek the sword with help from Merlin's strange and magical map. It is known that there are some dangerous foes lurking somewhere in the wood ....

* * *

It is early Spring, and there is little life in the forest and now comes fresh news that the Spring Maiden is held prisoner by the Winter King. Until she is rescued nothing can flower. Only one hero can loosen the iron grip of the Ruler of Ice and Darkness: the golden sun-hero, Mabon; and even he will need help. But Mabon too is lost, imprisoned in the Greenwood by a witch who may be reluctant to release him. He must be found and set free, then the Adventurers must help him put Winter to flight with an ancient and near-forgotten ceremony so that the Spring Maiden can bring the Greenwood back to life and all can celebrate in a Festival of Spring.

* * *

The hunters, in loin-cloths and war-paint,and bending low with bows and arrows at the ready, follow an almost invisible trail through the trees in silent file, eyes and ears strained for evidence of the dragon they are hunting. Gormand the dragon has stolen all their food while they were training, and they must find him if they are not to starve to death. Then someone spots a trail of enormous dragon-prints, and the hunters spring forward into action. Suddenly there is a great roar behind them, and they turn to face the dragon ....

* * *

There's news that elves and fairies have been seen in the Wildwood, and we're going to look for them. As we sit under an old oak tree drinking some delicious magic liquid that the Enchanter brought along, we hear soft giggles and the faint tinkle of little bells above our heads, then we look up and see four green faces laughing down at us: elves! The Enchanter persuades them to come down and meet us. They're a bit bigger than we are, and they say they are guarding the naughty Pixy Prince, who ran away from his underground palace to play with the fairies. He then arrives with two fairies and asks us to play too, and soon we are enjoying woodland games organised by the Enchanter and helped by a friendly witch and the elves and fairies. We're also going to make a hiding place for the Prince. They're real fairies: we asked them.

* * *

We use the word Adventure rather loosely - it may, indeed often does, take the form of an exciting wide game, but it can be a journey of discovery, or the building of huts or a totem, or it may be a festival or drama.

F/G Exploring
Plato, in 'The Laws', argued that the country should be divided into twelve roughly equal divisions and that each should be explored and patrolled for a month at a time by one of twelve tribes of youths who then move on to the next division until they had become familiar with the whole country, its fauna and flora and all the secret byways. Following this lead we divide the children into small groups, each with a well-briefed adult. They are encouraged to get to know the area intimately so that they won't get lost and they can identify possible camp-building sites and hiding places as well as all that is strange and beautiful. As an additional stimulus to look hard we sometimes plant a few un-natural objects for them to discover.

G Wide games

There are five basic forms of wide game, each of which can be
adapted to any number of story-lines:

(i)   The raid - one team defends a base which contains a
        trophy (their own or one belonging to the opposing
        team), the other team tries to break through and
        capture or re-capture the trophy (two to four teams;
        each could be guarding a trophy);

(ii)   Cordon-breaking - one team attempts to escort a
        person or an object through 'enemy lines' from A to B.
        The other team tries to waylay them and capture the
        prize;

(iii)   Search and rescue - a more positive version of (ii): one
        or more teams attempt to find and rescue a victim of
        kidnap. The victim and kidnappers could all be adults
        so that all the children have a positive role to play;

(iv)   Treasure hunt - teams compete to find the treasure
        with help from a map and/or clues;

(v)   Man-hunt: one or more (adult or older child) fugitives
        have to be found and captured by the rest.

These are only the basic forms. They only come to life if they
are cloaked in *romance* - the essential element. Draw on
myths and folk-tales for a story-line: Robin and the Sheriff of
Nottingham, dragon hunting, finding Excalibur, etc.

Good organisation is obviously essential for both quests and
wide-games:

1   Carefully plan the activity beforehand - and be prep-
        ared to cope with the unexpected! There's many a
        slip ....

2   Clearly define the playing area to avoid children
        wandering too far afield and getting lost. Depending
        on age and the terrain an area of a quarter to a third
        of a mile square is enough for young children.

3   Check the playing area beforehand for possible dangers.

4   Make sure that everyone (especially the adults!) clearly understands the objectives of the game and the rules.

5   Keep the rules simple.

6   See that everyone has a part to play all the time.

7   Insist on children staying with their tribes - individuals must not wander off on their own: remember, these are young children.

8   For the same reason attach an adult to each tribe - not necessarily to travel with them, but to be in agreed place (such as their base) where the tribe can locate them. It's a good idea if these people carry first aid kits.

9   Tell the children beforehand the time they have available, and stick to it.

10   Have an agreed signal for starting and calling everyone in.

11   Identify the teams with coloured cloths tucked in at the back of belts.These are 'lives' and the children can be 'killed' when the cloth is snatched away. The adult with the tribe should have plenty of replacements so that no-one is 'dead' for long.

F/G Dreamtime Journey

This activity is based on the Australian aboriginal creation myth that describes how the Universe was formed. Almost every culture has its own creation myth and you may wish to look through the wide literature now available on the subject. An excellent short account of the Aboriginal version is given in Bruce Chatwin's novel *'Songlines'* (Jonathan Cape 1987 - see section entitled *In the Beginning* between Chapters 14 and 15). Here is a brief synopsis of the myth:

Before creation time the infinite and eternal earth existed as a vast, uninhabited featureless plain. There was no sun, moon or stars, just a shadowy twilight. No hills or watercourses broke the surface, just a few hollows that one day would be waterholes. No plants covered its nakedness, nor did the calls of birds or animals disturb the quiet. It was a dead world. Yet far away, in their Paradise beyond the Western Clouds lived the Sky-dwellers.

Beneath the monotonous surface of the earth however, the Sun shone, the stars twinkled and the moon went through its cycle. There were also indeterminate forms of life that, when they awoke, would transform into the plants and animals which the aborigines know today.

As the ages passed, the sun and the other sentient forms grew restless and on the morning of the First Day the Sun was born - it burst through the surface of the earth flooding the land with warmth and light. The mythical Ancestors began to give birth to children - the Snake Man to snakes which slithered out of his navel, the Bandicoot Man giving birth to baby bandicoots from his armpits and so on ... Then the Ancestors began to emerge from their hollows beneath the plain and to wander haphazardly over its surface.

They cried out 'I am ... Snake, Bandicoot, Kangaroo...' This first naming was the most sacred moment. The Ancients then walked the earth calling all things into being and weaving the name of each thing and feature into songs and verses. These beings seem to have resembled creature or plants in appearance, but to have behaved like human beings. They camped, hunted, made fire, dug for water, performed ceremonies and fought each other, but wherever they went they left a trail, or more accurately, a web of song.

Then when the whole earth had been sung, creation time came to an end. The mythical creatures died, sank back into the earth, crawled into caves or went back to their waterholes. They went 'back in'. But each place that one or another of them had carried out a task or feat or had acted in some memorable way, is now marked by a natural feature.

The aborigines learn these songs of the landscape and by knowing the song of each thing or feature can navigate themselves across the land - often for huge distances.

Tell the children this story of the Dreamtime, describe songlines, and then explain that they are to go on a journey on their own based on these legends. The journey they make may be of any distance upward from a few metres - obviously you will need to set the boundaries for safety and supervision. Provide the children with two sticks which they can bang together to beat out a rhythm (or they may like to find their own if there is plenty of fallen wood around) and a set of face paint crayons (three or four colours are enough). Each child should then invent a simple rhythm of up to about ten beats that will be their own song. They should mark this rhythm in dots and dashes on the back of one hand using the face paint. They will be like the Ancestors in the myth and sign things into existence.

Explain that the distance travelled is not important but they will need to travel / explore for the amount of time you specify (we usually send them out for about 40-60 minutes depending on the site). Divide the group between the number of leaders you have, spread them out and tell them all to aim for a prominent feature as a finishing point. They should set out on

their songline journey and each feature they meet that interests them or is an important feature of the place should be sung to by playing their rhythm and then recorded by drawing a simple representation of the thing or view on their body (arms, legs, chests - as they prefer) using the face crayons. Continue to record the journey in this way until the end of the journey. Call them back in with a sound signal you agree to use.

As they return each child should be given a strip of cloth about 1-1.5 meters in length, some wax crayons, coloured pencils or felt-tips and asked to transfer the drawings from their body to the cloth in the right sequence.

There are a number of alternatives now depending on the time available:

Children can pair up and try to follow each others journey by 'reading' the paintings on each other's body or the cloth strips. Alternatively, the cloth strips may be attached to a figure made of withies or fallen wood and this is paraded back to your starting point accompanied by songs and rhythms beat out on their sticks.

Afterwards they can plunge into a river / lake / shower / bath to scrub off the paintings from their bodies - or keep them on to show proudly to their families!

F/G The Seven Talents of the Dragon Hunter
The aim of this programme is to help the children to learn to move quickly and quietly through the natural world, to use cunning and teamwork to trap the 'dragon', and to be able to solve riddles and puzzles. The final meeting with the dragon is to make them aware of the need to address the chaotic, untamed parts of their own personality.

(G) One reasonably athletic adult is selected to be the dragon and is dressed in the dragon's cloak - an old coat to which many card 'scales' are loosely attached by thread. The person may be one of the helpers made up to look as much like a dragon as you can achieve; the area in which the dragon can roam should be defined and the dragon should play the role carefully so that it is neither too hard nor too easy to catch. A number of 'dragon lairs' are marked off with coloured wool where the dragon may rest and not be approached. The tribes then set off to chase the dragon and remove the scales one at a time. As each group wins a scale they return to a central point where they are given a task by the leader. The tasks set will obviously depend on the nature of your site, the time of year, your policy on collecting/picking and the time available for preparation. Such things as these have worked well:

Recognise the work of **the Dragon of the East** (see p19): make up a four line poem about the something you think beautiful in the area;

Discover the richness of **the Dragon of the South**: find eight different types of grasses and draw them;

Challenge them to make a picture of a dragon on paper using only the natural materials around them;

Find one of the treasures of **the Dragon of the West**: plant one or two examples (e.g.a lump of coal, a can of oil, a lump of potter's clay, some gravel) in a hiding place, the 'dragon's lair', with some big paper cut-out 'dragon's footprints' for them to follow to the 'lair' as a simple trail;

Discover the power of **the Dragon of the North**: report back on evidence of the effect of the elements on the surroundings (i.e. the sun, the wind, the rain or a stream, subsidence); Face 'the most dangerous dragon you will have to conquer before you can call yourself grown-up'.

Do not give away the secret of what they are about to encounter!: warn them that it is one of the most destructive forces on the planet. Take them one at a time to look through a secret 'window': a mirror, covered with a cloth and mounted in a tree, hedgerow or other appropriate place. Lift the cloth quickly so that they get just a glimpse of the dragon - *themselves* ! (i.e. **the Dragon Within**). Then ask them to sit quietly on their own and reflect on the meaning of the revelation, and their own impact on the planet. Maybe they can think of a goal to set themselves - a goal that will help them to live more lightly on the planet and care for all life.

When a group has successfully completed a task they are given a card with a letter printed on it and when they have collected all seven letters they must compose the hidden word which will tell them what they need to help them deal with the last dragon: BRAVERY.

Finally they can be awarded their 'Dragon Hunter' certificate.

Quests and journeys

> *(The traditional quest's) conclusion is always one and the same. Whether the hero happens to gain a princess, a kingdom, a healing medicine, a talisman, or some other reward appears immaterial. He actually earns self-integration, balance, wisdom and spiritual health..... Final success spells the conclusion of an initiation into eternal mysteries.*
>
> ALEXANDER ELIOT [15]

Enchanters should be aware that all Quests in myths and fairy tales take place not in this world, but in the Otherworld, Fairyland, the Dreamtime or, if you prefer, in the

imagination. Most children have the gift of being able to enter and leave that magic kingdom, as in Celtic stories, suddenly, without being conscious of the transformation: for them no barriers exist.

For the Adventures, however, which inevitably take place in a real location, we first need to transform it into an Enchanted Realm with a magical threshold, defined by a ceremonial crossing of a boundary, or by stepping between two trees, or by a spiral dance at the beginning and end of the experience, in order to mark it off from ordinary life (see pp 75-6).

The traditional quest was not an activity of an afternoon; it entailed a lengthy adventure covering months, sometimes years, even (if it was a true spiritual quest) a lifetime. Our quests can only be primary training, hopefully to give children a direction in life; and this needs to be explained to them.

So we do have brief quest-type activities, but it is well-worth make it more substantial if you can work with the children over a period as in school or even during a camp.

The quest is the quintessential task of the mythical or folk-tale hero and it was invariably the final test of the traditional initiation process. Quests can have a variety of objectives:

(i)   **Recovery** of a special object (e.g. a sword, a sacred stone, a goblet);
(ii)   **Discovery** of a secret or some essential information;
(iii)   **Rescue** of a person or object from a wicked foe;
(iv)   **Overthrow** of a tyrant, or a dragon;
(v)   **Adventure** - a series of challenges and obstacles.

and we draw on the traditional elements and participants:

> **the Great Mother**: not much used in practice, but useful as representative of the Earth and Nature;

the Flower Maiden has to be rescued to bring in Summer;

the Divine Child also has to be rescued, then he leads the Quest (normally a sensible older child);

the Hero/Heroine: represented by the children themselves;

the Wise Guide: a role normally taken by adults;

Guardians of the Enchanted Realm (Robin Hood, the Green Man, Pan): normally played by an adult or older child;

Dangers, hazards : where these are personified they are always played by adults and, while they may seem fearsome in anticipation, they always prove to be fun when face-to-face.

Animal helpers: traditionally folk-tale heroes often encountered magical talking animals who challenge then help them. We use adults and older children wearing animal masks as the challengers, and we try to make the tasks appropriate to the story and animal.

Like the many Quests found in Arthurian literature, our quest activities normally takes the form of a journey through the woods, following clues, meeting challenges, or finding objects or restoring a lost or forgotten god (e.g. Mabon, the Spring Maiden - see below). Sometimes it incorporates a integral wide game and, always, the Achievement of the particular quest.

We start with an atypical example related to the seasonal cycle - and therefore covering an extended period:

G The Quest for Mabon and the Maiden
This quest is really a series of preparatory exercises that encompass many of the necessary talents traditionally required in a mythic hero quest. Many of these features can therefore be incorporated in any quest programme.

The Quest for Mabon and the Maiden is an amalgamation of two story-lines: 'Culhwch and Olwen' in the Mabinogion, that magical collection of Celtic stories that date back into the Dark Ages, and the Grail Quest to restore the Waste Land, centred on the Arthurian heroes Gwalchmai (Gawain) and Peredur (Parzifal or Percival).

A little background to each of these is required:

Mabon ap Modron - which is a title: it only means 'Son of the Mother' - is the quintessential Divine Child or Wondrous Youth, cognate with Apollo Maponos, worshipped in Britain and Gaul, with the Norse Balder, and with the Irish Oenghus Mac Og of the Tuatha Dé Danann, as well as Gwair, Lleu and Pryderi, and many others in the British Celtic tradition. He is a typical sun hero, born of a virgin goddess associated with the earth or water, who disappears ('stolen' or 'imprisoned' in the Underworld or Winter) for initiation while an infant, to reappear in the Spring in radiant glory as a golden-haired youth to herald a new age. As a sun god he alone can rescue the ugly Winter Hag with a kiss, which immediately transforms her into the beautiful young Flower Maiden of the Spring. At the same time the Waste Land springs into life.

The Holy Grail and its accompanying symbols - spear, sword and stone - were originally talismans which the descendants of Danaë, the magical Children of Don / Tuatha Dé Danann (who came from northern Greece via Denmark and northern Britain) brought with them to Britain and Ireland: the Stone of Destiny (our coronation stone) from the great northern city of Falias, the Spear of Lugh (Lug, Lleu) from shining Gorias in the south, the Sword of Nuada (Nodens, Nudd) from Finias in the east, and the Cauldron of Plenty from rich Murias in the west. These were transformed into Christian symbols in the 13th century. The cauldron became the Holy Grail, which is often described as a cup but sometimes as a dish or a stone, feeds the Wounded King, and the hero must ask a single question: 'Whom does the Grail serve?' for the king and the Land to be restored to health.

The Land was laid waste when King Amangans raped the Maidens of the Springs and out of greed stole the golden cups which they used to dispense sustenance from the Cauldron to all who asked for it. This is an eloquent symbol of what human greed and selfishness has done to our earth during the past two centuries: is there not increasing evidence that we are now living in a Waste Land? A symbolic childhood quest to restore the Land may help some to address the problem when they grow up - if there is still time!

Our quest is primarily based on the story of Culhwch (Kill'ooch, 'ch' as in loch'). His mother, a queen, lost her reason as his nativity approached, and gave birth to the boy in a pigstye - 'Culhwch' means 'pigstye' - before dying. After a time the father remarried, and the stepmother cast a spell over the boy so that he would fall in love with Olwen, daughter of the giant Ysbaddanen (Isba-thad'en, 'dd' like 'th' in 'the').

Culhwch, a nephew of Arthur, asked the king for help in finding Olwen and, after a long search the young hero, with six companions, came face to face with the giant who was not exactly welcoming - see the game at the end of the previous section, 'The Training of Heroes'.

Eventually the giant gave them 39 impossible tasks of which the most immediate was to locate Mabon, 'who was taken from between his mother and the wall when he was but three days old'. First he had to be found, so the heroes had to seek out the five oldest animals to help them: ouzel, stag, owl, eagle and the oldest of all: a salmon who had heard somebody crying in the castle of the Nine Witches of Gloucester. The heroes then gathered Arthur's army and attacked the castle while Cei (Kay) broke through the walls and carried off Mabon on his back.

And that was only one of the impossible tasks! Eventually all were completed, Cylhwch got his bride and the giant his come-upance. So much for the Culhwch story.

The other element of our quest is the task of our young heroes, led by 'the sun hero Mabon' (an older, ideally blond, boy) to find and release or transform the Flower Maiden so that Summer can be welcomed in.

The Seven Tasks of the Quest

1   It is important that the young heroes should be aware
       of their ancestry and their relationship with the
       Land. Before the Quest proper starts they should
       be encouraged to find out when and where their
       families were last in a working relationship with the
       land, and why they left it (assuming they did).

2   They should encounter a wizard (Merlin?) who will
       teach them Shape-shifting. This practice, borrowed
       from shamans, can not only draw children into total
       rapport with other elements in nature; in the hands of
       an expert it can even influence their actions. It is the
       method used by rain-makers to affect the weather.

       The technique must start with close observation of the
       target of your practice, whether it is an animal, an
       insect or a cloud. Start with domestic animals, cats
       and dogs, then go on to something more difficult. Let
       us assume it is semi-domesticated deer in a park -
       truly wild deer will be much too difficult until you are
       very expert. Get down-wind of a herd and approach as
       close as you can (see 'Stalking' on page 81), then, in
       stillness and silence, watch. What sort of habitat is it?
       What do they do? How do they move? How do they
       relate to each other? Once you have developed a
       degree of understanding you should then, in your

mind, try to imagine yourself a deer, browsing with the herd, sensitive to every scent and movement around you.

Note: if you do try it with deer bear in mind that they are exceptionally highly strung creatures, so any stalking should be done in small numbers under firm discipline and for a very limited time.

As a preliminary exercise with the children hand round slips of paper naming something for them to imagine. Relax them (see 'The Dreaming Tree' on p135), then give them a few minutes to become one of the following (drawn from a list in one of Taliesin's 6th century poems):

a wind on the sea	a standard-bearer before Arthur
a fire on the hearth	a mist in the forest
a mountain stream	a night wind
a hawk on the cliff	running with the deer
a wave on the long shore	a seed in the husk
a salmon in the torrent	a leaf in the wind
a bird in the nest	a blackbird on the tree-top

Too difficult for children?

> *..Let the subjects be as difficult as you like. Nothing is too difficult for the innocent .....Remember they've generally got plenty of visual imagination even if we have not.*
>
> ERIC GILL [16]

3 PATH-FINDING
This is an opportunity for some map and compass training - and learning to draw maps, then testing each other on their efficacy.

It can also incorporate an appreciation of the Seven Directions, something that was an important part of sacred ceremonies across the world. The seven directions are North, East, South, West, Up and Down, and Within.

NORTH, traditionally coloured blue, representing Winter: this is the time when life seems to decay and die, and when Nature appears to sleep, yet, amid the decay new life is stirring, growing out of the dead. On a winter expedition invite the children to explore amid the decaying leaf debris beneath the trees and they are sure to find signs of new life burgeoning. Remind them to replace the protecting cover again.

EAST, coloured Green, represents Spring, the young Sun, and new beginnings of every sort. There are few things more delightful than to observe young animals - lambs, baby birds - and young children. Invite your children to go out and observe other young creatures and how they beg their parents for food - ask them if that's how they behave - and how protective the parents are at this stage.

SOUTH, coloured Yellow, representing Summer and the joy of life. Invite the children to study the beautiful colours and patterns of the flowers and insects, and comparing the number of petals on different flowers, and to look upwards through the patterning leaves of a tree in sunlight.

WEST, coloured Red, represents the dying year, dreams and visions. Traditionally at death souls 'go West' or rather travelled to Otherworldly 'Isles of the Blessed' or 'The Land of the Ever Young' somewhere out beyond the sunset over the western seas. Among the more beautiful signs of this season are the wonderful colours of the fallen leaves, and the childen can be invited to collect and arrange a spectrum of autumnal leaves.

UP, coloured Violet, carries our eyes up to the sky and the stars. Children should become familiar with the most obvious stars: the Pole Star and the Great Bear (called 'Arthur's Wain' by the Celts), Venus - the Morning and Evening star, Orion stretching for the Pleiades, as well as the Milky Way. You could also use the introductory section of our Appendix, 'The Wheel of the Year' as a basis for talking about the skies.

DOWN, coloured Black, represents the earth itself, leading to an exploration by the children of the variety and forms of rocks and stones and how they were shaped. They can also explore the sources of the life-giving waters, the patterns they make on the sea and in streams, and the textures and patterns of tree-bark and wood-grain.

THE CENTRE (Within) brings all the colours together, so it is White, the most sacred of colours.

A SHORT 'SEVEN DIRECTIONS' GAME can introduce the subject or celebrate its completion.

Set out in the woods four posts about 100 metres apart, with each post accurately placed in one of the four cardinal directions and hung with an appropriately coloured cloth.

Gather the children in the centre of the square, point out compass North, then invite the children as a group to seek the Eastern post, collecting something on the way. When they have gathered again draw their attention to the infinite range of greens in nature.

Next set them off in search of the South post, looking for natural objects that are yellow on the way, first reminding them about not destroying rare flowers. When they have found and gathered round the post, see who has collected the best yellow object.Remind them too of what the South symbolises - as outlined above.

Searches for West and North, and their colours should follow. They can then look for blues outside the square, and blacks within it. Finally remind them that they are each the centre of their own world, and that they should try to 'Know Themselves'.

4. JOURNEY THROUGH THE FOUR ELEMENTS: A 'Know Thyself exercise'.
Ancient peoples reduced the world to four elements: Earth, Air, Fire and Water, and the Neoplatonists said that we are all made up of different proportions of all four, if only in character:

EARTH: people with more of this element in their make-up have a stolid character, and are reluctant to change their minds; they are reliable and keep their feet on the ground.

AIR: these people are highly imaginative and like to use their brain; they are not always in touch with reality, dreamers.

FIRE: these are keen enthusiasts, rushing into things, quick to fire up. Handle with care!

WATER: gentle, changeable in nature, drifting from one interest to another; they are often difficult to pin down.

Much more can be said of each of the above characteristics, and it is well worth meditating on them, and inviting children to become more self-aware by considering which element predominates in their own make-up.

A passage through the elements was a feature of many initiations, and this can easily be adapted to form an Adventure. Here are some ideas:

EARTH: Collect seeds and nuts for potting up at planting time; Clay-modelling;

AIR:	Search for air-born seeds and study them closely; Set up a rope Tarzan-swing - first check it's safety yourself;
FIRE:	Explore how plants are affected by the sun; Teach the children how to make a woodcraft fire (see illustration);
WATER:	Pond-dipping, and discovering the life of ponds and streams; Bucket Battle (see Chapter VI)

5. CUNDRY'S MESSAGE.

In the search for the Grail Cundry was the fearsomely ugly woman who appeared from time to time and berated the young questor Peredur for neglecting the suffering of his mother when he left her. She is a reminder of the way we humans have ignored the suffering of our mother the Earth and of the harm we have done to her.

This should lead to a search for evidence of human damage to the environment in the vicinity, and a discussion about what individuals can do to start restoring our 'Waste Land'.

6. THE SECRET OF THE INITIATES

While we cannot be certain, there is a good deal of evidence to suggest that the secret unveiled at the completion of initiation ordeals in many cultures was some sort of revelation about the eternal cycle of Birth - Life - Death - Rebirth demonstrated in the seasonal cycle and human life. Traditionally this invariably incorporated a dramatic presentation, sometimes with dance.

Following a discussion the children could be helped to create their own interpretation, perhaps to show to their parents.

7. THE SEARCH FOR THE FLOWER MAIDEN

The quest period can culminate in a Wide Game in which the children first seek Mabon, 'imprisoned' in a hidden cage of branches, with help from a series of animal helpers which they can meet in turn or rotation:

> **Hare** (speed): some form of race with purpose, e.g. to convey a message;
> **Fox** (ingenuity): a challenge that requires good thinking: e.g. to rescue an object from an almost inaccessible place;
> **Bear** (domesticity): to create a place for hibernation;
> **Deer** (senses): a scent trail by e.g. rubbing wild garlic or mint on certain trees at nose height.

Once they have found Mabon he can lead them in a search for the Flower Maiden who is held by Arawn, grey-cloaked ruler of the Otherworld in Winter, who will 'kill' any young hero or heroine whom he catches (by snatching a 'tail' hanging from their belts). Once the maiden is found and carried off she can be crowned with a garland of flowers.

F/G Robin and Marion's Greenwood Adventure

The Greenwood band is traditionally associated with the arrival of summer, and our 'Robin and Marion' adventure is usually linked to the May Games (see below), though much of it can be accomplished by a family group.

Most of the time is spent in building a Bower of natural materials and preparing the Festival, but we usually include one or two wide games.

(G) The children can be divided into a team of 'Sheriff's Men' (usually some of the older children) who must find a site for the Bower, and three teams of 'Merry Men' who must set up three hiding places.

While they are doing this, and because we are fortunate in having a traditional hunting horn, we hang this on a tree and challenge the teams, without their adult minders, to find and blow it to call everyone together. As an additional challenge during this search the children must keep out of sight of all adults (a penalty if spotted). A bell could be used instead of a horn.

F/G In the stories Robin often challenged newcomers to a fight on a bridge. We place a plank over a ditch and and arm a pair of young volunteers with sacks filled with polystyrene foam chips. They can then try to dislodge their opponent without serious damage to each other. Alternatively they can be challenged to try to ambush the adults.

G In the wide game the Sheriff's Men can attempt to escort a rich abbot (an adult) and a sack of 'treasure' from one end of the activity area to the other, while the Merry Men try to capture the prizes. Then the Sheriff's party can attempt to hunt down the Merry Men and find the Abbot and the stolen jewels. See page 93 for advice on organising Wide Games.

The May Games: welcoming Summer
May Day, when Summer is brought in, was traditionally one of the most important festivals of the year, and it is still about the time that most schools and holiday schemes start to move to outdoor activities.

While we work with children in the woods from time to time throughout the year, we always make the most of the warm summer months up to the harvest and beyond.

How was the arrival of summer welcomed traditionally? What can we make of the event?

While it usually took place on May Day it was sometimes delayed until Whitsun or any time up to Midsummer. Trad-

itionally the proceedings began with a Battle of Winter and Summer.

In many parts of the country folk would build a 'Robin Hood's Bower' at a sacred site (often in the churchyard) for the wedding and coronation of Robin, King of the May, and Marion, his Flower Bride.

G. Building Robin Hood's Bower: in order to prepare for the main ceremony it is necessary to build and decorate a 'bower' or hut for the May King and Queen. With permission from the owner or the warden of the site, take the children to collect some long branches, sprays of young leaves and, if possible, some May-blossom (hawthorn). These should be cut off with a knife or secateurs. Before starting explain that in many traditional societies people always asked permission and forgiveness of a tree or plant before taking anything from it, and they never take the whole plant because they want it to continue growing. Ask the children to do the same. See that

116

they remove only a little of anything so that there will be little or no sign that they have taken anything. Traditional peoples recognised that all living things, including trees and flowers, possessed Soul (or a protecting fairy), so they always thanked the plant when removing any part of it. Invite the children to do the same because there is scientific evidence that plants feel pain.

Construct the bower in an appropriate place - between some trees or in a small hollow - by sticking the branches firmly into the ground and attaching the spays of leaves and vegetation. On page 118 we offer a few hints, but the type of construction will depend on your place and available material. For ideas for a May Day festival see Chapter V.

May is also the time when the Green Man appears - he and Robin are really identical but we like to make the most of the Green Man.

G. Meeting the Green Man
The Green Man was the ancient European spirit of nature and fertility. His image, peering out of a forest of leaves, can be found on roof-bosses in many churches. The current increase in environmental awareness seems to be bringing him back into human consciousness so the children should meet him. See a way to do this in the appendix (The Wheel of the Year) - Midsummer Day activity. Also the game 'Green Man Arise! in Chapter VI.

Farewell Summer, welcome Autumn and Winter!
As we greet the Summer months on or around May Day, so it is appropriate to greet Autumn and Winter, for every season has its pleasures. This should start at Lammas - Harvest Time.

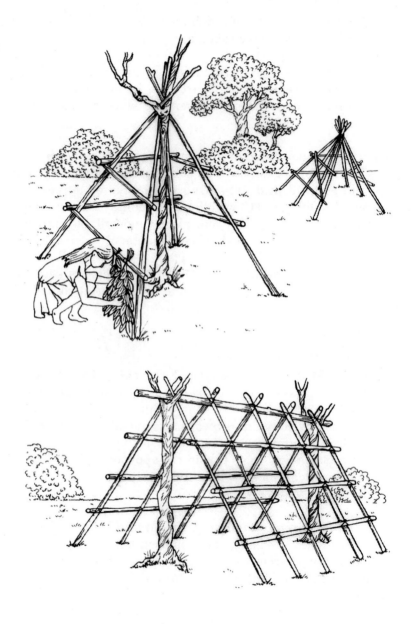

Hut construction

120

Robin and Marion
welcome
to the
Freedom of the
Greenwood

GREENWOOD RIGHTS

To enjoy the wonders of the woods

To befriend the freeholders of the woods:
Deer, Badger, Squirrel, Mouse
Woodpecker, Tree-creeper, Owl
Ground beetle, Ladybird, Woodlouse
Oak, Ash, Beech, Holly
Fern, Bluebell, Primrose, Fungi
and all other rightful denizens
of the forest

GREENWOOD RESPONSIBILITIES

To protect and care for all woods and trees,
and all the creatures that depend on them

G. Crying the Kern

This custom can be traced into the remotest past throughout Europe, Asia and North Africa, and it probably symbolises the death of the Corn Spirit (John Barleycorn). Hone's Year Book (1845) claims it is a relic of the gift the Hyperboreans sent from this island to the Greeks in honour of Apollo. Once the last sheaf had been cut the oldest reaper would take a few stalks and tie them into a simple corn-dolly (variously named the 'Knack', 'Neck', 'Kern', 'Churn', or `Mare'). In the meantime the other reapers went off to the farthest shouting distance. Once the Kern was made the old reaper would shout 'I've gotten it!' The others would shout back, 'What hast gotten?' 'I've gotten the Kern!' The reapers then ran forward and gathered round the dolly on the ground and chanted three times over 'A Kern, a Kern, a Kern! Well bound! Well shocked!' They would then sing 'John Barleycorn' or another harvest song. The dolly is then thrown into the air, and the reapers struggled to take it, the 'winner' running with it back to the next farm or field where harvesting was scheduled.

There was three men came out of the west,
Their fortunes for to try,
And these three men made a solemn vow,
John Barleycorn should die.
They ploughed, they sowed, they harrowed him in,
Throwed clods upon his head,
And these three men made a solemn vow,
John Barleycorn was dead.

Then they let him lie for a very long time
Till the rain from heaven did fall,
Then little Sir John sprung up his head,
And soon amazed them all.
They let him stand till midsummer
Till he looked both pale and wan,

And little Sir John he growed a long beard
And so became a man.

They hired men with scythes so sharp
To cut him off at the knee,
They rolled him and tied him by the waist,
And served him most barbarously.
They hired men with the sharp pitchforks
Who pricked him to the heart,
And the loader he served him worse than that,
For he bound him to the cart.

They wheeled him round and round the field
Till they came unto a barn.
And there they made a solemn mow
Of poor John Barleycorn.
They hired men with crab-tree sticks
To cut him skin from bone,
And the miller he served him worse than that,
For he ground him between two stones.

Here's little Sir John in a nut-brown bowl,
And brandy in a glass;
And Little Sir John in the nut-brown bowl
Proved the stronger man at last.
And the huntsman he can't hunt the fox,
Nor so loudly blow his horn,
And the tinker he can't mend kettles or pots
Without a little Barleycorn.

Alternatively you could centre a programme round the death
of Robin Hood, the Summer King and willing sacrifice, or the
abduction of Persephone. The latter is the more positive story
as it holds the promise of her return in the Spring.

JOHN BARLEYCORN

Sung by 'Shepherd' Haden, Bampton, Oxon. (C.J.S. 1909)

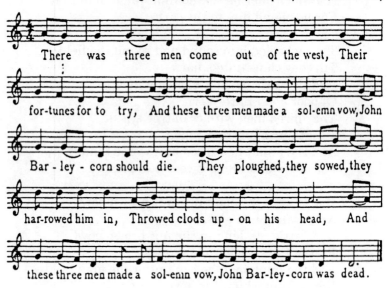

There was three men come out of the west, Their
for-tunes for to try, And these three men made a sol-emn vow, John
Bar - ley - corn should die. They ploughed, they sowed, they
har-rowed him in, Throwed clods up - on his head, And
these three men made a sol-emn vow, John Bar-ley-corn was dead.

124

Many farmers welcome children on farm visits. Why not try to arrange a visit at the end of harvesting, and asking if you can make it a Harvest Home celebration. Invite the farmer and his family.

After exploring the farm, go to one of the harvested fields and explain the celebration and rehearse the song. The children can re-create this ancient ceremony with a few grain-straws collected from the field-edge. The final struggle and race could take the children to the picnic site for their 'Harvest Feast'.

Fairy Frolics: some nature activities using a fairy theme (6 to 9 year-olds)

As nature spirits fairies and elves offer an attractive way to teach younger children woodland skills. Adults sometimes forget how ready young children are to believe. On one occasion we asked a class of 4/5 year-olds if any had ever seen a fairy; nearly every hand went up. And when we do invite younger children to look out for fairies in the woods, several invariably claim, quite sincerely, to have seen some by the end of the day.

First you need to be clear about your underlying aims, apart from any curriculum objective. We would suggest that with young children you should be helping them to feel comfortable in the woods; awakening their sensitivity to and compassion for it's fauna and flora; and helping them to discover the 'magic' of Nature in the beauty of both the very small (flowers and insects) and the very large (tall trees).

At this stage in their development they naturally anthrop-omorphise, giving human characterisitics and feelings to animals and objects, and we make use of this: we tell them that everything in Creation, even rocks and rivers, has a guardian spirit who cares for it. We usually call them elves or fairies. These are very shy, so few see them, and generally they are friendly if mischievous, though they can punish those who hurt nature. They are working all the time to make nature more bountiful and beautiful, and we should try to help them.

If rationalists worry about misleading children with 'lies', they can be reminded that the belief of young children in Father Christmas, encouraged by most adults, seems to do no-one any harm - except to parents' pockets!

After an introduction which calls on the children to be gentle and to harm nothing, one of the first things we do is to explore the area in small groups with an adult, to look for beautiful and interesting things as evidence of the fairies at work. It is not essential for the adult to know much about nature: the aim of the exercise is to open the perceptions of everyone, adults included.

It is of course essential to make a preliminary survey of the area that you plan to use: to look for possible hazards and potential opportunities that can be exploited - ancient trees or rocks that might beome disguised dragons or witches, 'magical trees' (an oak-ash-thorn combination, hazel, apple, oak) or in which human 'wizards' or 'wood elves' could hide; pools, wells, streams or waterfalls; fairy hills' (tumuli or rounded or conical hills); flints in chalk country - so you can look for 'elf-shot (arrow-heads), etc.

Second you need to think what the children can do on their way from the arrival point to the main activity area. If it is some distance the journey needs to be broken into stages with a variety of activities and pauses for a brief story or piece of information.

Here are a few ideas:

F/G tell them that every flower has a fairy that cares for it and who doesn't like it's flower being crushed; so as you walk try to avoid stepping on any flower; you might also warn them that,as an Enchanter, you will hear any crushed flower squeak!

G divide the children into teams then, within the team, give each child in order a different field animal to immitate, e.g. rabbit, fox, squirrel, hare, blackbird, hawk, butterfly. Make sure that each child knows how the animal behaves (e.g.the fox runs low along hedges, the blackbird hops, head on side, listening for worms), then send some helpers ahead as judges before setting off all the 'rabbits' to make their way to the helpers, then the foxes, and so on. The judges can then comment (constructively) on their efforts. It may be helpful to discretely prime your judges beforehand. As an extra bit of fun you could also quietly tell the foxes to try to catch the rabbits - without forewarning the latter;

G as you approach the 'fairy wood' you could do the fairy dance (p. 163);

F/G as you enter the wood you might lead the children between a pair of trees, representing the threshold to the enchanted realm;

F/G in the initial walk through the wood, get the children to follow you in complete silence while they keep their eyes skinned for elves and dragons; its a good idea to stop suddenly at one point as though you had spotted something: this should keep them alert;

F/G the children should leave a really beautiful present for the fairies for allowing you to use their wood: the children in their teams, under an adult, should set out to collect beautiful objects that can be arranged into a little display; if there are enough common wild flowers they might be allowed to pick *one flower only* from a plant - after asking permission from both the adult and its protecting fairy. If you plan to allow the picking of wild flowers you should also provide jars of water; the children, in their teams, could also collect dry, dead sticks for a small lunchtime camp-fire (make sure you have the owner's permission to have one);

F/G you could tell the children one or two fairy stories and/or invite the children to make some up (see notes on story-telling, Chapter V).

F/G 'Woodland Whispers': annoint each child's ears with 'fairy ointment' (water plus vegetable colouring in a magic-looking bottle) 'to help them hear better'; then each individual and the adult leader should move well away from each other before standing for a few minutes in silence with eyes closed, listening for bird-song, the sound of the wind, etc. They should point silently towards every sound they hear, counting them on their fingers.The variety of sounds can then be discussed;

F/G build a 'nest' for a small bird or animal (in pairs or threes);

F/G 'Leaf Hunt': collect beforehand six different leaves from nearby trees, lay them on the ground, then challenge the children, in pairs, to collect similar ones;

G there is a witch in the wood, and she changes children into animals; to avoid this happening to them, they should be prepared to act like an animal in order to fool her; the 'witch' should then appear to test them;

G the witch might also be used for a game of 'What's the time, Mrs Witch?' - as in the better know form of this game, the 'witch' stands at one end of a glade, the children at the other; the children shout 'What's the time, Mrs Witch?', and she answers, say, 'Three o'clock'. The children take three paces forward. Other times of day can follow, with the children getting closer to the witch until she suddenly answers 'Dinner time!' then runs to catch children for her dinner, before they can return to the starting point;

F/G 'The Fairy Bells': all the children blindfolded, then one adult, with a string of bells, leads a chase - make sure there is nothing for the children to trip over;

F/G the Fairy Queen has lost her crown, so the children, in pairs must try to make a new one for her; she might then appear and judge which is the best;

F/G the children could make 'magic wands' of fallen hazel or apple branches, then try to enchant each other (see Matthew's Game in Chapter VI);

F/G 'Visit to Fairyland': get the children to lie relaxed on the ground, eyes closed, and magic wand ('as protection from any monsters they may meet') in hand; then talk them into imagining themselves passing through a fairy door and down a tunnel to visit a wonderfully beautiful fairyland where lovely things happen to them. Leave them to stay and dream for as long as they want, then when they have seen enough, they are to return through the tunnel, open their eyes and get up silently in order to avoid disturbing the others, and come to you for art materials to draw a picture of their adventure;

alternatively, as some are bound to have seen fairies in the wood (if you have created the right atmosphere), they could draw them.

F/G Elven Treasure. Each adventurer should collect a number of natural objects such as pine cones, grasses, leaves, dead branches, etc., return to a central point and fashion them into a small sculpture (string, coloured wool, Blutack can be made available if you wish). An appropriate name for the sculpture should be written on a small card label and then carefully placed in an appropriate niche. The group then views each sculpture. Subsequent groups will be able to search the area for previous groups' treasures - indeed, if the same area is used over a period of time with other groups, a whole store of treasures will build up! (You may need to specify that no living species is collected).

The programme can be filled out with games drawn from Chapter V.)

Some small adventures, particularly suitable for family groups

F The Key
This is based on an episode in Algernon Blackwood's 'The Extra Day' and is suitable for a small mixed group of sensitive and receptive adults and children. It is essential for everyone to be in the right mood - anyone being 'silly' can ruin it. Much will depend on the personality of the leader.

Site: a quiet beautiful area with some woodland and freedom to roam.

It's one of those special days; there's magic in the air, and Someone is calling you to follow. Who is the 'Someone'? Perhaps it is Pan or some other forest god. First it will be helpful to find and carry one of nature's monitors - a soft downy feather: watch it for movement, signal that you are getting 'warm' on his trail, for 'he' will leave clues if you watch and listen: he will make himself know through tiny signs: things deep, gentle and beautiful. Each individual in the group must follow their own trail, looking for 'signs' that he has left for you. It may be beautiful little snail shells, or fungi hiding in the bushes; it may be amazing tree-bark, or the song of a particular elusive bird; it may be the scent of the earth, or the dance of wild grasses. The important thing is not to hurry: you have a lifetime ahead to seek him.

'I think,' he stated shyly, 'I think - he's - hiding.'

Nothing more wonderful fell from grown-up lips. They had heard it said before - but only said. Now they realised it.

'Hiding!' They stood up; they could see further that way. But they waited for more detail before showing their last approval.

'Out here,' he added.

They were not quite sure. They expected a disclosure more out of the ordinary. It might be true, but -

'Hide-and-seek?' they repeated doubtfully. 'But that's just a game.' They were unsettled in their minds.

'Not that kind,' he replied significantly. 'I mean the kind the rain plays with the wind and leaves, the stream with the stones and roots along its bank, the rivers with the sea. That's the kind of hide-and-seek I mean!'

He chose instinctively watery symbols. And his tone conveyed something so splendid and mysterious that it was impossible to doubt or hesitate a moment longer.
'Oh,' they exclaimed. 'It never ends, you mean?'

'Goes on for ever and ever,' he murmured.

ALGERNON BLACKWOOD [3]

(By the way, if you enjoy sensitive, beautiful books about children and nature, we would strongly commend to your attention the following by Blackwood, still occasionally to be found in antequarian bookshops:

'The Education of Uncle Paul' [Macmillan 1910] *'A Prisoner in Fairyland'* [Macmillan 1913] - In 1915 this was made into a popular play called *'Starlight Express'*, with incidental music by Elgar - nothing to do with the Lloyd Webber extravaganza. *'The Extra Day'* [Macmillan 1915] Also *'The Centaur'* [Macmillan 1911] - nothing to do with children, but a powerful presentation of the idea, now fashionable, that the Earth is itself a living entity.

F Variation: The Trail of the Wild Goose Feather

Truly a wild goose chase! The children should be divided into groups of two to four, accompanied by an adult. Each child should have a clip-board, paper and pen of pencil. The group should carry a feather (which they should find for themselves) as a 'compass'. Their task is to explore the wildwood and record anything wonderful, beautiful, or magical that they find, as a drawing, a song or a poem. The feather is thrown in the air as often as they wish - usually at the junction of paths - and they follow wherever it points when it lands.

F/G The Hands of the Wood People

'Just look at your soft, white hands! The Woodwitch will not share the secrets of the wood if she thinks you aren't one of the woodpeople. So we had better do something about it'.

This activity started because one of the woodland sites we use has rich outcrops of clay and the children just couldn't keep

their hands - or in some cases bodies - out of it! So, never ones to stop children getting in touch with the earth, we tried to build on the experience. Having covered their hands with clay the children added leaves, thorns, gorse stems, bones, feathers etc. so their hands became beautiful or grotesque sculptures. They loved it!

So, if clay is available on your site, or you just happen to have a bucket full of wet clay hidden behind a nearby tree , then let the children cover their hands in it and as you move off invite them to collect bits and pieces to stick in and on it.Some children (and adults!) will inevitably want to go one better and cover their arms and face - this is up to you, but you should supervise this carefully. If clay is not available then a water based glue painted on with a large paintbrush will work just as well - in fact this 'times' the activity well as the glue dries quite quickly and limits the amount they can stick on. Remembered to warn parents about wearing old clothes!

F/G The Place that Forgot its Name

Children are invariably aware of the *feel* of a place - the *Genius Loci* - but rarely think of putting their feelings into words. In preparation for this activity select a number of Places that seem to you to have a strong character, one for each tribe, then mark them on a decorative map of the area, or lay simple trails to each site. Assign each tribe to one of the sites and invite them, with guardian adult, to find it. Explain that each of these Places once had a name but the Genius or Spirit of the Place has forgotten it. The tribes have the task of exploring the place thoroughly, then agreeing on a name and preparing a story to explain the name. They should 'write' the name with dead twigs or leaves on the ground then report back to base at a predetermined time. When all the tribes have gathered, the whole group should make a tour of the Places and be told the story by a member of the tribe that named it.

F The Dreaming Tree

Find a decayed tree with plenty of holes and cracks in it. First, ask the children to explore the tree with their eyes, then give each child a stone that you claim to have 'magicked' beforehand (by drawing a rune or some other symbol on it with a felt-tip pen), and invite them to lie beneath the tree but not touching each other. Then lull them with your voice (a quiet, even tone) into a state of total relaxation, inviting them to day-dream themselves into one of the holes to discover what adventures await them there. Tell them that if they do meet anything they don't like they will be perfectly safe: they have only to point the stone and tell the threat to disappear, and it will obey. They can also ask the stone to take them back to safety if they feel the need. At the end of the experience draw them back to full wakefulness very gently and give them time to stretch their limbs and readjust. They may take the stones home with them as a gift.

F/G Relaxing

Tree Dreaming works best if the children are totally relaxed. How do you achieve this? First, talk about the activity in a hushed voice while they are sitting on the ground. If any children feel they cannot be quiet invite them, without criticism, to leave the group and go for a little quest with one or two adults, perhaps looking for strange and wonderful things to show the others later. Ask the others to lie on their backs, out of reach of anyone else while you gently talk them into relaxation:

1. Stretch and tense the muscles of your hands as tightly as you can - then relax!
2. Ditto with - arms, then legs, the neck, then face, then whole body at once.
3. Breath deeply and evenly: in-two-three, out-two-three, several times until you are totally relaxed. You should now be ready.

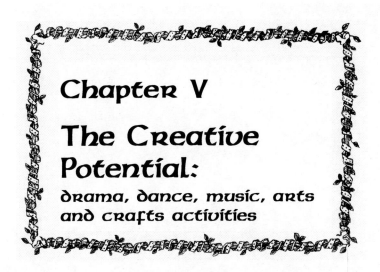

Chapter V

The Creative Potential:
drama, dance, music, arts and crafts activities

We have already indicated that the arts have always played an important part in the initiation process: telling stories, the role-playing or dramatisation of the Hero's adventures, and the ritual dances. Arts and crafts are involved too, as we shall see.

Here are some ideas and hints that may help you bring the arts and creative expression into your programmes.

F/G Poetry
If we are to reinforce children's sensitivity to the natural world, there is nothing better than poetry. We sometimes encourage the writing of Haiku, the Japanese three-line, five-seven-five syllable free-verse form in order to heighten the children's sensitivity to aspects and incidents of the seasonal changes in the natural world.

When the breeze goes by   (5 syllables)
Each time upon the willow   (7 syllables)
Shifts the butterfly.   (5 syllables)

Basho (1644-94), tr. Shoson

We also use the ancient Celtic "Pleasant Things" format, based on a poem by Taliesin (which we have very freely adapted below):

Sweet is the cuckoo in Maytime,
and pleasant when weather get's better.

Sweet is the sun in the blue sky,
pleasant are long days of summer.

Sweet is the scent of old roses,
and pleasant to meet deer in the woodland.

Sweet are the fruits of the autumn,
and pleasant is wheat in light breezes.

Sweet is the moonshine on water,
and pleasant are seagulls when gliding.

To create the right atmosphere start by inviting the children as a group to throw into a common pool their own ideas about the delights to be found in the natural world, then invite them as individuals to compose their own nature couplets on paper, summoning up a pair of pleasures for each of the four seasons or five senses. Remember to encourage them to present their thoughts rhythmically and with a steady metre.

G Story-telling

Children love stories, and there is no easier way to get them settled quietly, especially if you can confidently tell the story in your own words, and it lasts normally not more than about 15-20 minutes per session. Professional story-tellers can hold an audience aged from six to sixty-plus spellbound with a single story for an hour and more. Reading to children is very much second-best.

Traditionally stories were told after dark, with the listeners huddled together in a circle round a fire. Try to get near to this ideal if at all possible.

Make an effort to discover the original form of the story. There are many updated versions in libraries and bookshops today, but they have often been so distorted out of their primordial form that their magical, transforming purpose has been lost. See the bibliography at the end for sources close to the original.

Go for visual detail: as you tell the story try to see it in pictures - it makes it far easier to follow if the action, characters and places can be visualised in the listeners' minds - it also makes it easier to hold the sequence in your own memory too.

Keep your voice as varied and colourful as you can: try to imitate the different accents and tones of the characters.

Never rationalise the events, or you destroy the transforming power of the story - see Chapter III for more on this.

Among the stories we tell are:

GREEK: Apollo and Python
Persephone
The Labours of Herakles

	Jason and the Golden Fleece
	The adventures of Theseus
	The story of Perseus
CELTIC:	Peredur (from the Mabinogion)
	Culhwch and Olwen (ditto)
	Branwen, daughter of Llyr (ditto)
	Manawydan, son of Llyr (ditto)
	Pwyll, Prince of Dyfed (ditto)
	Merlin and the two dragons
	Arthur and the sword in the stone
	Gawain and the Green Knight
	The saga of Cu Chulainn
	Exploits of Fionn Mac Cumhaill
	The Sorrows of Etain
NORDIC:	The death of Balder
	The Ragnarok
	Sigurd the Volsung
	Beowulf
FOLK:	East of the Sun, West of the Moon (Norwegian)
	Tsarevich Ivan, the Firebird and Grey Wolf (Russian)
	Vasilisa the Beautiful and Baba Yaga (Russian)
	Fenist the Falcon (Russian)
	Chestnut Grey (Russian)
	The Fern Flower (Polish)
	Beauty and the Beast (French)
	Iron Hans (German)
	Thorn Rose (German) or Sleeping Beauty (French)

G Story-telling by the children

Children should be given every encouragement to express themselves verbally, but story-telling is an art, and *discipline* is an essential element of every art. This is certainly not to say that children should be discouraged from story-telling, but they do need a good deal of help.

In the first place most children have few resources to call on other than television. As a result most unguided child-tales, especially by boys, tend to be at the level of cops and robbers, with endess shoot-outs, murders and chases. Furthermore some children get so carried away into their personal fantasy that the story can go on and on endlessly, often incoherently and so quietly - after all they are really only talking to themselves - that the audience dies of boredom.

Discipline then: first, children need exercises, ideally in the form of games, to encourage them to speak loud and clear, and to modulate their voice; secondly, time to prepare the story; thirdly, unless a child proves to have a real talent, you should impose a strict time-limit - say 2/3 minutes per story to start with; fourthly, it will help if you provide them with something around which to weave their story: a piece of landscape or three objects which must be included; finally, tell them lots of myths and folk-tales yourself, and encourage them to borrow books of them from the library.

F/G Costume, make-up, drama and role-play

'We ought to be something,' said Mark discontentedly.
'Of course we ought,' said Bevis. Things are stupid
unless you are something.'
'Lions and tigers,' said Mark, growling, and showing
his teeth.
'Pooh! '
'Shipwrecked people on a desert island.'
'Fiddle! They have plenty to do, and are always happy,
and we are not.'
'No; very unhappy. Let's try escaping - prisoners
running away.'

RICHARD JEFFERIES [20]

144

Children learn through role-play and always enjoy it, so we involve them in role-play as often as possible, not only to re-create the great myths but to get the children to create their own stories.

Let us concern ourselves first with ways to make the role-play more vivid, and this is mainly a matter of costume, make-up and props.

F/G Costume and make-up (face- and body-painting)

Just as they enjoy trying out other roles, so children love dressing up as someone else. If they can all be in costume it can bring an extra degree of realism into the Adventure: it becomes a richer experience if they can look round at each other, and the Enchanters too, if they are all in appropriate costumes. But what about the expense?

The Enchanters' may well have to spend some money on their own costumes (see illustrations for ideas), but the children's costumes can be very simple: it need not be elaborate, requiring meters of cloth and hours of sewing. We have used bark, grass, leaves, newspaper, tissue and crepe paper.

LOIN- CLOTHS (boys only - though some smaller girls like to wear them too!): in these warm summers, when they are being a primitive tribe in the woods, the boys are encouraged to bring swimming costumes over which they can wear loin-cloths (see photographs). No child should be compelled to dress like this - a few may be too shy: they, and the girls, can wear tabards instead, but we strongly encourge them all to wear either swimming costumes or short shorts as we want them to make as much whole-body contact with the earth and growing things as possible. Children are intensely physical and they do not confine their enjoyment of tactile experiences to their hands. Naturally we try to avoid taking them among

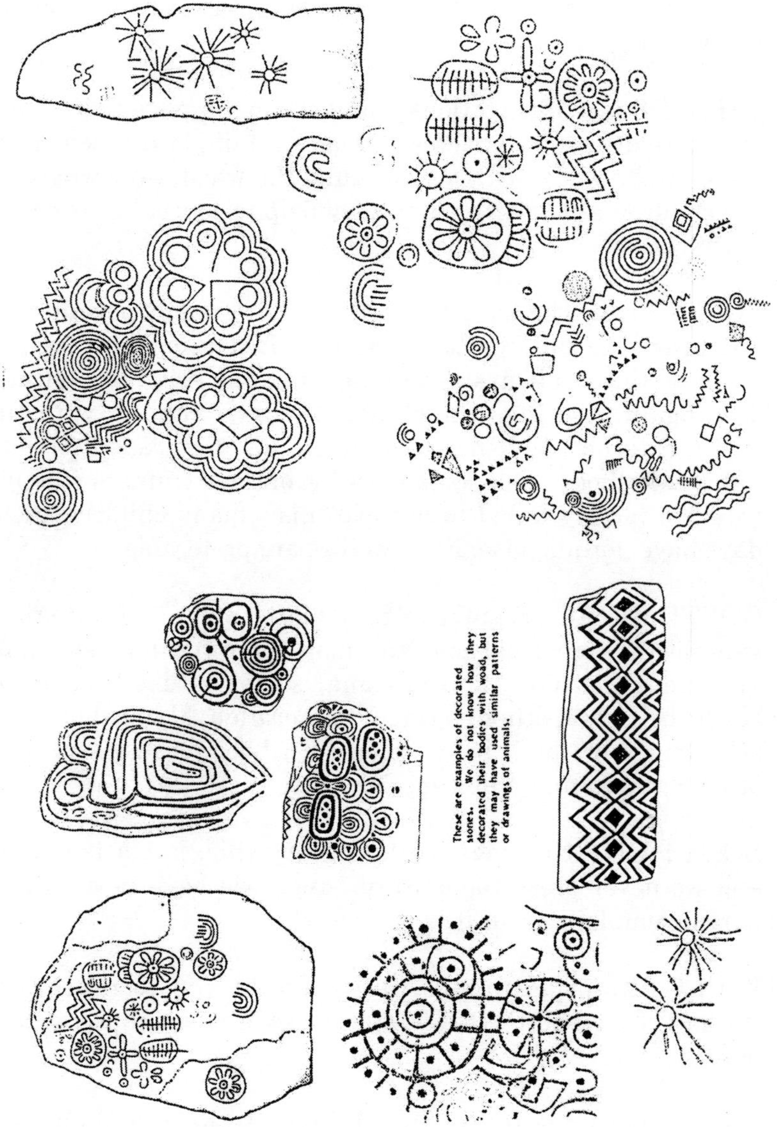
These are examples of decorated stones. We do not know how they decorated their bodies with woad, but they may have used similar patterns or drawings of animals.

Celtic patterns

nettles, brambles and bracken (often a home for deer-tics which seem capable of reaching the skin however much you wear).

TABARDS (see illustrations and diagram on page 219): these can be relatively inexpensively made out of plain green cloth. They can be worn, with a cord round the waist, over whatever the children are wearing, and they help to conceal over-bright teeshirts.

FOOTWEAR: wherever the state of the ground permits, we encourage the children to go barefoot. Like everything we ask of them, this is always a voluntary matter. It is far healthier and, again, it brings the child into direct contact with the earth. Alternatively the child should be encouraged to wear light, soft shoes or sandals - preferably not trainers (though we have largely failed to achieve this - many children these days have nothing else. Even wellies are preferable).

COSTUME ACCESSORIES: a visit to the ethnological galleries in your local museum may show you how shamans and medicine men in traditional societies used feathers, beads, bells, and other objects for decoration. Many shops now sell strings of small bells, colourful ribbons and items from other cultures that add a special touch.

BODY-PAINTING: most children love this, but a few don't and we never press them. Surprisingly we have never had a parent complain about it.

With Celtic programmes we generally aim to reproduce "tattoos" based on the Celtic spiral - see the examples offered here.

Alternatively we invite the children to design their own pattern and colours, usually shared by the whole tribe; they can also decide where they want to be painted. After one or

Mummers costume

two messy and expensive disasters when a few children used up all the paints making a glorious mess of themselves, we now do not permit the under-tens to paint themselves - the adults or older children do it for them. We also limit each tribe to two colours only, so they can be identified by their colours. Our advice is to keep the patterns simple and quite rough like those of their ancestors - it can take a long time to decorate two or three dozen children.

Either use water-based face-paints, expensive but readily available from fancy-dress shops, or the traditional material - earths (reduced to mud). Paint with brushes, fingers or twigs.

PROPS: these have an important role in almost every story, and they inevitably cost money. Several can be home-made; others can sometimes be found on market stalls or in junk shops - if you are very lucky! A few, like toy bows and arrows, swords, crowns and masks, can be bought in fancy-dress shops, but they tend to be very fragile, and it is far better for the children to make them.

We have found the following props particularly useful:

swords	a (hunting) horn	a goblet
bows and	a cauldron	a ring
arrows	spears	a crown
(hazel sticks or canes)	shields	jars, bottles
ancient-looking boxes	cloaks	

G Drama

We use drama, as such, sparingly with this age-group: just for the main seasonal festivals; and we offer examples below. Some have been adapted to our needs by the singer-songwriter and playwright, Tim Laycock, who was a leading member of our team during the initial trials of the project.

A PLAY FOR CHRISTMAS: THE DOLBURY MUMMERS' PLAY (adapted by Tim Laycock from traditional versions).

The Mummers traditionally performed this slapstick play during the Twelve Days of Christmas. It has a strange fascination for children, especially the less able. We have found that they want to keep repeating it, perhaps because the lines are so easy to remember.

Traditionally the costumes were very simple - a potato sack (conveniently available now in stout paper - you may be able to beg some for nothing from an agricultural wholesaler), hung all over with overlapping narrow strips of newspaper, plain or painted, plus a paper hat and wooden or cardboard swords and shields. For other props you can use your imagination and have fun - e.g. the dragon's armour can be large saucepan lids tied on with string back and front.

The characters: Room, Father Christmas, Beelzebub, Big Head, St. George, Dragon, and Doctor. Beelzebub carries a club and a frying-pan, St George and the dragon have wooden swords and shields, and the doctor usually wears a top hat and carries a beer bottle of 'medicine'. Not all the characters are essential, so you can adapt it to a group of almost any size.

Room (*entering backwards, broom or besom in hand*):
  In comes I, old Hind-before.
  I comes fust to open your door;
  I comes fust to kick up a dust,
  I come fust to sweep your floor.
  Now we're ready, I've had my say,
  So step in Father Christmas and clear the way.

Enter Father Christmas.

Here comes I, old Father Christmas.
Welcome or welcome not,
I hope old Christmas
Will never be forgot.

Beelzebub: In come I, Beelzebub.
Over my shoulder I carry a club,
In my hand a dripping-pan,
Don't you think I' m a jolly old man.

Big Head: In comes I as ain't been yet,
With my big head and little wit.
My head so big, my wit so small,
I'll dance a jig to please you all.

Big Head dances.

Room: Now we're ready,
We've had our say;
So step in St. George
And clear the way.

St.George: Here come I, St.George!
From Britain I did spring.
I'll fight the dragon bold,
My wonders to begin.
I'll clip his wings,
He shall not fly,
I'll cut him down,
He shall die!

Dragon: Who's he that seeks the dragon's blood
And calls so angry and so loud?
That English dog, will he before me stand?
I'll cut him down with my courageous hand.

Here am I, bold Dragon.
My back is made of iron;
My belly's made of steel,
My hands are made of knuckle-bones
And that I'll let you feel.

They fight and St. George falls. The dragon struts around triumphantly.

Room: What has he done! What has he done!
 He's killed England's champion.
 I'll give five pounds for a good doctor ....
He appeals to the audience
 I'll give TEN pounds for a doctor.

Doctor: I'm a doctor.

Room: How came you to be a doctor?

Doctor: By my travels.

Room: Where have you travelled?

Doctor: Italy, Tittaly, France and Spain,
 And round to Grandmother's door again.

Room: What can you cure?

Doctor: Itch, titch, gallop and gout,
 If a man has nineteen devils,
 I'll cast twenty out.

Room: What is your fee?

Doctor: Ten pounds is my fee,
 But as you've an honest face
 I'll make it twenty-three.

The doctor kneels by St. George and produces a bottle.

Doctor: Here, take a little of my bottle;
                    Let it run down your throttle.
                    Rise St. George, and fight once more,
                    But don't do as you did before.

St. George rises, and fights and slays the dragon.

St.George: The dragon is killed,
                    The dragon is gone!
                    I am the hero,
                    So join in my song.

All: Hurrah!

St.George: Number one, number one,
                    Some stand still, but I go on.

All: To my rum, tum taddler, Old Jack Saddler;
                    Oh what merry lads are we.

Room: Number two, number two,
                    Some can harrow, but I can plough. (chorus)

Father C.   Number three, number three,
                    Some are blind but I can see. (chorus)

Beelzebub: Number four, number four,
                    Some go through but I get o'er. (chorus)

Big Head: Number five, number five,
                    There's lots are dead, but I'm alive. (chorus)

Dragon gets up and hobbles round with sticks as support.

| Dragon: | Number six, number six, |
| | Some use crutches, but I use sticks. (chorus) |

| Room: | Number seven, number seven, |
| | Some go to hell, but I'll go to heaven. (chorus) |

St.George: Number eight, number eight,
Lots can spar, but I can fight. (chorus)

Doctor: Number nine, number nine,
Some like beer, but I'll drink wine. (chorus)

All: Number ten, number ten,
If you want any more you must sing it again.
(chorus)

Father C.:   We wish you all good health
And a happy Spring and Summer.
If you don't like our play
You must find another mummer.

A PLAY FOR MAYDAY: THE PLAYE OF ROBYN HOODE

Robin Hood was the elected Summer Lord (and Lord of Misrule) who presided with his Queen of the May, Marian, at the traditional May Day celebrations and other folk festivities from May to the end of July, and especially at Pentecost (Whit Sunday), to the scandal of the clergy. Marian, who only appears at the end to dance with Friar Tuck, was originally performed either by a pretty girl dressed like a lady of rank or by a boy or man in comic drag.

The May and Pentecost Games centred on a large 'Hall' or 'Bower' made of boughs decorated with flowers, which was built near the May-pole, sometimes in the churchyard. The games, which included processions, archery contests, Maypole, morris and social dancing, and a performance of a play by 'Robin Hood and his Company', always culminated in a riotous banquet in the 'Hall'.

The play was performed to raise money. This was made by selling paper 'liveries' (badges) which were copies of the larger badges which the players wore on their costumes. The performers always dressed in green and yellow with this large badge (of unknown design) on it.

No Robin Hood plays are known to have been played in or near Sherwood or the north of England. Records show regular performances in the late Middle Ages at a scattering of places from the south Midlands (especially the Severn and Thames valleys, through Somerset and Devon to Cornwall, with one each in Norfolk and Kent. Robin Hood ballads, however, were recited all over England and Scotland, and there were also versions in France.

The following example, which Tim Laycock has amended for performance by children, was first printed in about 1562. No stage directions have survived, but it is assumed that Robin's throw into the water was represented by douching him with a bucket of water or confetti made of torn newspaper. The 'dogs', Cut and Bouse, probably wore masks, though they fought with clubs and staves. So we offer this skeleton of the play for you and your children to present as they wish.

Robin Hood: Now stand forth, my merry men all,
                  And hark what I shall say:
                  Of an adventure I shall tell
                  Which befell the other day.
                  As I went by the highway
                  A stout friar there I met,
                  With quarter staff in his hand,
                  In front of me he lept.

Still he bade me stand;
There were knocks two or three,
But I cannot tell who had the worse,
After he lept on me
Though he took away my purse.
Is there any of my merry men all
That to that friar will go
And bring him forth withall
Whether he will or no?

Little John: Yes master, I make good avow
To that Friar I will go
And bring him to you now
Whether he will or no.

*Friar Tuck steps forward to address the audience. He is
accompanied by three players dressed as dogs.*

Friar   God save all this company.
Jolly Friar Tuck is here.
The quarter staff I can weild,
And shoot both far and near,
And handle sword and shield.
I come to seek a yeoman good,
His name is Robin Hood
And if he is better than I
His servant will I be.
But if I be better man than he
By my truth, my knave shall he be
And lead these dogs all three.

Robin jumps out and seizes the friar by the throat.

Robin   Yield thee, friar, in thy long coat!

Friar   Beshrew thee, knave, thou hurtest my throat!

Robin	I trow, Friar, thou starts to dote.
	Who made thee so impudent and so bold
	To come into this forest here
	Among my fallow deer?

Friar	Go louse the ragged knave!
	If thou want words I'll box thy ear,
	Though I be but a poor friar.
	To seek Robin Hood I came here.

Robin	Thou lousy friar, what would thou with him?
	He never loved friars nor none of their kin.

Friar	Avaunt, ragged knave, this is but a mock,
	If you say more you shall have a knock.

Robin	Hark, friar, to what I say here,
	Over the river I'm pledged to go,
	But the bridge is broken, so
	Over this water thou shalt me bear.

Friar	I will not say nay
	To break thine oath were great pity and sin
	But if you go on a friar's back
	Not over the river you'll go, but in.

Robin	Nay, I'll go over.

Robin climbs onto friar's back.

Friar	Now the water I am in and thou, Robin, art out;
	But now I'll lay thee IN I have no doubt!

The friar throws Robin into the water.

Robin	For that thou wilt pay.

Friar	Why, wilt thou fight today?
Robin	And god send me good luck!
Friar	Then have a stroke from Friar Tuck!

They fight with staves

Robin	Hold thy hand, friar, and hear me speak.
Friar	Say on, ragged knave, methinks you sweat.
Robin	In this forest I have a hound Which l would not lose for a hundred pound. Give me leave my horn to blow That my hound may know.
Friar	Blow on, ragged knave, without any doubt Until both thine eyes start out.

Robin summons his company.

Friar	Here be a sort of ragged knaves come in, Clothed all in Kendal green. I gave thee leave to blow at thy will Now give me leave to whistle my fill.
Robin	Whistle, friar, evil might thou fare Until both thine eyes start there.

The Friar summons his dogs

Friar	Now 'Cut' and 'Bause,
	Bring forth thy clubs and staves,
	And down with those ragged knaves.
	    *(Bause: animal with white mark on
	    face)*

The outlaws fight the dogs. After a while Robin halts the fight.

Robin   How sayest thou, friar, wilt thou be my man
                      To do me best service that thou can
                      Thou shalt have both gold and fee
                      And serve my Lady Marian and me

Marian appears and presents herself.

Marion   Come, Friar, my charge,
                      And my chaplain I thee make,
                      So serve me for my sake.

Friar   Go home ye knaves and lay crabs in the fire
                      (crabs = crabapples)
                      For this lady and I will dance in the mire
                      For very pure joy.

The Friar dances with Marian. Robin and his Company join in.

NOTE: the original text and full background information may be found in *"The Early Plays of Robin Hood"* [39]

G Role-play: ancient rituals for May Day and Midsummer

THE BATTLE OF WINTER AND SUMMER
This mock battle took place at the May Games every year. The version that follows was performed in Wales as recently as the 19th century.

Divide the children into two groups. One group, representing the forces of winter, should be dressed as for winter (or they could make up their faces and hands with some mud and white face-paint) and arm themselves with straw and dead leaves.Their leader, Arawn, wearing a grey cloak, should carry a black shield. The rest of the children representing Summer, should wear green with their faces made up with leaf or flower patterns. They should be armed with grass cuttings from a lawn. Their leader, Hafgan, wearing a white shirt, should be garlanded with leaves and carry a hazel wand decorated with flowers and ribbons. After some horseplay with the leaves and grass the Master of Ceremonies (Little John?) should declare that the forces of Summer have won. At the end of the battle the defeated Arawn should be given the privilege of selecting someone to be Robin, the May King, while Maid Marion should be elected by the whole company.

THE WEDDING OF ROBIN AND MARION

Robin should be dressed in green, decorated with leaves, Marion in white, decorated with flowers. They should process to the Bower to be enthroned, then crowned with garlands of leaves and flowers. After maypole dancing the royal couple can be entertained with a performance of the Robin Hood play, and games and sports; ball games were particularly popular as the ball, often painted gold, represented the sun.

As a simple alternative to dancing round a maypole, the children could follow an alternative tradition, hold hands and dance in a spiral round an important tree until they have wound themselves tight up to the tree, then jump up and down - mostly on each other's toes! As they wind they should chant "The old oak (or other) tree gets thicker and thicker!", then as they jumped they shouted "A bunch of rags! A bunch of rags!" This refers to the tradition of tying rags to a tree's boughs as a thanks offering. Jumping and stamping dances round trees were to awaken it into fertility.

G RITUAL DANCES

Shake off your heavy trance!
And leap into a dance
Such as no mortal used to tread:
Fit only for Apollo
To play to, for the moon to lead,
And all the stars to follow!

FRANCIS BEAUMONT (1584-1616)

Dance was probably man's earliest form of creative expression, and amazingly some of the most ancient dances have been preserved, because they were believed to have been invented by the gods and heroes. They are all very simple, without complicated steps, so children enjoy performing them.

MIMETIC DANCING: Perhaps the earliest form of 'dance'; our ancestors would rehearse a hunt or a battle beforehand, or celebrate its success afterwards, with a mimetic performance.

A STALKING DANCE (Baden-Powell's 'Bagheera Dance'): form the children in a large circle, with a ball of newspaper - the 'prey' - at the centre. Their instructions are to strictly follow the leader who will start 'stalking' the prey, at first on his feet, then crawling round in a circle, but keeping well out from the centre all the time. The children must copy his mime then, at a signal from him, they all pounce on the paper, tearing away what they can, and squatting, pretending to eat it.

PROCESSIONAL DANCES: best performed to music or drum-beat; sometimes wild and bacchic, with pipes and tambourines; alternatively slow and formal, with drums, banners and torches.

CIRCLE DANCES: danced to a rhythmical drum-beat with the children stamping hard on the ground or, borrowing from the Native Americans, putting the ball of the foot down first, then the heel, three steps forward, one step back: left-right-left-left, right-left-right-right, ...

FAIRY DANCE: the 'Good People' traditionally dance in a circle, hand-in-hand, facing outwards. We created the following version, using the tune of the ancient sacred tree dance which, long ago, decayed to become 'Here we go round the mulberry bush'.

The children form a ring, holding hands and facing outwards. They step sideways, slowly at first, then faster and faster until the circle collapses - 'because they are only humans'. It is wise to have an adult leader to control the pace.

Clockwise: This the way the moon goes round,
                    The moon goes round, the moon goes round;
                    So we follow it round and round
                    In our merry mad dance-a.

Anticlockwise: This is the way the stars go round,
                    The stars go round, the stars go round;
                    Now we follow them round and round
                    In our merry mad dance-a.

Clockwise: This is the way the sun goes round,
                    The sun goes round, the sun goes round;
                    So we follow it round and round
                    In our merry mad dance-a.

Children drop Now we all turn and turn about
hands and   In our ring, in our ring;
turn round   Now we all turn round about, round about,
and round   In our merry mad dance-a.
on the spot,
then collapse:

MUSIC

Music should play an important role in the adventures. You may be fortunate, as we were during the pilot trials, and have an accomplished musician who can help you. Failing that you must make do with percussion and/or the voice. You could even fall back on a tape-player.

And what sort of music? Here is Tim Laycock:

> I'm a great believer in taking existing songs and reworking them to fit whatever storyline or situation you invent for yourselves. It's really only an extension of the 'folk process' whereby songs were made and then honed and adapted by subsequent singers. For example, we've had some splendid new verses for 'Turn, turn, turn' contributed by the children, and on another occasion I introduced them to the Cornish Wassail Song, and they made their own verses dedicated to the local apple orchard.
>
> It is possible to find versions of traditional folk songs in every region of Britain. Nowadays there are lots of collections of songs published, very often by the English Folk Dance and Song Society (Cecil Sharp House, 3 Regent's Park Road, London NW1), and there are also many recordings available,including songs and music recorded by the BBC from country singers in the 1950s, as well as more recent versions by younger 'revival' singers. Other useful sources are *Scout, Guide, Woodcraft Folk* and *Forest School* song-books.

F/G ROUGH MUSIC: the children are sent out to collect sticks and stones which make a clear note when struck against each other. These can be used to make a rhythmic sound as a background for chanting and processing.

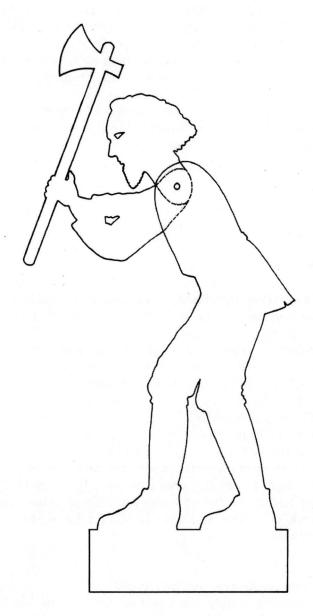

Shadow puppet

F/G Woodland Instruments: the children, in tribes accompanied by an adult, are sent out to create a xylophone - a series of logs graduated by size resting across others. These can then be played by hitting them with another stick. They could also make some woodland 'chimes': smaller branches, again graduated by size, hung from a branch with string. A blade of grass or a leaf squeezed between the balls of the thumbs then blown through the lips and other wild instruments could also be created.

ARTS AND CRAFTS

There are many ways to incorporate art and crafts into programmes:

F/G Drawing Tree Spirits: First explain to the children that traditional peoples and children all over the world have seen the nature spirits that inhabit trees. If they haven't already seen some invite them to try and imagine what they must look like. The Spirit would have the same character as the tree it lived in, so find a tree, study it's character carefully:

> Is it young or old?
> Is it ugly or beautiful?
> Powerful or graceful?
> Cheerful or threatening? ..... and so on.

Give the children clipboards, paper and pens and/or pencils and invite them to select a tree they like, then try to draw what they think the Spirit looks like. Emphasise that it should look tree-like and that it should have the same character as the tree.

F/G Shadow puppetry by Tim Laycock
This is a thriving, highly developed art form in the Far East and Turkey, and it enjoyed a vogue in France and Britain

during the nineteenth century, when the entertainment was known as the 'Ombres Chinoises' ('Chinese Shadows'). Puppets can be made relatively easily from cardboard, bamboo and wire, or you can use actors as puppets. In both cases, the technique involves creating moving silhouettes by placing the puppet or actor between a light source and a screen. Shadow puppetry works very well out of doors.

Erect a large screen, made from thin white cotton; an old sheet will do. We used a piece 6' by 8'. It was tied between two tripods made of ash poles, but could equally well be tied between two trees. The screen should be as taut as possible. You can use evening sunlight as your light source, but this is rather unpredictable in Britain. Victorian showmen used candles or oil lamps. Indoors you can use electric light; outdoors we have used a 'Camping Gaz' lamp, which produces a warm, constant light. It should be placed on a tree stump or box at least two meters behind the screen (you will have to experiment with the distance). The actors then mime the story in between the screen and the light source. The audience sits on the other side of the screen. The actors will need to get as close as possible to the screen to produce a clear image. When rehearsing someone needs to direct proceedings from the audience side, and it is a good idea to have at least two 'teams' performing the story, so that one team can learn by watching the other, and vice versa. The shadow effect obtained is often rather different to the effect the actor imagines she is producing; and of course swords can be passed through bodies, monstrous meals can be eaten, and strange objects miraculously produced in shadow merely by moving the object just behind the actor.

MAKING SHADOW PUPPETS: shadow puppets are beautiful and satisfying objects to make, which then magically come to life through the medium of light and screen. You could start by making cardboard silhouettes, and then progress to puppets made from natural objects - there are plenty of strangely-shaped sticks, leaves, bark and feathers around in the autumn! You can use the same screen, decribed above, for the human shadows. If you put a long sheet of thick card or thick fabric about 1.3 metres high across the bottom of the screen on the inside (i.e. the side away from the audience), the puppeteers will not be seen. If you prefer, you could use a smaller screen, and mount it on a table, with a cloth to cover the front of the table down to the ground. There are two basic types of shadow puppet: those operated by vertical rods, and those operated by horizontal rods. For outdoor use, using the big screen and a Camping Gaz light source, shadow puppets with vertical rods are recommended. The advantages are that the puppets do not need to be pressed against the screen, as is the case with horizontal-rod shadow puppets; and the operators can make the puppets move in opposite directions simply by turning the puppet. The vertical rods are of course visible to the audience, but this does not matter in the least, because the rods are part of the puppet, (and in no way spoil the pictures created).

Shadow puppets can be made from many different materials. Very effective puppets can be made from cardboard salvaged from cardboard boxes, and leaves, grasses etc. can be attached with tape or glue. The main thing is to work out beforehand how many puppets are needed (e.g. it may be best to have several John Barleycorns to represent the different stages of the story), and make the shapes as simple and striking as possible. Moving limbs, mouths, etc. can be made from separate pieces of card, and attached with clips as fasteners; but it is always best to keep moving parts to a minimum, as each part will require a separate rod to make it work, and most people only have two hands! In any case, shadow puppets have their own inbuilt sense of movement, and delightful effects can easily be achieved with apparently rigid puppets.

Shield construction

Remember that the shadow cast by the puppet will be black. If you want colour for eyes, fiery tongues, etc., you can cut a hole in the puppet and cover the hole with coloured tissue paper or gel. A thin wash of PVA glue will strengthen the tissue paper.

To operate the puppet you need thin rods. These can be made of wire, thin garden canes or sticks. The rod is attached with tape or glue to the body of the puppet. Moving joints require a rod attached to the end of the limb or moving part, tied in with string or a thin wire. The length of the rod will depend on what the puppet is required to do. If you have puppets that need to fly (birds, clouds, dragons) you may need to use the 'fishing rod' method; simply suspend the puppet on string from a bamboo or stick.

Allow plenty of time for rehearsal, as the children will want to observe the effect of the puppets, and it takes a while to find out how each puppet works most effectively. The main things to remember are (1) keep the puppets as close to the screen without touching as you can (except when you want a special effect) and (2) slow movement is much more effective that fast, jerky movements. You will need to have tables or groundsheets laid out on either side behind the light so that puppets and operators can wait their turn without being seen.

There is a lot of preparation involved in producing an effective shadow puppet play, but the work is absorbing, and the results can be very satisfying. Shadows are the most atmospheric of all the forms of puppetry, and a shadow show in a woodland setting at dusk will be magical in the best sense of the word.

F/G Shield making
In many cultures shield making was an important skill. They were very powerful spiritual objects in the Native American

tradition, and were made with care and ceremony.

Make the shields from cardboard (cut from old cardboard boxes) or make a hoop from willow or hazel branches then stretch and tie cloth across the hoop. Make arm bands or handles so that the shield may be carried easily. Try to discourage children from making them too large if resources are scarce or if they are to take them into thick woodlands for the activities. 30 -50 cm diameter is about right. All sorts of things that the children find can be hung on to the shield.

What was painted on the shield was of great importance and it was this symbol, rather than the material of the shield, that protected the carrier. The children could simply paint their shields with the symbol of the nation's patron saint, or a totem animal, or they can create of their own private symbol.

The children will not need much encouragement to take their shields home or back to school with them.

F/G Clay
MODELLING PARADISE: if you are in clay country, make the most of the opportunity: children love playing with clay (we can recollect one eleven-year-old, on a very wet but warm day, sitting in the rut of a clay track and, in evident ecstasy, covering himself, literally head to foot, in wet clay; not all are quite that enthusiastic!). If it is a wet day, and you have some cover, you can collect some clay, then get the children to model their ideal landscape, then furnishing it with streams or coastline, miniature trees, huts, etc.

TREE SPIRITS AGAIN: another thing you can do with clay is to reveal the faces of the tree spirits by pressing a lump of clay onto a tree-bole, then modelling the face of what you think the tree spirit looks like. The features can be decorated with seeds, grasses, bracken fronds, and so on.

Arborics

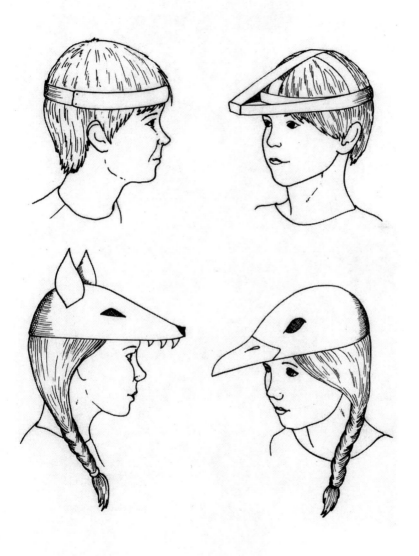

Mask making

F/G Arborics

The term 'Arborics' was coined to describe artistic presentations obtained from working with twigs, branches and roots of trees. It is perhaps one of the oldest art forms going back hundreds of thousands of years.

You can make full-size 'forest gods' or monsters out of assembled brushwood and greenery, or you can carve individual pieces of wood. Sometimes the pieces just call out to you, sometimes you have to search for just the right shape for the image you wish to create. We have often seen people retrieve pieces of wood from the campfire because they are just right for a sculpture or carving! If you are going to whittle or carve you need the right tools: you cannot cut and carve safely with blunt knives or chisels. High quality knives which are very sharp are essential. Teach them how to use, sharpen and look after them. Inevitably someone cuts themselves, but usually only once, so do have the necessary first aid to hand. The only serious cuts we have ever had were amongst the grown-up helpers who weren't obeying the rules!

Have a few examples to show, go through the safety rules, explain some of the techniques and divide into small groups with a helper to supervise each group and go foraging for material to work with.

F/G Mask making

Masks are very powerful tools and even the most simple design can transform an activity.

Chapter VI
Make It Magical!

THE ENCHANTER'S MAGIC BREW
Exciting stories to act out, hunting games in the woods, building camps and hide-outs in the woods, dressing up for other roles, ... The mix is almost complete. For the recipe to be a real success, however, it wants but two more things: a pinch of the spice called Romance, and sound preparation and the right ordering of the ingredients.

Part I: ROMANCE: MAKING IT WONDER-FILLED

> *Wondering, listening,*
> *Listening, wondering,*
> *Eve with a berry*
> *Half to her lips.*
> RALPH HODGSON: Eve

The beginning of widom is surely - wonder.
                    ALGERNON BLACKWOOD [3]

Love of knowledge begins in wonder.
                    ARISTOTLE (C.360BC)

Childhood ceases at the moment when things cease to astonish.
                    EUGENE IONESCO:*Journal en miettes*

Here are a few ideas that can add to the romance of the experience:

Badges
Provide each child with a badge with their first name written in large enough letters to be seen from a reasonable distance. Then, if you do not know the children you can immediately create a friendlier atmosphere by using their real name instead of, 'You with the brown hair!' If you know the children well, or you have arranged it with the teacher, you may like to give them mythic names to suit the programme. To make the badges we use off-cuts of canvas decorated with gold paint and fixed with a feather, or sections of branch cut diagonally on a band-saw, drilled and threaded with some string, or a laurel leaf backed with adhesive tape and fixed with a safety pin. Use a gold or silver pen to write their names and be creative how you give them out. Sometimes we hang them in the bushes for them to find and this acts not only as a good first activity, but gives you a chance for a quick check on numbers, a chat with the teacher/leader or to write extra badges. Sometimes, before they meet us, they are taken along a path and discover the names scattered on the ground. While their attention is distracted, looking for their own name, we 'magically' materialise in their midst.

Magical maps

Another nice introduction - particularly if you have to walk some distance from the coach / car-park / Centre to where the first activity is to begin - is for the children to make their own amulets. Give out pieces of card cut to an appropriate shape for the day to which is fixed a safety pin on one side and a strip of double-sided sticky tape on the other. You may decide to write their names on the cards before they arrive or let them do it at the end of the activity. Invite them to collect things with as many hues of green as they can find. When you are ready to start tell them to peel the backing off the tape and as they walk collect small natural items (grasses, feathers, dead leaves, petals etc. - but remember to tell them what they can't pick if you are in a sensitive area) which they stick onto the tape. As they arrive let them share their collections and write their names on the card if you didn't do this earlier. They can then wear their own special badge for the day and add things to it if they wish.

Maps and Messages: Any letters to the children or maps and messages for the programme should continue the mythic theme. Off-cuts of canvas soaked in cold tea and the edges singed with a candle make magical, durable and waterproof media (remember to use waterproof ink!). Good, stiff 'parchment' paper is equally good, and multiple copies can be made by photocopying from a master. Remember to photocopy before you treat the paper with tea!

Bark and leaves inscribed with gold and silver felt-tip pens ('sun-' and 'moon-writing') make wonderful messages. Smooth bark (e.g. birch and beech) and most leaves will do, but vine leaves gathered as they turn colour during the autumn, then pressed, offer a large and colourful surface for writing on.

Ancient alphabets: the druids did not put any of their secrets in writing, but for other purposes they used Greek - perhaps a vestige of the Greece / Hyperborea connection (see

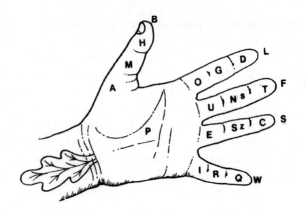

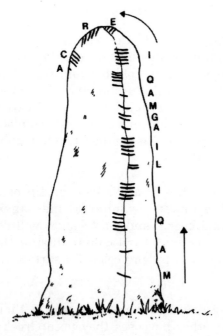

Secret language

Chapter III). They did however also have another way of conveying messages - the tree alphabet: they used a tree to represent each letter, so they could send short messages by threading appropriate leaves on stick. They also used hand-signals. The Picts, in what is now Scotland, used another alphabet called Ogham, which could be carved on the edge of a stone or piece of wood, or by using their fingers against the nose, while the Vikings used carved runes which had a magical potency, so they were sometimes engraved on swords and other weapons.

Many children enjoy private messages of this sort. See the accompanying chart.

Magical script: Children love codes and strange scripts - some will spend hours de-coding and writing messages written in them. If you are left-handed you will probably find it easy to do 'mirror writing' or ....

The 'Ancient and Magickal Art of Fire-writing' which is a romantic way to produce a message for an adventure. Write your message with lemon juice on paper - when this is placed close to a flame the lemon juice scorches more quickly than the paper so the writing is gradually revealed as if by magic.

Finally, the messages can be hidden (but easily found) in special places or old, mystical looking boxes.

Some educationalists warn of 'letting the medium get in the way of the message', which is often true, but in our adventures the medium is very often a crucial part of the message so let your imagination fly and MAKE IT MAGICAL.

Bull roarer construction

Language: For ceremonial occasions and messages try to use high poetic language, antique forms of speech, and terms and phrases borrowed from Arthurian or Shakespearean literature.

Magic fire: Coloured smokes, sparkling firing powders and puffs of smoke for sudden appearances can be bought at most theatrical costumiers. Obviously ensure that they are used with care by an adult and at some distance from the children.

Flaming torches and lanterns: these can add to the atmosphere of night events, and you and your children can make your own at very little expense - see the diagrams.

The bull-roarer: primitive tribes have always use the bull-roarer to alarm children during the process of initiations. It was usually used at night and always kept secret from them. It is very simple to make (see diagram): a short piece of wood attached to a string, then swung round above the head. It makes a weird throbbing buzz.

Using the potentials of the environment: try to cultivate a romantic eye, and use your memory of childhood adventure stories. What features did you find exciting? They will still appeal to children today: secret hiding places such as a hollow tree, or a 'haunted ruin', or a deepcut ditch to make a 'hidden trackway', or a mysterious ancient stone, and so on.

Can you manufacture a magical happening? On one occasion we gathered the children round a vast and ancient stag-headed oak, and made a circle round it to do a dance. Then as we started strange music came from the tree itself: we had hidden a piper - our colleague Tim - up in the foliage. Eventually he emerged in his strange wildwood costume. The children were truly enchanted by the experience.

Part II : GAMES FOR FUN AND ENCHANTMENT

> *Virtually all young things find it impossible to keep their bodies still and their tongues quiet. They are always trying to move around and cry out; some jump and skip and do a kind of gleeful dance as they play with each other, while others produce all sorts of noises. And whereas animals have no sense of order and disorder in movement ('rhythm' and 'harmony' as we call it) we human beings have been made sensitive to both and can enjoy them. This is the gift of the same gods who are given to us as companions in the dance: Apollo and the Muses, from whom education originally comes.*
>
> PLATO [32]

A note on team games

As a matter of policy we change the constituents of teams fairly frequently so that the children don't become too clannish. To start all races we use the silent ancient Greek method: one arm help out sideways means 'Get ready!' The arm dropped to the side means 'GO!' As a discipline we also emphasise that the winning team is the first to be sitting cross-legged and silent in a straight line (i.e. not necessarily the first back). Obviously when the ground is wet we let them stand.

Sense training games

Observation

F/G DRAGONS IN TREES: this is an exercise in imagination as much as in observation. The branches of some trees can be very serpentine, and children can be challenged to see how many 'dragons' pretending to be branches can be spotted. (6+)

F/G WATCH THE WIZARDS/WITCHES: the children hide in the wood to observe a spot where two sorcerers are expected to meet. Two adults - the 'wizards' - then meet in full view and together perform a more or less complicated visual 'spell'. The children are then challenged to report back, reproducing the 'spell' in detail. (8+)

F/G THE ELVEN HOARD (a form of 'Kim's Game'): twelve small natural objects (e.g. an acorn, a stone, a feather, a leaf) are placed together on the ground under a large leaf or frond. This is removed for one minute while the children observe and memorise. They must then recite from memory what they have seen. (8+)

F/G LANDSCAPE SEARCH: the children are taken to a high point in the landscape where they compete to see who can first spot a series of features previously noted by the Enchanter. Alternatively they are given time to visually explore a view then, with backs turned they are challenged to answer questions on their observations. (8+)

Hearing

G THE ENCHANTED GAME (based on 'Gereint and Enid' in the Mabinogion and 'Erec and Enide' by Chretien de Troyes): In the Forest Gereint/Erec comes upon a mysterious Otherworld garden surrounded by a wall of air. Inside, in a wonderful apple orchard, he finds a fairy maiden sitting on a golden throne surrounded by skull-crowned stakes and another stake with a horn hanging from it. He is then challenged by a Red Knight, whom he defeats. The Knight than bids him blow the horn. When he does this the Red Knight (who turns out to be Mabon, again imprisoned by enchantment) is released from his enforced confinement and everyone is filled with an intense joy. The fight is called 'The Enchanted Game' and the strange result 'The Joy of the Court'.

Our version: one child, the 'Red Knight', is blindfolded and placed beneath a hanging string of bells. The other children are in teams placed at the Four Directions, about 30 metres away. At a signal each team sends one child to *creep* forward (anyone running is disqualified) to try to ring the bells without being 'killed'. The 'Knight' must listen intently, and if he hears anyone approaching he claps his hands and points to 'kill them. The first child who succeeds in ringing the bells takes his place. The next four children then attempt the task. (8+)

Scenting

F/G SNIFF TRAIL: rub some mint or wild garlic leaves at child-nose height on trees to make a short trail which the children can sniff their way round. Good also for getting a group from one activity to another. (7+)

Touch

F/G TREE-SEEKING: the children are organised in pairs with one of the two blind-folded. The sighted partner then conducts the other to one of many trees some distance away (depending on the age of the individual), taking care that the blind child does not trip or knock against anything and stopping beside significant objects (e.g. tree-roots, rocks) to allow the sightless one to explore the object with his hands. At the destination a more thorough investigation of the target tree takes place: the conductor should guide the partner's hand to discover unique features. The sense of smell can sometimes be utilised too. The pair then return to the start and the blindfold is removed. Where is the tree? Which way did we go to get there? Strangely - or significantly - the blind child invariably not only locates the target tree, but subsequently seems to feel a special relationship with it. (8+)

Empathy

F/G SHAPE-SHIFTING: this can be done in several ways - initially the children should be invited to think of an animal then try to mime it for the others to identify by guesswork. The next stage is to encourage the children to observe another animal, perhaps a pet, closely in order to mime its actions as closely as possible. A fun alternative is to divide the children into clumps of four or five, then ask each clump to form themselves, as a group, into a single animal form which the others must try to identify.   (8+)

F/G STILL LIFE: a one metre long piece of wool or string is given to each participant. Tie the ends together then lay this on the ground in a place that appeals to them to act as a picture frame. Within the picture they should compose a story about the plants that grow there, how they came to be there, where they originally came from, who or what bought them or their seeds here etc. They should talk about the animals that live there, travel over the picture, drop things there etc. They should also talk about the land or the rocks below the picture - how did they get there what has the last few million years been like for them etc. (7+)

PERIOD GAMES

Medieval Games

G 'GREEN MAN, ARISE!' - the children form a circle, and a volunteer, the 'Green Man', lies down in the middle, covered with grass or leaves. The rest then chant 'Green Man, arise!'

189

repeatedly until suddenly the 'Green Man' jumps up and tries to catch one of them. The one caught then becomes the 'Green Man'. (7+)

G BARLEY BREAK, for six children, was traditionally played in the farmyard which has to be divided into three adjacent spaces: two children holding hands are in each space. Those in the centre space (called 'Hell') shout out 'Barley Break!' and the two other pairs have to try and cross 'Hell' as many times as possible without being caught. They may, if pressed, release hands, but those in 'Hell' must not do so. They must try to tag the others, taking prisoner whichever individual they touch, until two remain. These then take over 'Hell' and the game starts again. (8+)

G JOUSTING: a popular team relay game to train young squires for knighthood: a rope is stretched above head height between two trees with a rope quoit or rubber ring suspended from it by string at head height opposite each team. Each team is armed with a long 'lance' (a garden cane). The children, in turn, have to run up to the ring and pass their lance right through it before returning to pass the lance to their successor. Older children can try it riding pick-a-back. (7+)

G HOODMAN'S BLIND is the medieval version of Blindman's Bluff. One child is blindfolded (traditionally they wore their hood back-to-front) and the other children have to try to touch the Hoodman as often as possible without being caught and held by him. It can be adapted as a team relay to see how many times the children in each team can touch without being caught. (7+)

G JINGLING MATCH: another medieval game - all are blindfolded except one who has a bell or string of small bells who tries to avoid being caught by the blind chasers. Care should be taken to see that the space is clear of roots that might cause someone to trip. (6+)

F/G BUCKET BATTLE (an adapted medieval fun game which requires a hot day and access to a plentiful supply of water): a bucket full of water is hung, just above head-height, from a branch. One group of one to three children have responsibility to defend the bucket. A second group of the same number must try to empty the bucket by tipping it, hopefully on everyone's head. Swimming costumes essential! (8+)

F/G RING SNATCH: a rope quoit or rubber ring is suspended by string from a long stick held above the children's heads by an adult. The children are in pick-a-back pairs. The riders compete to snatch the quoit which is moved around by the adult. (7+)

A Viking game

F/G ARM WRESTLE: children, in pairs, lie on the ground face to face. Each places the right elbow on the ground touching their opponent's and clasping hands. The contestants must then attempt to press their opponent's arm back until the hand touches the ground. At all times they must keep their elbows together and in contact with the ground.
(9+)

GAMES LINKED TO MYTHS

Our version: one child, the 'Red Knight', is blindfolded and placed beneath a hanging string of bells. The other children are in teams placed at the Four Directions, about 30 metres away. Each team sends one child to creep forward (anyone running is disqualified) to try to ring the bells. He must listen intently, and if he hears anyone approaching he claps his hands and points to 'kill' them. The first child who succeeds in

ringing the bells takes his place after the four children have all had a go. The next four then attempt the task. If you have a horn a child from the team with most success can attempt to blow it. (8+)

G SNATCH THE SHEARS FROM TT'S EARS (based on the chase after Twrch Trwyth, the evil king-turned-boar in 'Culhwch and Olwen' - from the Mabinogion). One reasonably athletic (and brave!) adult (TT) wears a band or kerchief round his head to which is attached by easily breakable wool a pair of round-ended children's scissors with the blades taped together - these should hang down the back. TT is supported by one or two adults or older children as his 'army' who defend him. All the other children have a cloth 'tail' (representing their life) hanging from the back of their waist. Their task is to evade the wicked king's army, who will try to snatch their lives, and capture the 'shears' from the running and dodging boar-king. (9+)

FUN GAMES

G CHASE IN THE GLADE: this has proved to be a popular warm-up game with no winners or losers. We emphasise that it is just a fun game to get them warm. It normally takes place in a grassy woodland glade without too many things to trip over.

Start by pointing out that there are lots of creatures in the woods if they keep their eyes open. The leader then points up at a tree and says 'Oh look, there's an owl. Can you see it?' (Of course the owl is entirely imaginary). The leader then makes the sound of an owl hooting. Then turning to another tree he might say 'Ah, look, there's a poor little kitten trapped up on that branch there: Miaow!' The children are beginning to catch on by now. Then, pointing in another direction: 'Look here come some ducks: Quack! Quack!' And again: 'Look, under that bush is a great fierce rabbit attacking a poor little Alsatian dog: Bow-wow!' 'In a moment I'm going to see who is first - and last! - to go and see these things..... But sometimes you get deer in the woods, so if I shout 'Deer!' you must immediately freeze; and where there are deer there may be poachers, so if I say 'BANG!' you must all lie flat on the ground.'

The children will almost certainly have played variations of this game before so they enter into the spirit of it very quickly. We keep everyone playing - no 'out' if you're last - the point is to get them all warm and relaxed. The game can be as well played indoors as out; and there are many variations: for example they can be defending the walls of Troy, with the Greeks attacking from the North, South, East or West, with 'Spears coming over!', and 'Hector!' - everyone stands to attention for the Commander. (6+)

G DODGE THE DRAGON: another variant of the above: four trees - or walls - are designated 'Animals', 'Birds', 'Fish', and 'Insects'. At the centre, in a marked area, is a 'Dragon' in her lair. The Enchanter calls out the name of a creature, and the children have to run to the appropriate tree or wall without being caught by the Dragon. If caught they too become dragons and help to waylay the others until only one child, the 'winner', is left. (6+)

G 'MATTHEW'S GAME' : THE MAGICAL SHAPE-SHIFTER (invented by a   six-year-old): we had been making 'magic wands' out of apple twigs, and the children were dying to use them. Matthew suggested waving his wand over himself to change him into a cat with the word 'Abracadabra!', then waving it over the other children to change them into mice. He then chased them until someone was caught. The victim then became the new magician, choosing to become a different predator and selecting the name of appropriate prey before chasing the others again. We made sure that every child had the opportunity to become a 'magician'. (6-9s)

G THE WICKED WIZARDS/WITCHES AND THE PETRIFIED PRINCESS: first, clearly define a relatively small area, such as a glade, in a wood, then rope off a small 'castle' and a Hero's Base. Three children - wicked necromancers - have captured a princess who now lies, petrified (turned to stone) in their castle. All the other children are heroes and heroines trying to release the princess within a limited time. If they are tagged by the necromancers they must freeze, petrified, where they are caught. To release the princess they must evade the wizards, enter the castle and bring the princess back to life by taking her hand and leading her, hand in hand, back to the Hero's Base. If they succeed all the petrified heroes are revivified; if the wizards catch her, she must return to the castle. (7+)

Chapter VII
Some Practical Advice

G Organisation

Wherever you plan to take children it is wise to familiarise yourself with the site beforehand. Prepare more activities than you are likely to be able to use: if something goes wrong you will not be floundering, wondering what you can do to fill time. Have some wet weather alternatives ready. Normally you should be working outdoors, whatever the weather: most children don't mind.

See that there is plenty of variety in the programme, both in content and pace, and that there's lots of fun. Then ensure that you have planned the sequence of activities carefully so that there is a flow from one activity to the next and that the atmos-phere is maintained, so check that all props are to hand or in position, helpers understand their roles and things happen at the right time. Something may well go wrong - but it's easier to cope with the unexpected if you are confident of the overall structure - and anyway the odd mistake often adds to the fun! Be ready for any real emergencies. Make sure all normal safety measures have been taken and all the appropriate people have been informed as to where you are and what you are doing.

A good rapport and mutual affection between the adults and the children is important. The children should feel totally safe in every sense of the word. Choose your helpers carefully and remember that there must always be more than one adult present at all times and, unless they are close relatives, they should avoid being alone with individual children.

Schools, leisure services, and study centres always check on the moral probity of anyone involved in such programmes as these; so should other groups. Keep parents fully informed of what is going to happen. Encourage them to join in - subject to their children's permission! Nothing should be secret from parents, but secure their co-operation in making the programme a surprise for the children. With this age-group it is wise to recruit as much adult/student help as possible. If possible you should aim to have at least one adult to every six children - you are advised to have a ratio of at least 1:8 for children under eight and 1:10 for age eight and over.

G First impressions

First impressions are crucial. Research has shown that children retain the first impression of a visit longer than just about anything else. If you are welcoming a group of children for the first time then conspire with their teacher or leader beforehand so that she knows where to meet you, then you can make that important first encounter dramatic and memorable. We normally wait for the leader to disembark the children from the coach and organise bags, boots, coats and food before making our appearance - usually in costume and sometimes literally with a bang, and a puff of smoke! If you are going to lead the activities as the group's 'normal' teacher or leader then think carefully how you can be creative with the role - maybe by telling a story of how you have had a spell put on you.This spell gives you a dual personality which enables you to slip in and out of the role of 'teacher' and "enchanter'.

F/G Starting out

Sometimes you need to move the group some distance from the coach/car-park/ Centre to where the first activity is to begin. Having made a brilliant introduction it would be a great shame to loose the focus during a long slog to the first activity where you have to start all over again! Make sure the group knows where to go and has something to focus on or something to do whilst they walk so that they stay 'enchanted' and don't start mentally reverting to their mundane concerns. Either use the badge-making exercise described above or try something like this:

Explain that each person should take something as an offering to the dragon or spirit of the place. So on the walk to the first activity they must collect five things. They do not necessarily need to collect them in their hands, they can collect them in their minds.

The five things could be:
1. Something which changes within minutes.
2. Something which changes with the centuries.
3. Something which never changes at all.
4. Something that can't be photographed.
5. Something beautiful (this could be a feather, a beautiful leaf etc.).

Share the groups ideas when you arrive and leave the offerings at that place.

G Talking to the group

Establish some working patterns for the day; e.g. rather than talk to the group in one large rabble, arrange them in a circle. If, as often happens with this age-group, boys and girls are reluctant to hold hands - shout "Sticky elbows!' - tell them to lick their fingers then rub their elbows so that they will 'stick to their neighbour's' elbows. You should end up with a near circle fairly quickly - the few children standing in the middle with elbows flailing will soon catch on with some gentle words of encouragement. You might like to try 'sticky knees' or 'sticky shoulders' to add a touch of variety during the day.

At some time during the programme you will need to gather then in to listen to a story or instruction. Rather than shout or whistle, use an animal call (if you can't make one naturally, then buy one from a sports shop).

If you want quiet, once you have gathered them together raise your hand and explain that this is a signal for them all to raise their hand, stand still and zip their mouths up. They will very soon catch on and its worth trying out a few times during the first part of the programme.

A judicious use of the emotions can make the experience memorable: e.g. a frisson of fear at the prospect of meeting a dragon can be enjoyed by most quite young children as long as they are confident in adult protection, but you need to be sensitive to the reactions of insecure or nervous children who may need support and reassurance.

Avoid formal initiation ceremonies or rituals: they are likely to make the children feel exclusive, wanting to keep others out. They should rather be encouraged to feel that they are one with the whole world. Any bonding between children should arise out of shared adventures.

G Tribes

For most activities the children will work best in small groups - 'tribes', normally of no more than six children, with an accompanying adult. Few children in the age-group are capable of leadership and it can be a burden to the individual selected - better to let the adult guide them.

We like to keep changing the composition of the tribes so that the children can mix thoroughly and really get to know everyone; otherwise, because the children are reaching the 'gang' stage, there is the danger of developing an unfriendly rivalry between groups. At all times we like to encourage them to work co-operatively together. This does not preclude competitions which children enjoy.

Wet weather

Normally you should be working outdoors, whatever the weather. If it is pouring with rain, and it's warm enough, invite the children to change into swimming costumes and play some vigorous games: they will love it - but remember to have towels handy so that they don't get a chill afterwards. Alternatively, if you feel you really have to be indoors, there are several activities in this book that can easily be adapted, or you could all go out and collect some sand, mud or earth, plus acorns, pine cones, grass, twigs, etc. and make model landscapes.

Accidents and emergencies

As long as you are sensible and in command you should have few problems beyond minor scratches and grazes; however accidents can always happen in the safest environment. Always carry an emergency aid kit with you - and know how to use it! St John's Ambulance (see your local telephone directory for initial contact) run day courses to introduce basic techniques. Ensure that you are up-to-date with current

Health and Safety practice. Also know the whereabouts of the nearest doctor and hospital emergency department. If you have one, carry a mobile phone with you.

Hazards and risk assessment

These days, when a growing number of people rush to litigation on the least excuse, it is wise to ensure that you are covered by personal risk insurance, even if you are working for an organisation that already has cover. You also need to check the safety and assess the risks of the site and any equipment you use. However, despite their adventurous image, our wildwood adventures do not have a high risk factor: and it is important that you, the children and their parents are not deterred by possible risks. Just be observant and take every possible care: the children are your responsibility while they are with you. For the record, over very many years working with children we have never had to deal with anything beyond minor cuts and bruises.

Some risks to keep in mind:
> **sunburn:** in the woods the children are pretty well protected, but advise them to cover up if they spend any time in full sunlight.
> **dehydration:** ensure that you have a good supply of drinking water.
> **exposure to cold:** encourage children to put on something warm if they feel cold.
> **snakes** (only in certain parts of the country): get the children to wear wellies.
> **deer-tics** (a growing problem in some areas): keep away from bracken, and learn how to remove them safely and painlessly. Advise parents to check the children over when they get home.
> **tetanus-infection** from deep cuts: inform parents and take child to hospital.

poisonous plants: warn the children not to eat anything from the wild without first consulting a knowledgeable adult.

Infection from dead animals: keep children away.

Bee and wasp stings: ask parents beforehand if you may use a pain-killing spray - in case of possible allergic reaction.

Allergies (e.g. hayfever, asthma): ask parents to advise you beforehand.

Appendix

The Wheel of the Year

THE WHEEL OF THE YEAR: through the seasons

*Man only repeats the act of the Creation; his religious calendar commemorates, in the space of a year, all the cosmogonic phases which took place **ab origine**. In fact, the sacred year ceasely repeats the Creation; man is contemporary with the cosmogony and with the anthropogony because ritual projects him into the mythical epoch of the beginning.*

MIRCEA ELIADE [14]

Each new day is very different, and has its own special magic! This fact, more than anything, has generated innumer-able stories, myths and theories through-out human history. People have marvel-led, puzzled and argued over the lengths of the days, the positions of sun, moon and stars and the reasons for the changes in weather since the beginning of communication - and each culture has had their own explan-

Wheel of the year

ations. Creation myths, stone circles and complex architectural structures have been built around our day dreaming and nightwatching. Some ancient peoples believed that there was a new sun born every day and each person should strive to make a good world for it to live it's one day in. What an inspiring thought for us to live by today!

But why should every day be so different? What proportion of humans alive today know the answers? How many of us are any wiser than a hunter/gatherer 25,000 years ago? We would venture to say that there is a majority in the 'developed world' of today that are in many ways less conscious of the turning of the year than any culture before us - despite our science and expensive education! Well, that's part of the reason for this book - to help people get in touch with the natural elements.

If our earth were to spin like a top around an axis that was completely upright at 90° then our days, nights and seasons would be very different. We have the wonders of the seasons because as the earth orbits the sun it spins on an axis tilted over at an angle of about 23.5°. This means that for half the year the north pole is closer to the sun and for the other half of the year the south pole has its turn - whichever hemisphere is tilted towards the sun is having its summer.

But that's not all, if Earth's yearly orbit around the sun were a perfect circle then again things would be very different. It's orbit is eccentric and elliptical - which also means the planet will be travelling faster when it is nearest the sun (called **Perihelion**, around the 2nd or 3rd. January) and more slowly at its furthest point from the sun (**Aphelion**, around the 2nd. of July). When the Earth is nearest the sun it just so happens that the northern hemisphere is having its winter and so it follows that the southern hemisphere has its winter when the earth is furthest from the sun - this means that northern winters are warmer than southern ones. But before you northern dwellers get too smug, remember that the converse works - the southern summers are warmer than the northern summers!

The difference in speed due to distance from the sun explains why the seasons are different lengths. In January the Earth is travelling at a zappy 19 miles per second, whilst in July it is orbiting at a much more sedate 18 miles per second. This may not seem much of a difference, but it is the reason why the seasons are different lengths.

So just how long is a Summer? In countries of high latitude like Britain it can sometimes seem like it only lasted a few weeks and sometimes (for children especially) it can go on for ever! Astronomically, Summer in the northern hemisphere lasts from the summer solstice to the autumn equinox - a period of 93.7 days; Autumn lasts from autumn equinox to the winter solstice - 89.6 days; winter lasts from winter solstice to spring equinox - 89 days and Spring from spring equinox to summer solstice 92.9 days. Remember that these are astronomical dates - not climatic. An astronomer will tell you that the northern winter begins on 21st December - the winter solstice - but if you live in Scotland and are already up to your elbows in snow, you may have another opinion!

A few words about equinoxes and solstices must be included - because they are the real turning points of the year and very important markers in many cultures. The Summer solstice is when the Earth's axis is leaning as close to the sun as it will go - June 21st in the northern hemisphere, December 21st. in the southern. These will also be the longest and shortest days respectively. The equinoxes (21st March and 23rd. September) are marked when the Earth's axis is at right angles to the sun and on these days both poles receive equal day and night and the sun is exactly overhead at midday on the equator.

The moon is crucial to our story. It's 28 day cycle exerts an influence not only on our orbit and tides, but on all living things, their rhythms and psychology. It is another important symbol in our stories, myths and legends. It has been observed that crops and the vegetables in your garden will be healthier and produce higher yields if planted in tune with the moon's rhythm. We really don't know why, but it serves to remind us that there are still many secrets of the natural world for us to explore.

Together the rhythms of the skies and the biological clocks that have become synchronised with them rule our lives - though we too often forget it these days. Light and dark, warmth and cold, moisture and drought have formed and re-formed our landscapes, and all of the living things on this planet have learned to live with the seasons. Our species, but one of millions, has learned this too - but as our numbers grow many of us are forgetting this important lesson. There are many stories that will help people live with the seasons, understand them, enjoy them, and most importantly become a real part of them.

The festivals of the year

As part of our aim to make children more aware of the natural world, we try to incorporate as many of the seasonal festivals as possible, as they all arose from man's response to the ever-changing face of nature. Of course awareness of the seasons was more acute in the past, but the turning of the year is an important part of that greater cycle of birth-life-death-rebirth from which none of us escapes.

In ancient times most calendars, like that of the Celts, were based on the thirteen lunar months, though the Greeks and the northmen had a twelve-month lunar-solar year.

The start of the year varied from culture to culture, some-times even from tribe to tribe. The Greek year started from sunset before the new moon preceding the Summer Solstice; the Roman year started at midnight at the Spring Equinox; the Celtic year started at Samain - sunset on 31 October; while the Nordic year started at sunset of 20 December (24 December, Old Calendar) - the Winter Solstice. As it is nearest to our modern custom we shall follow the northmen.

Note that there are far more festivals in the first half of the year when the growth of the young sun god / Divine Child - and the crops - was being encouraged by age-old rituals.

WINTER

December - Holy Month (Anglo-Saxon)

20/1   WINTER SOLSTICE: the birth-day of the Divine Child - Dionysos, Mithras and, of course, Christ. In the old Julian Calendar (Roman), the solstice took place on 25 December.

24   CHRISTMAS EVE: the day to put up holly and mistletoe (ever-greens to reassure everyone that life continues, even in winter), to decorate the Christmas tree (a Victorian introduction from Germany), and sing carols.

25   CHRISTMAS DAY was only fixed on this day in about AD 530, to follow the pagan custom (e.g. Mithras was born on this day). The northmen called the occasion Yule, and they lit fires and candles to encourage the return of the sun. What was left of the great ash yule-log, preserved from the previous year, was put on the fire on the day to ensure continuity. This is the first day to eat mince pies.

26   BOXING DAY; this is the day when the mummers go round the houses. For a simple mummers' play see Chapter V.

January - Wolf Month (Anglo-Saxon)

1   NEW YEAR'S DAY: First Footing - shortly before
F   midnight on the last day of the Old Year, everyone leaves the house with the doors and gates left open to allow luck to enter. Once midnight has struck, all living things, animals and plants, on the property are visited and wished good luck, then any outside gates are shut, and the youngest member of the company,

208

representing New Year and carrying a branch of evergreen and some mistletoe, leads the way to the open door and 'first foots' it into the house. Everyone follows in silence and waits for the branch to be put on the fire; then the young 'New Year' turns and wishes everyone a happy New Year. Then after sweetened ale, egg flip and triangular mince-pies, everyone partakes of spiced ale and greets each other with 'Waes hail' (All-heal).

6
F/G

TWELFTH NIGHT: wassailing the apple trees - if you have access to an orchard (or even a single apple tree) you should visit it after dark with a jug of cider (or apple juice), some metal buckets and sticks, and a piece of cake. After making 'rough music' with the buckets and sticks (to frighten away evil spirits), everyone should take a cup of cider, drink some, and pour the rest over the tree-roots, then sing or chant:

> Here's to thee, old apple tree.
> May thou bud, may'st thou blow,
> May'st thou bear apples enow!
> Hats full, caps full!
> Bushel, bushel, sacks full!
> And my pockets full too! Huzza!

The cake, soaked in cider, should be lodged on a branch for the birds to eat.

"Twelfth Cake" is a small fruit cake with one bean and one pea in the mixture, garnished with icing-sugar stars, castles, palaces and churches, dragons, flowers, crowns, kings and queens, etc. The finders of the bean and pea are respectively crowned King and Queen with home-made crowns.

February - Mud Month (Anglo-Saxon)

2   CANDLEMAS was originally a Roman, then later a Christian festival of light and purifiction. It was also a Celtic festival called Imbolc, celebrating the childhood of the god, which was sacred to the Great Mother goddess, Bridget. It was the custom to decorate houses with snowdrops and candles on this day. It was also a day to present gifts to field and garden to ensure fertility. In Scotland a boy and girl, dressed in green, paraded round the town as 'King' and 'Queen'.

G   Two children could be elected King and Queen and dressed in green, then carried or led clockwise (i.e. sun-wise) round a school garden, a field or a planting of young trees, with songs and dances. This would be an appropriate day to turn over the garden and dress it with organic compost.

14   ST VALENTINE'S DAY: the sending of anonymous cards started in Victorian times, but the celebration of the formation of love bonds goes back much further, and its roots are lost in time. This is the time when birds are beginning to build nests and find their mates, so it is not surprising that many mating ceremonies took place at this time of year.)

G   SHROVE TUESDAY: rather than sit at home and eat pancakes, organise a pancake race. A golden pancake tossed in the air is a symbol of the returning sun.

March - Many Weathers Month (Old English)

1   ST DAVID'S DAY (Wales): remember to wear a leak or daffodil.

17   ST PATRICK'S DAY (Ireland) - Patrick was a one-man environ-mental disaster: in his battle against the druids he is said to have turned a good part of a fertile Ireland into bog, he cursed the rivers so that they would have no fish, and he banished all reptiles from the country! Remember to wear a shamrock.

SPRING

21   SPRING EQUINOX

GOOD FRIDAY: hot cross buns are the descendants of loaves marked with a sun-wheel to welcome the returning sun.

20/23   VERNAL EQUINOX which the Angles and Saxons called EOSTRE, after their goddess of Spring and the

F/G   dawn. The arrival of Spring should be celebrated with flowers, song and dancing.Eggs were always very important at this time as they symbolise regeneration. In Chester Cathedral at this time the ocassion used to be celebrated by an egg-throwing match between clergy and choristers as an integral part of the Easter service!

G   A simple ceremony could be created by appointing a fair-haired boy dressed as the young sun-god to welcome a girl dressed in light green and decorated with flowers, representing Virgin Spring, with a poem written by the children.The two could then lead everyone in a sun-wise circle dance and songs.

G   Traditional Easter games include football, bowls (both representing the sun), jumping and wrestling. In many counties someone would be seated on a chair and lifted three times head-high then turned about sunwise (i.e. clock-wise).

G   Children's games included "Thread my Needle": two children form an arch with their hands and the others ran through in pairs then immediately formed a new arch. This would continue through the streets of the town. It could of course be adapted to become a competitive race between two teams.

F/G   Another widespread custom, dyeing or painting hard-boiled eggs and giving them as presents, provides an enjoyable and engrossing activity for adults and children.

F/G   Another appropriate activity for Easter Sunday morning is to rise before dawn and go to a hilltop to see the sun dance for joy as it rises over the horizon.

April - Eostre's Month (Anglo-Saxon)

1   ALL FOOLS' DAY: be sure you think up some really good tricks -   but only before midday, or *you* will be the fool!

23   ST GEORGE'S DAY (England): who St George was remains something of a mystery, but his name may be derived from the Greek (Ge = earth goddess; orgias = secret rites). His connection with England is a mystery too, but he is closely linked to the Green Man legend in Europe, and he often battles with a dragon. His story is an uncomplicated version of the universal myth - the male sun hero penetrating the female chthonic dragon with a 'spear' to promote fertility in the Spring. The St George of the mummers' plays is, like almost all sun heroes, 'killed', then resurrected into new life. The 23rd is also Shakespeare's birthday.

30   THE RITE OF SPRING: on the eve of May Day fires were lit on hilltops, and young people ran between two

fires to be purified of the sickness of Winter and receive some of the sun god's fertility before taking off into the woods (see May Day).

SUMMER

May - Merry Month (Norse)

MAY DAY or GARLAND DAY or ROBIN HOOD'S DAY or BELTAIN: 'Bel' is the ancient root name of the sun god, 'tan' means 'fire'.

G   *Against May all the yung men and maides, old men and wives, run gadding over night in the woods, groves, hils,and mountains, where they spend all night in plesant pastimes; and in the morning they return, bringing with them birch and branches of trees, to deck their assemblies withall .... But the chiefest jewel they bring from thence is their May- pole.... which is covered all over with floures and hearbs, bound round with strings from the top to the bottome, and sometimes painted with variably colours. And this being reared up, with handkerchiefs and flags hovering at the top, they straw the ground round about, binde green boughes about it, set up sommer haules [halls], bowers, and arbours hard by it; then fall they to daunce about it....*
PHILIP STUBBES: *Anatomie of Abuses, 1583*

This vivid account, by a rabid puritan who condemned the raising of the maypole ('this stinkyng Ydol, rather') as the heathen worship of 'Sathan, Prince of Hel', is surely enough to make one want to join in bringing in the May.

F/G   In the early morning of May Day many people washed
      themselves in the dew - May dew has special powers to
      beautify - and carried may-blossom home to decorate
      the doors.

      For activities see chapters IV and V.

      ROGATIONTIDE (fifth week after Easter) was the
      traditional time for 'Beating the Bounds' From the 8th
      century it became the custom to take the children
      round the parish boundaries and to duck or beat one
      at each marker to ensure that the next generation
      would never forget the boundaries. If there was a holy
      well in the parish the children would be 'baptised' in
      it. They would then again leave rag thanks token on
      the nearest tree.

      For our fun version of Beating the Bounds see Chapter
      IV

      WHITSUNTIDE (7th Sunday after Easter): the Morris
G   Dancers are invariably out at Whit. In the past it was
      the custom to dress in finery and elect a 'Lord' and
      'Lady' who were dressed in white, plus a Mace-bearer
      and a Fool to attend them. These four presided over
      the festivities, which included dancing and games, a
      hobby horse and, sometimes, a dragon too.

29   OAK APPLE DAY: in 1644 the Commonwealth
      government forbade the celebration of both Christmas
      and May Day as pagan festivals. Many of the May Day
      activities were revived in 1660 to celebrate the
      restoration of King Charkes II. The festival, which
      survived here and there for some two centuries, was
      marked by the decoration of houses with oak branches,
      and the wearing of oak leaves. It was said to be a
      reminder of the king's escape from Roundhead troops

by hiding in an oak tree.

June - Fallow Month (Norse)

23   MIDSUMMER EVE (ST John's Eve.): a night of great
       magic. People decorated their doors with birch, fennel,
F/G St John's Wort, orpine and lilies. Many of these plants
       were thought to have magic properties. Some people
       would go out at midnight with a plate to catch some
       fern seed without touching it, for it was said that it
       could make you invisible, and able to understand what
       the birds and animals say!
       Unfortunately we cannot let you have the correct spell
       to achieve this ....!

       As on May Day, bonfires were lit on hilltops to help the
       sun on its course, and young people would run
       between two purifying fires.

24   MIDSUMMER DAY: this is another morning to wash
F/G in the dew as it has the power to make you beautiful.

       This a good time to introduce children to the Green
       Man, the ancient spirit of nature and fertility: take the
       children deep into the woods in order to collect
       materials for a 'Beauty Feast' - a competition between
       pairs to produce later the most beautiful display of
       foliage and flowers - obviously this will need close
       supervision to ensure that the plants are treated with
       respect. In the meantime, out of sight of the children,
       dress an adult as the Green Man - a green or grey-
       brown costume and make-up and a net over the head
       and upper part of the body, heavily decorated with
       foliage. If possible he should be accompanied by
       someone with a flute, recorder or pipe (also in
       woodland costume). The piper's soft music should start
       in some place out of sight of the children, then the

two characters should drift slowly towards the group, coming to a standstill in their midst. The piper should stop playing, then quietly invite the children to weave some of their leaves and flowers into the netting. Once they have done this the piping should resume and the Green Man can drift silently away into the wood. This can provide a truly magical experience for the children.

July - Hay Month (Norse)

15   ST SWITHIN'S DAY: if it rains today it will continue for forty days.

G   WELL-DRESSING: at this time of year the holy wells were decorated with patterns and pictures made from flower petals pressed into a tray of soft clay.

August - Harvest Month (Norse)

1   LAMMAS (Harvest Home): once the harvest was
G   completed here in Britain the workers joined in games and a feast. For details of what you might do, see 'Crying the Kern' in Chapter IV and the game 'Barley Break' in Chapter VI.

September - Wood Month (Frankish)

AUTUMN

21   AUTUMN EQUINOX: the time of the Harvest Moon, when the full moon rises at round about sunset, giving bright nights for several days, ideal for harvesting well into the evening.

29   MICHAELMAS: St Michael the dragon-slayer is the Christian successor to Apollo, and many hilltop sites

originally used for sun worship were re-dedicated to St Michael and crowned with a church with tower or spire representing his spear.

October - Hunting Month (Norse)

31   HALLOWE'EN: this night was the first of the Celtic New Year. It was also the night when ghosts were abroad. All but the bravest stayed at home and lit candles to keep the sun alive.

G   Of all the festivals, this must be the one most widely celebrated as a pagan rite, and it provokes strong opposition from some Christians. It should therefore be approached with sensitivity. Unquestionably children love it, and they normally give no thought to its pagan significance. If your children do celebrate it with pumpkins, masks or make-up in order to scare neighbours, they should be reminded not to frighten nervous elderly people.

November - Sacrifice Month (Anglo-Saxon)

5   GUY FAWKES NIGHT: the bonfires and other fire festivals really belong to the Celtic New Year but the date changed with the revision of the calendar in 1752. In the years of the Common - wealth the only way to continue the ancient festivities was to pretend that the fires were celebrating the discovery of the plot against Parliament.

22   ST CECILIA'S DAY: St Cecilia is the patron saint of
F/G   music, and this provides an excuse to enjoy a musical celebration at this time.

F   STIR-UP SUNDAY (The Sunday before Advent): this was traditionally the day when the Christmas pudding was made, and everyone was expected to give it a stir. In fact the name is derived from the first words of the Collect for the day: 'Stir up, we beseech thee, O Lord, the will of thy faithful people ....'

30   ST ANDREW'S DAY: remember to wear a thistle.

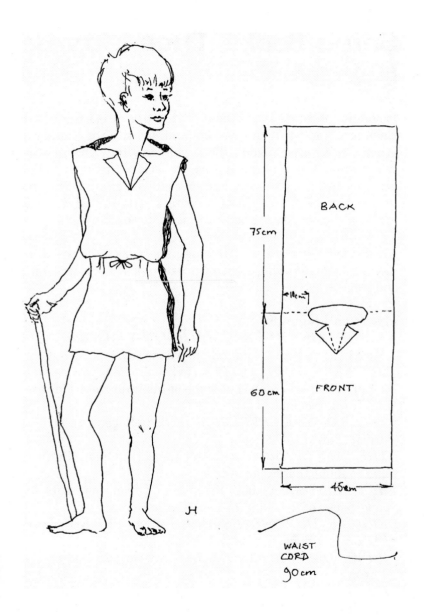

BACK

75cm

18cm

FRONT

60 cm

45cm

WAIST
CORD
90cm

Making a tabard

Some Books That May Be Helpful

It should, of course, go without saying that it is essential that Enchanters must themselves be familiar with the literary and other sources that inspire the adventures they choose to run. If you are not sure of the stories, go back to them: they should give you infinite pleasure, and more ideas: after all they have inspired some of our greatest writers, artists and musicians for hundreds of years, and continue to do so.

All the following are available as paperpacks and are almost always in print. Those with an asterisk (*) are written for children.

Myths and legends
A HANDBOOK OF GREEK MYTHOLOGY : H J Rose (Methuen) - a sound comprehensive survey.
THE GREEK MYTHS : by Robert Graves (Penguin) - a comprehensive account but some of his interpretations are highly questionable.
* *TALES OF THE GREEK HEROES* : by Roger Lancelyn Green (Puffin)
* *THE TALE OF TROY* : by Roger Lancelyn Green (Puffin) - this is about the Trojan War
THE MABINOGION : both Penguin and Everyman publish paperbacks of these myths from Celtic Britain.
* *KING ARTHUR AND HIS KNIGHTS OF THE ROUND TABLE* : by Roger Lancelyn Green (Puffin)
* *IRISH FOLK AND FAIRY TALES* : by Gordon Jarvie (Puffin)
* *IRISH LEGENDS FOR CHILDREN* : Y. Carroll (Gill and MacMill)
* *IRISH SAGAS AND FOLK TALES* : Eileen O'Faolain (Oxford)

THE TAIN : Thomas Kinsella (Oxford)
* *THE ADVENTURES OF ROBIN HOOD* : by Roger
 Lancelyn Green (Puffin)
* *MYTHS OF THE NORTHMEN; THE SAGA OF ASGARD* :
 by Roger Lancelyn Green (Puffin)
THE NORSE MYTHS : by Kevin Crossley-Holland (Penguin)
*HEROES, MONSTERS AND OTHER WORLDS FROM
RUSSIAN MYTHOLOGY* : by Elizabeth Warner (Peter Lowe)
KALEVALA: translated by K Bosley: (Oxford 1989)

Folk tales
THE PENGUIN BOOK OF WESTERN FAIRY TALES : Jack
 Zipes
ENGLISH FAIRY TALES : Joseph Jacob (Bodley Head)
CELTIC FAIRY TALES : Joseph Jacob (Bodley Head)
THE PENGUIN BOOK OF ENGLISH FOLKTALES : Neil
 Philip (Penguin)
THE PENGUIN BOOK OF SCOTTISH FOLK TALES ; Neil
 Philip (Penguin)
* *CELTIC WONDER TALES* : Ella Young (Floris) - this and
 the two following books by Ella Young are told in delightfully
 simple but highly poetic language.
* *THE TANGLE COATED HORSE* - Ella Young (Floris)
* *THE WONDER SMITH AND HIS SON* : Ella Young (Floris)
BEAUTIES, BEASTS AND ENCHANTMENT: Jack Zipes
 (Meridian)
WONDER TALES : Marine Warner (Chatto and Windus)
GRIMM'S FAIRY TALES : (Routledge)
SCANDINAVIAN FOLK TALES : Jacqueline Simpson
 (Penguin)
RUSSIAN FAIRY TALES : Aleksandr Afnasev (Pantheon)
ITALIAN FOLKTALES : Italo Calvino (Penguin)
* *A BOOK OF DRAGONS* : Roger Lancelyn Green (Puffin)

Nature activities

SHARING NATURE WITH CHILDREN, Book I and II: Joseph Cornell (Dawn Publications, available from Deep Books Ltd, Unit 13 Cannon Wharfe Business Centre, 35 Evelyn Street, London SE8 5RT): these books provide an exciting range of nature appreciation activities and games for all ages and all group-sizes, including families.

EARTHWALKS: Steve

TALKING TO THE EARTH: Gordon Maclellan (Capall Bann)

Reference

THE ENCYCLOPEDIA OF MYTHS AND LEGENDS : Stuart Gordon (Headline) - a good general reference book.

THE HERO WITH A THOUSAND FACES : Joseph Campbell (Paladin) - the late Joseph Campbell, the greatest mythographer of the late 20th century, published many books ranging across the myths of the world: always worth reading.

THE GODS OF THE GREEKS : C Kerenyi (Thames and Hudson) - this and the following title are probably the best studies of the subject.

THE HEROES OF THE GREEKS : C Kerenyi (Thames and Hudson)

THE DICTIONARY OF CLASSICAL MYTHOLOGY : Pierre Grimal (Blackwell) - an excellent comprehensive guide.

DICTIONARY OF CELTIC MYTHOLOGY : James MacKillop (Oxford) - a first-class detailed work for reference.

CELTIC HERITAGE : Alwyn and Brinley Rees (Thames and Hudson) - a good background study.

MABON AND THE MYSTERIES OF BRITAIN : Caitlin Matthews (Arkana) - this and the following book are perceptive interpretations of the Mabinogion stories, though we would differ from her over the significance of Mabon.

ARTHUR AND THE SOVEREIGNTY OF BRITAIN : Caitlin Matthews (Arkana)

THE WESTERN WAY : John Matthews (Arkana) - Matthews,

often in association with his wife Caitlin, has produced a long list of titles on Celtic and Arthurian, topics. They are always illuminating and well worth reading.

DICTIONARY OF NORTHERN MYTHOLOGY : Rudof Simek (D S Brewer) - an excellent, scholarly and comprehensive handbook.

THE WELL OF REMEMBRANCE:Ralph Metzner (Shambala) - a useful sourcebook about Nordic myth.

THE OXFORD COMPANION TO FAIRY TALES : Jack Zipes (Oxford) - apart from a bias to American entries, it is a useful reference handbook.

A DICTIONARY OF FAIRIES : Katherine Briggs (Allen Lane) - the standard work, with many stories included.

STORYTELLING AND THE ART OF THE IMAGINATION: Nancy Mellon (Element). A useful introduction.

Index of activities and games

Note: Activities presented in Chapters IV, V and VI that are suitable for families or very small groups are preceded with **F**. Those for groups of ten or more are marked **G**. Most are suitable for both types of group. These are marked **F/G**.

GAMES FOR FUN AND ENCHANTMENT

References

1 Berenson, Bernard — *Sketch for a Self-Portrait*: Constable 1949

2 Bhave, Vinoba — *Thoughts On Education*: Sarva Seva Sangh Prakahan, India 1964

3 Blackwood, Algernon — *The Extra Day*: Macmillan 1915

4 Buchan, John — *Midwinter*: Nelson 1923

5 Carson, Rachel — *The Sense of Wonder*: Harper (US) 1965

6 Clark, Kenneth — *Moments of Vision*: John Murray 1981

7 Cobb, Edith — *The Ecology of Imagination in Childhood*: Spring (US) 1993

8 Cooper, J C — *Fairy Tales, Allegories of the Inner Life*: Aquarian Press 1983

9 Cornell, Joseph — *Sharing Nature with Children*: Dawn Publications (US)

11 Crossley-Holland, Kevin — *The Norse Myths*: Deutsch 1980

12 Duer, Hans Peter — *Dreamtime*: Blackwell 1985

13 Eliade, Mircea — *Rites and Symbols of Initiation*: Harper (US) 1975

14 Eliade, Mircea — *The Myth of Eternal Return*: Arkana 1989

15 Eliot, Alexander — *The Universal Myths*: Meridian 1990

16 Gill, Eric — *Art in Education in Essays*: Cape 1948

17 Graham, Kenneth — *The Wind in the Willows*: Methuen 1908

18 Hillman, James — *Senex and Puer in Puer Papers*: Spring (US) 1989

19 Hillman, James — *A Note on Story in Loose Ends*: Spring (US) 1986

20 Jefferies, Richard — *Bevis, the Story of a Boy*: Cape 1943

21 Jefferies, Richard — *The Dewy Morn*: Macmillan 1990

22 Jung, C G — *Man and his Symbols*: Aldus 1964

23 Jung, C G — *Introduction to a Science of*

24 Jung, C G — *Mythology*: Routledge 1951
The Conjunction in The Psychology of the Transference: Routledge 1989

25 Lawrence, D H — *A propos Lady Chatterley*: Mandrake 1930

26 "Macleod, Fiona" — *Poems and Plays*: Heinemann 1933

27 Markdale, Jean — *Merlin, Priest of Nature*: Inner Traditions (US) 1995

28 Matthews, Caitlin — *Mabon, the Celtic Divine Child in Merlin through the Ages*: Blandford 1995

29 Otto, Walter — *The Homeric Gods*: Thames and Hudson 1979

30 Paul, Leslie — *The Folk Trail*: Noel Douglas 1929

31 Pindar — *The Odes of Pindar*: Penguin 1969

32 Plato — *The Laws*: Penguin 1970

33 Raine, Kathleen — *Back to Blake in Resurgence* No. 101 1983

34 Russell, George (AE) — *The Candle of Vision*: Macmillan 1918

35 Russell, George (AE) — *The Dream of Angus Oge in ImaginationsandReveries*: Mansel (Dublin) 1915

36 Sukhomlinsky, Vasily — *To Children I give my Heart*: Progress, (Moscow) 1981

37 Traherne, Thomas — *Poems, Centuries and Thanksgivings*: Oxford 1966

39 Wiles, David — *The Early Plays of Robin Hood*: D S Brewer 1981

40 G Winfield Digby — *Paul Nash in Meaning and Symbols in Three Modern Artists*: Faber 1955

41 Virgil — *The Pastoral Poems*: Penguin 1954

42 Zimmer, Heinrich — *The King and the Corpse: Tales of the Soul's Conquest of Evil*: Princeton UP (US) 1971

Acknowledgements

This book is dedicated to the many people who helped with the project:

Tim Laycock, singer-songwriter, actor and playwright, our Bard and principal co-experimenter;

The National Trust staff at the many properties we have used, especially Bill Lambshead, Denise Melhuish, Paul Sharman and Sally Twiss at Killerton; Marcus Brown and David Smith at Kingston Lacy; and John Turner, Fred Hunt and Richard Higgs at Stourhead; as well as the staff at the many privately owned properties that we have used over the years;

Tracy Cooper and East Dorset Leisure Services, who has provided encouragement and many opportunities to try out our ideas, as well as lots of keen helpers;

Our fellow-Enchanters: Anna Dyer, Stewart Edmondson, Philip Hull, Sian Goodfellow, Juliana Montgomery, Steve Mellor, Ros Orwin, Pip Shaw, Karen Smith, Edward Thompson, Nigel Watson, Jo Wermig, and other, occasional, helpers;

And the original Dragon Questers from whom we learned so much: Hayley Abdullah, Beth and Laura Allen, Becky Calvert, Jenny Debenham, Tom and Zoe Dyer, Phillip Elston, Kane Fowler, Edward Gore, Sophie Hare, Hannah Hocking, Madeleine Hodgkins, Alex Hookway, Ben Jenkins, Lucille Johnson, Laura Jones, Gabriel, Polly and George Laycock, Sally Megee, Ben Palmer, Simeon Paskell, Hannah Patterson, Daniel Shaw, Edmund Standing, Philip Symes, Jo and Lizzie Wiltshire, and Dominic Wood;
And, not least, the Dragon of Dolbury!

Thanks also to Joseph Cornell and Gordon MacLellan for inspiration and sharing ideas from their own experience, and to the many story-tellers and mythographers, past and present, who have kept the myths and folk-tales alive.

The project was made possible by generous financial support from :

The National Trust
Rolle School of Education, Faculty of Arts and Education - University of Plymouth
Enterprise in Higher Education - University of Plymouth
South West Arts

Other environmental education books from Capall BAnn:

Celebrating Nature Gordon MacLellan

A practical handbook of celebration. For a small youth group, a class of school children, a family or a community gathering of several hundred people, this book offers guidelines and a range of ideas for designing and leading celebrations that will grow from people's own imaginations and their perceptions of the places where they live and play and from the issues that are important to them. Activities are generally short and might stand alone as small celebrations in themselves or can be combined to create longer and more spectacular events. A number of ways of exploring the natural world and the sorts of celebrations that might arise from these adventures are presented. Different structures for celebrations are described and how to make the most of the enthusiasm and creativity of the participants. The many topics covered include: The importance of celebration; Historical celebrations and their survival into current times; Celebrations as ways of sharing experiences; Principles and activities to use in finding ideas; Inspiring a group; Personal celebrations; Working with natural materials; Working with stories; Developing storytelling skills; Animated Trails: an application of story work: creating performance pieces: activities include puppets, twig people, foam toadstools, and more. Plotting and planning a trail with a group; Activities for making and working with flags, banners, standards. Planning and leading a procession, Working with music; Performance and presentation skills: movement activities for puppets, masks and costumes, working with the spoken word, telling stories, creating characters; Working with groups of people of various sizes and minimal equipment: mumming plays, instant meditations, leading dances; Behind the scenes planning; Putting it all together: structures of celebrations: atmosphere and activity, mapping out a whole celebration, managing your participants, keeping people involved, practical tips. An immensely practical, inspiring book for everyone - another masterly work from Gordon the Toad! ISBN 186163 1685

Talking to the Earth Gordon MacLellan

This book welcomes the reader onto an adventure of creativity into the wild that hides in the corners of park and city: a chance to explore the world around us and express discoveries in exciting ways. "Talking" is a collection of activities to let the artist out in everyone:- using natural, recycled or cheap materials, here are chances to explore new ways of expressing the relationship between ourselves and the natural world. Ranging from the dramatic potency of "Masks" to banners and story boards, activities are presented with easy to follow guidelines, practical notes for teachers, parents and group leaders and handy hints for a smoother run. Designed for use by children of all ages from infant to ancient, "Talking to the Earth" is an invaluable manual for anyone working in environmental art - from the experienced art-worker to the cautious beginner. A set of A4 work sheet masters is available at a cost of £7.50 including p&p.
ISBN 1898307 43 1   £10.00

FREE detailed catalogue
Capall Bann Publishing, Auton Farm, Milverton, Somerset, TA4 1NE
www.capallbann.co.uk